BOTANY
IN 8 LESSONS

A complete curriculum for ages 8-14

by Ellen Johnston McHenry

Ellen McHenry's Basement Workshop
State College, Pennsylvania

Published by **Ellen McHenry's Basement Workshop**
State College, Pennsylvania, 16801
www.ellenjmchenry.com, ejm.basementworkshop@gmail.com

Printed and distributed by Lightning Source, a premier print-on-demand publisher with worldwide distribution services. www.lightningsource.com

ISBN 978-0-9887808-0-4

HOW TO USE THIS CURRICULUM:

TEXT: The text is organized into two levels. All students do level 1. For younger students, academically challenged students, or those with very limited interest in science, this might be enough. Most of the activities in the activity section can be used if you do only level 1.

Level 2 adds extra information for students who are older, who read quickly, or who are very interested in science. However, there may be some level 2 sections that you want use even with your level 1 students. (For example, level 2 of lesson 7 gives information about carnivorous plants, which most students find very interesting.) You are welcome to pick and choose which level 2 sections you want to use.

NOTE: If the paperback binding format of this book is less than ideal for you, and you would prefer a loose-leaf format, don't hesitate to cut off the binding, 3-hole punch the pages, and put them into a 3-ring binder.

EXTRA STUDENT BOOKLETS can be ordered on Amazon. ISBN 978-0-9887808-1-1

MAKING COPIES: You have permission to make extra copies of pages for your student(s) or your group. For example, you might need extra sets of cards for the games. You have the author's permission to do whatever copying is necessary for your students or your small group.

DIGITAL COPIES: If you would like to print out copies of activity pages using your computer printer, you can download a digital copy of these pages (free) by going to www.ellenjmchenry.com and clicking on FREE DOWNLOADS, then on PLANTS, then on "Printable pages for *Botany in 8 Lessons*." These files won't contain any instructions, just pattern pages that you can print out. This book contains all the instructions.

VIDEO LINKS: A special YouTube channel (www.YouTube.com/TheBasementWorkshop) contains most of the video links that are recommended at the end of each lesson. As with all YouTube channels, The Basement Workshop has no control over the basic format of the channel, including comments posted as part of the original video posting, and video thumbnails that pop up in the side bar. The Internet provides a forum of free speech not be equaled anywhere else on earth, but this does mean that indiscrete persons are within their rights to post their stupidity for all the world to see. But we have the right to ignore them. Fortunately, inappropriate comments are not frequent, and on most computer screens you can't see the list of comments unless you scroll down. You can also go to full screen mode right away.

The videos that are part of the playlist have been previewed and specially selected because they are age-appropriate and high-quality (not a waste of your time). They add a dimension to the curriculum that would not be possible otherwise. Please don't shy away from using them simply because they are on YouTube. They are wonderful resources. Parents and teachers will enjoy watching these videos along with their students.

ACTIVITIES: The activity section provides instructions and patterns for many game and craft activities. These are often ideal for use in a group situation, but can be adapted for use with a single student. You may skip any activities that won't work for your situation.

USING THIS CURRICULUM WITH A GROUP: If you plan to use this curriculum with a group, I would suggest assigning all the reading and activities in the student booklet as at-home work to be done before coming to class. Use class time for follow-up discussions and for the games, experiments and crafts listed in the activity guide. (Some of the experiments might need to be done at home, however, as they involve long-term activities such as watching fruit ripen.) Activities that don't suit your situation can be omitted. You are the best person to make decisions for your student(s) or group, so it's up to you to decide how to use your class time.

You may want to consider asking the members of your group to purchase individual student booklets. They relatively inexpensive and are easy to order on Amazon.com. ISBN 978-0-9887808-1-1

CONTENTS

BOTANY
In 8 Lessons

STUDENT TEXT

LESSON 1: PLANT CELLS

LEVEL ONE

What is a plant? A quick answer might be "something that is green and has leaves." But are all plants green? There's a type of maple tree that has purplish-red leaves. Obviously it is a plant because it is a tree. So being green can't be a requirement for being a plant, though most plants are indeed green. What about leaves? Do all plants have leaves? Think about a cactus. Do those sharp needles count as leaves? Or what about the "stone plant"? It looks like a rock. (No kidding--it really does!) What makes a plant a plant?

The answer is... a plant is a plant because it can make its own food using a process called *photosynthesis*. Plants can use the energy from sunlight to turn water and carbon dioxide into sugar. ("Photo" means "light," and "synthesis" means "make.") Wouldn't it be nice if you could make your own food from sunlight? No more going to the grocery store or planting a garden. You could just stand in the sunshine, take a deep breath, drink a glass of water, and make your own food. Sounds funny, but that's exactly what plants do. They take water from the ground, carbon dioxide from the air, and energy from light and turn them into food.

Photosynthesis is a very complicated chemical process. The exact details of how a plant takes apart the molecules of water and carbon dioxide and turns them into sugar is so complicated that you need a college degree in chemistry to really understand it. Since you probably don't want to learn about "photophosphorylation" and "chemiosmosis," we'll just stick to the basics of photosynthesis.

To understand the basics of photosynthesis we need to start by looking at a plant cell. A *cell* is the basic "building block" of a plant. A plant is made of individual cells in much the same way that a building is made of individual bricks.

Here is a simplified drawing of a typical plant cell.

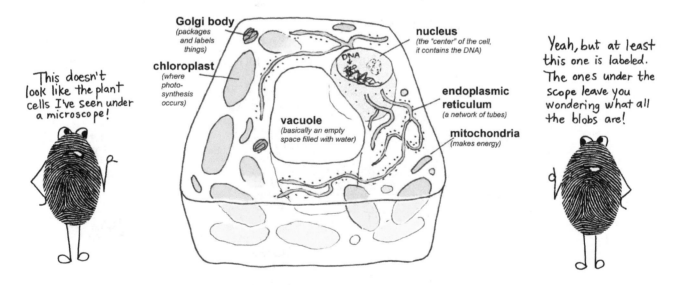

Not all plant cells have exactly this shape. Some are very long and thin, some are flat, some are round, and some are curved. The shape of a plant cell depends on where it is in the plant. A root cell will look different from a leaf cell. However, all plant cells are at least somewhat similar to the one shown here. Most plant cells have organelles called *chloroplasts*. (Some cells, such as root cells, are specialized for tasks not related to photosynthesis, so they don't have chloroplasts.) Real chloroplasts are green, just like the ones in our diagram. Other organelles have no color, but we added a bit of color to our organelles just to make the diagram look more interesting.

1

The things that look like stacks of pennies (or maybe pancakes) are called **thylakoids**. Chlorophyll molecules are located on the surfaces of the thylakoids.

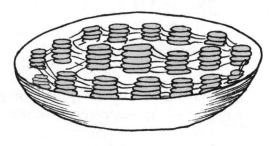

inside a chloroplast

Hmm... reminds me of a football filled with pennies.

It is inside the chloroplast that photosynthesis takes place. The chloroplast's job is to use the energy in the sunlight to make sugar. The chloroplasts contain a special chemical called **chlorophyll**. This chemical happens to reflect green light, which is why most plants look green.

One molecule of chlorophyll is so small that you can't see it, even with a microscope. It's made of five different kinds of atoms (carbon, hydrogen, nitrogen, oxygen, and magnesium) linked together to make this shape:

This long part is called the "hydrocarbon tail."

This molecule has the amazing ability to transform light energy into chemical energy. The light energy is used to tear apart molecules of water and carbon dioxide. The plant takes six carbon dioxides and twelve waters and turns them into one **glucose** (sugar) molecule plus six oxygens and six waters.

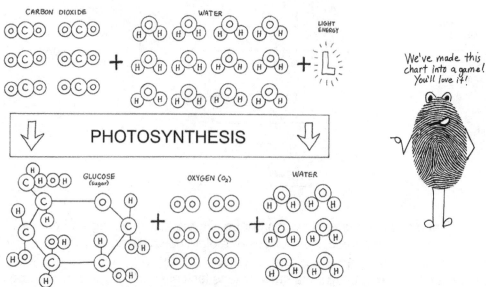

We've made this chart into a game! You'll love it!

The water molecules on the bottom are **not** the same water molecules from the top. The plant tears apart the original water molecules and makes totally new ones!

Without drawing each individual molecule, the formula for photosynthesis looks like this:

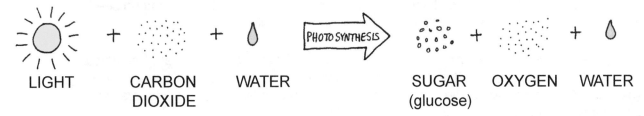

LIGHT + CARBON DIOXIDE + WATER → PHOTOSYNTHESIS → SUGAR (glucose) + OXYGEN + WATER

This says in pictures what we've already said in words: plants use sunlight, carbon dioxide and water to make sugar. In the process of making sugar, oxygen and water also are produced. Oxygen and water are called "by-products" of photosynthesis. (A by-product is something extra that is produced along with what you intended to make.)

Now let's do something interesting with this formula. Let's flip it around:

SUGAR (glucose) + OXYGEN + WATER → RESPIRATION → CARBON DIOXIDE + WATER + ENERGY

This "backwards" photosynthesis is called **respiration**. Respiration is what all cells do (both plant and animal cells) to get energy from sugar. Plant cells use the sugar they make, plus oxygen and water from the environment, to make energy that keeps their cells alive and growing. Animals use the sugar they eat (made by plants), water they drink, and oxygen they breathe in, to make energy for their cells. Both plants and animals breathe out carbon dioxide and water vapor. (You can see this water vapor in your breath on a cold winter day—it looks like a cloud of steam.)

Both these processes—photosynthesis and respiration—go on at the same time in plants. (Animals do only respiration.) Photosynthesis and respiration complement each other nicely. The waste products of one process become the raw materials for the other. We could draw it like this:

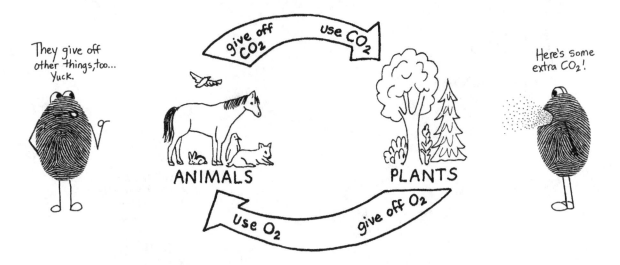

Animals depend on plants not only for putting oxygen back into the air, but also for supplying food. All animals are dependent upon plants whether they eat plants or not. Even carnivores such as lions depend on plants, because the prey that they eat (zebras, for instance) are usually plant eaters. Without grass for the zebra to eat, the lion would starve.

Could plants survive without animals? Perhaps some could. But what would happen if there were no bees or butterflies to pollinate flowers? What about plants that depend on seed-eating animals to spread their seeds? Plants do benefit from animals.

Let's wrap up this section with a brief review of what goes on in a leaf. See if you can follow along with this paragraph, putting your finger on the appropriate words or arrows in the diagram as you read. Stop when you come to a comma or period and make sure your finger is in the right place before you continue.

The plant uses light, carbon dioxide, and water in a process called photosynthesis. This process results in the production of oxygen, water, and glucose (sugar). Some of the glucose is used by the plant as its own food. (This "eating" process inside a plant cell is called "respiration.") For respiration, the plant needs some of its sugar, plus oxygen and water. It produces energy, plus carbon dioxide and water.
Plants usually make more glucose than they need. The leftover glucose is packaged into starches or fats and is stored in the roots, seeds and fruits.

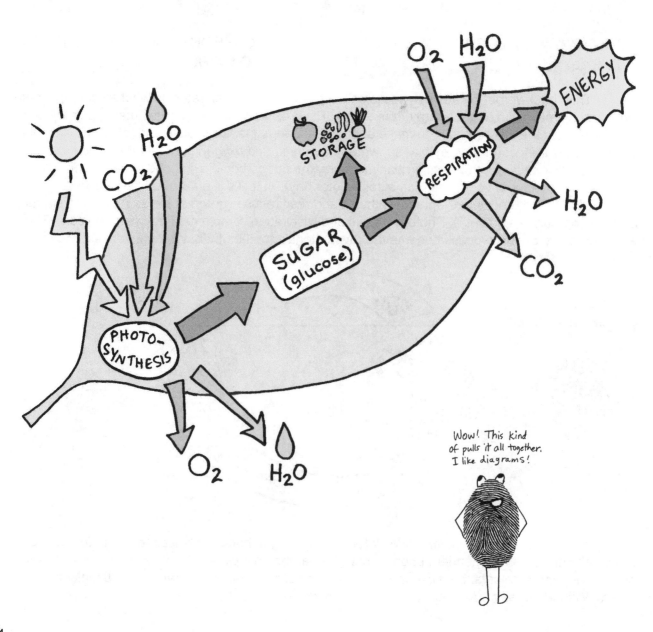

Wow! This kind of pulls it all together. I like diagrams!

And now for something completely different...

HOW CELLS DIVIDE

As a plant grows, it must increase the number of cells it has. To make more cells, plants use a process called *mitosis*. Mitosis is both very simple and very complex. It is simple because it just means that a cell splits in half, making two cells. That's it. The word mitosis just means splitting in half. However, in order to do this, the cell must go through some very complicated procedures.

First, the nucleus must prepare. If there are to be two cells, each new cell must have a complete copy of the DNA instructions. Also, each new cell will need a full set of organelles. Let's say a cell needs 10 chloroplasts to survive. That means that before it is ready to split in half, the "parent" cell needs to have 20 chloroplasts, 10 for each new "daughter" cell. (Sorry, there are no "son" cells, only "daughter" cells!) Each new cell will also need mitochondria, Golgi bodies, ribosomes and all the other organelles. So a cell has to keep busy making new organelles all the time.

When the cell has enough organelles to make two cells, the division process starts. Scientists have lots of complicated names for all these steps, but we're going to use ordinary words for our explanation. (If you want to know the complicated words, you can look them up on the Internet; just use the key word "mitosis.")

This is how the nucleus divides:

1) The DNA in the nucleus doubles, making two complete copies. Organelles called centrosomes go to the opposite sides of the nucleus and get ready to start pulling it apart.

2) The two copies of the DNA separate. At this point they look pretty organized. Usually the DNA looks like a pile of yarn, but right now it's all lined up neat and tidy. The membrane around the nucleus start to disintegrate.

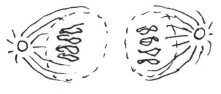

3) New membranes begin to form around the two new nuclei (nu-klee-i).

4) The membranes are complete. Now there are two separate, identical nuclei.

Now the whole cell prepares to split in half. Half of the organelles go to one side, and half go to the other. Each side has a nucleus. At this point the cell looks very long. In fact, this is sometimes called the "elongation phase" because the cell looks very long.

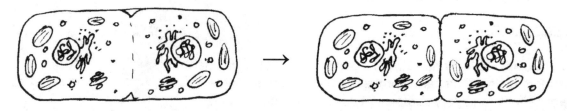

Now the cell builds a wall between the two sides. Usually the two cells stay stuck together, though, because that's the way a plant stays together. If the cells came apart, the plant would come apart. Then each cell starts all over again. As soon as mitosis is over, it's time to start making extra organelles again, to prepare for the next division. (And just think—this goes on billions of times each day, right in your own backyard!)

Wow--we made mitosis seem pretty easy to understand. Just be aware that if you go online and check out some Internet articles or videos about mitosis, you'll see words like "cytokinesis," "metaprophase," and "telophase." However, don't let these fancy words scare you off. For example, in cytokinesis, "cyto" means "cell," and "kinesis" means "movement." If you know what the Latin and Greek roots mean, the word becomes easy to understand.

ACTIVITY 1: LOOK AT SOME REAL CELLS

Use the key words "plant cell micrograph" in an Internet search engine (like Google) to see some actual photographs (micrographs) of real plant cells. The micrographs will be in black and white because the electron microscopes used to take the pictures don't use light to create their pictures--they use electrons. No light means no color.

ACTIVITY 2: SOME PLANT CELL VIDEOS

There are several short video clips related to plant cell mitosis posted on the Botany playlist at YouTube.com/TheBasementWorkshop.

ACTIVITY 3: WATCH CHLOROPLASTS "STREAMING"

Chloroplasts move around inside the cell in a very orderly way. They flow around in a circle, around the outside edge. They do this so that each chloroplast has an equal chance to absorb sunlight if the light is stronger on one side than another. You can see this in action by watching two videos posted on the Botany playlist (YouTube.com/TheBasementWorkshop).

ACTIVITY 4: ONE MORE VIDEO: THE DISCOVERY THAT PLANTS DON'T EAT DIRT

Until recent centuries, people assumed that plants "ate" dirt. It seemed obvious. You put a seed into the ground and it grew into a large plant. It seemed likely that the plant absorbed nutrition from the soil through its roots. In 1643, a scientist named Jan Van Helmont decided to test if this was true. He carefully weighed a pot of dirt before he planted a seed. He let the seed grow into a large plant then dumped out the dirt and weighed it again. Surprise! The dirt weighed almost the same at the end of the experiment! You can watch a short video that shows Van Helmont and mentions a few other scientists who contributed to our knowledge of how plants work. This video is on the Botany playlist.

ACTIVTY 5: PHOTOSYNTHESIS/MITOSIS CROSSWORD PUZZLE

ACROSS
1) The organelles where photosynthesis takes place
2) The nucleus is surrounded by a thin _____. (Hint: Read step 3 on page 5.)
3) The "parent" cell produces two "_____."
4) The process by which plants use light, carbon dioxide, and water to make glucose sugar
5) The phase in which a cell gets very long
6 The goal of respiration is to release _____.
7) Plants need this liquid for photosynthesis
8) The DNA of a plant cell is inside this organelle
9) The name of the chemical in the chloroplasts
10) Plants need this gas for photosynthesis.

DOWN
1) Plants use this source of energy for photosynthesis
2) When plant cells divide in half it is called _____.
3) Humans can't make their own sugar; we have to ___.
4) Glucose is a type of _____.
5) This is produced by plants during photosynthesis. It is also used by plants during respiration.
6) The instructions inside the nucleus are in the form of ___.
7) The empty "bubble" in a plant cell
8) The process used by both plants and animals to get energy from sugar and oxygen
9) The outer layer of a plant cell is called the _____.

ACTIVITY 6: FILL IN THE MISSING ATOMS IN CHLOROPHYLL

Use the chlorophyll atom in this chapter to help you fill in the missing atoms.

How many atoms of magnesium are in a chlorophyll molecule? _____
How many nitrogens? _____

ACTIVITY 7: LATIN WORD ROOTS

Many scientific words come from Latin or Greek. See if you can match the Latin or Greek word root on the left with its meaning on the right. To help you figure them out, think about the meanings of these words.

| chloroplast   vacuum   photosynthesis   chlorophyll   nucleus   respiration   repeat |

MATCH:

1) photo _____   A) empty
2) vacuus _____   B) to make
3) synth _____   C) again
4) chloro _____   D) light
5) nucula _____   E) breath
6) re _____   F) greenish-yellow
7) spiro _____   G) leaf
8) phyllo _____   H) little nut or kernel

(TIP: Do the ones you are sure of first, then use the process of elimination to try to figure out the ones you aren't so sure of.)

8

LEVEL TWO

A cell is sort of like a miniature factory. Real factories make products, store them in ware-houses, and ship them out to customers. Cells make things like sugars, proteins and fats, and they store them and transport them. In this diagram, the plant cell looks flat. Remember that in real life plant cells are three-dimensional.

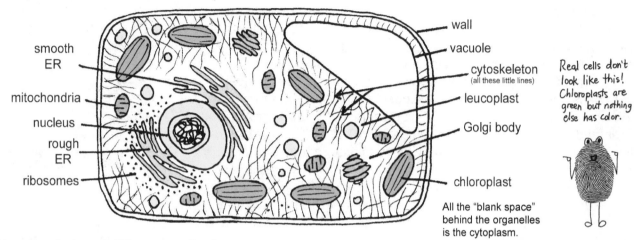

Real cells don't look like this! Chloroplasts are green but nothing else has color.

All the "blank space" behind the organelles is the cytoplasm.

Here is what each little organelle does:

Vacuole: This is like a water-filled bubble in the middle of the cell. Water from outside the cell constantly "leaks" into the vacuole, keeping it full. This water pressure inside the cell keeps the cell firm and healthy. If a plant can't get enough water to fill the vacuoles in its cells, the cells will shrink, causing the plant to wilt.

Cytoplasm: This is the jelly-like fluid inside the cell but outside the vacuole. It contains not only water, but proteins, fats, carbohydrates, and minerals. The cytoplasm circulates the chloro-plasts around and around, making sure they all get an equal amount of light.

Chloroplasts: This is where photosynthesis occurs. Chloroplasts contain the chemical chlorophyll, which can use the energy in sunlight to turn carbon dioxide and water into sugar (making water and oxygen in the process).

Cytoskeleton: This is a network of fibers that does two jobs: it helps the cell to maintain its shape, and it serves as a system of "roads" on which various things can travel across the cell.

Nucleus: This is sort of the "center" of the cell. It contains the instructions for how the cell operates. The instructions are in the form of a very long protein molecule called **DNA**. The DNA contains the "blueprints" for everything the cell makes.

Mitochondria: These are often called the "powerhouses" of the cell. Respiration takes place here. (Remember, respiration is how a cell gets energy out of glucose.) The mitochondria produce the energy the cell needs for its activities.

Leucoplasts: These are "storage tanks" for starches and lipids (fats). There are three different types of leucoplasts, the most common being the amyloplast. You will sometimes see the word "amyloplast" on a cell drawing instead of "leucoplast." ("Amylo" means "starch.")

Golgi bodies: These are often called the "post offices" of the cell. This is where proteins made by ribosomes are packaged and labeled for delivery to other areas of the cell, or to other cells.

Endoplasmic reticulum (ER): This seems to do several jobs. One type of ER manufac-tures protein molecules. Another type of ER makes lipids (fat) molecules. Both types of ER help the cell to maintain its shape by providing a bit of internal structure. ER also helps to transport things about the cell. Rough ER has ribosomes all around it; smooth ER does not.

Ribosomes: These little dots along the ER are a bit like the workers on an assembly line. They do the actual assembly of the plant's proteins.

9

Now for some info about the cell wall. It's not really an organelle, but it's still important. The outside wall of a plant cell is very tough. It is made of something called **cellulose**, which animals cannot digest. Only microorganisms (such as bacteria) can tear it apart. That is why animals that live on nothing but plants (herbivores) need lots of "good" microorganisms in their digestive systems to help them digest the plants. For example, a cow can live on nothing but grass because of the microorganisms living in the first of its four stomachs—the rumen. The microorganisms can tear apart the outer wall of the grass cells so that the proteins, fats and sugars inside of them spill out and are then available for the cow's body to use.

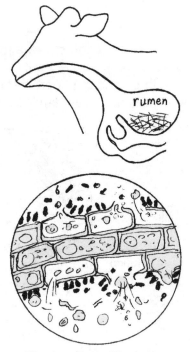

You don't have a rumen, so when you eat plant cells, most of them pass through your system undigested. This isn't bad for you, however. In fact, nutritionists call this plant material **roughage** or **fiber**, and they recommend that you eat plenty of it. The plants in our diet help to keep our intestines healthy even though they provide only some nutrition. (Cooking can help to break down the cell walls, and very thorough chewing helps, too.)

Just inside the cell wall there is a **cell membrane**. It is very thin and hard to see compared to the thick cell wall. Membranes are found in all types of cells, not just plant cells. They are fragile and come apart easily, but still have an important job. They control what

Plant cells spilling open

comes into the cell, allowing nutrients and water to flow in but keeping harmful things out.

Let's discuss the process of photosynthesis again, this time taking a closer look at it. Just how does a chloroplast produce sugar?

At the heart of photosynthesis is the chlorophyll molecule. (Interestingly enough, the ring of atoms around the magnesium atom can be found in other molecules, too. If you switch the magnesium atom for an iron atom, you get a "heme" molecule, an important part of the hemoglobin protein found in red blood cells. Hemoglobin carries oxygen to your cells.)

This long part is called the "hydrocarbon tail."

When a photon of light hits a chlorophyll molecule, it can super-charge an electron from one of these atoms, causing to become **excited**. (It's hard to track down exactly which atom the electron belongs to.) The excited electron has so much energy that it is forced to leave the chlorophyll molecule and go elsewhere. A regular electron comes in and takes its place so the molecule doesn't fall apart.

When a person jumps up, gravity brings him back down again. An excited electron "jumps"

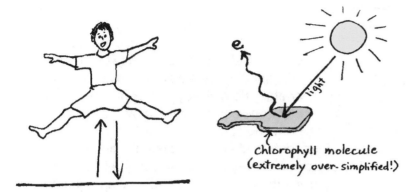

chlorophyll molecule
(extremely over-simplified!)

to a higher energy level, but it can't stay there any more than our jumper can stay in the air. The electron must come back down and return to its original energy level. On the way back down, though, the electron can pass its extra energy to other molecules, resulting in molecular "work" being done.

As it "falls," the high-energy electron passes through an assembly line made of tiny biological machines. The energy contained in the electron is used to power these machines. The goal of this assembly line is to re-charge the cell's biological batteries.

Floating around in the cell are millions of molecules called ATPs, which act like re-chargeable batteries. ATP is fairly simple, as far as biological molecules go. The A stands for **adenine**, the same molecule found in the rungs of DNA. Then there is a little sugar called **ribose**, which acts as a connector. The ribose holds on to three **phosphates**. (A phosphate is nothing more than a phosphorus atom with a few oxygen atoms attached to it.) In this diagram, the ribose is not shown separately because when adenine and ribose are joined together they are called adenosine, which also starts with the letter A.

The way this battery works is to pop off the phosphate on the end. When that third phosphate comes off, energy is released. You could think of it as a nano-sized pop gun. To re-load the gun, you simply stick the phosphate back on again. A cell has a few ways it can do this, but all of them require energy. Ultimately, the sun will provide this energy.

Each "P" triangle actually looks more like this.

$$O = P - O$$

There are two stages in the photosynthesis process. One stage uses the energy of sunlight and the other uses the energy stored in biological batteries. Sometimes these stages are called the "Light Phase" and the "Dark Phase." The Light Phase needs light, but the Dark Phase doesn't need darkness. The new-and-improved names for these phases are "Light Dependent" and "Light Independent." We'll look at the Light Dependent phase first, since it provides energy for the Light Independent phase. (We'll meet the Independent phase on page 13, disguised as a sugar factory.)

Each phase has its own little assembly line. A quick overview of the Light Dependent assembly line looks like this. →

We will look at each part separately and see how it works.

solar field

shuttle

pump

shuttle

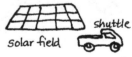
solar field   shuttle

generator

Have you ever seen fields full of solar panels? If not, go to Google, click "images," then type in "solar farms." You'll see huge, flat fields (usually in desert climates since they get a lot of sun) with hundreds of solar panels set up in neat lines. These solar panels collect energy from the sun and pass it along to a central collection area where the energy is then converted into electricity.

The plant cell's solar farms are embedded around the edges of the thylakoids (those pancake things in the chloroplasts). They are called **photosystems**, instead of solar farms, and they have chlorophyll molecules instead of solar panels. Like solar farms, photosystems have a central collection point where the energy is harvested. These central points are called **reaction centers**. Photons of light energy hit the chlorophyll molecule and energize them, causing them to vibrate. All the vibrations are passed along to the central chlorophyll molecule which then gets so energized

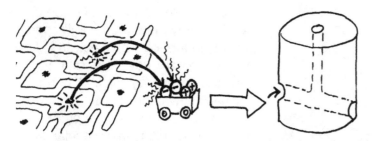

that an electron from its center goes flying off. While the electron is in this energized state, it can be used to do work. Quick! Get it to the pumping station! A little shuttle bus is waiting next to the photosystem, ready to pick up energized electrons and carry them over to the pumping station.

The shuttle bus has four seats and always picks up two electrons along with two protons. The protons also need to be transported to the pumping station, so the shuttle gives them both a ride. Off to the ion pump!

Hey - wait a minute! What about that molecule that lost an electron? Won't it fall apart or something?

Good question! What is going to happen to the chlorophyll molecule that lost an electron? That electron was part of the molecule. Without the electron, the chlorophyll molecule will begin to collapse. Fortunately, the chloroplast has a way to deal with this emergency. It has little chemical "scissors" (made of atoms of manganese, calcium and chlorine) that can chop apart water molecules. Water is made of two hydrogen atoms and one oxygen atom. The chemical scissor cuts the bonds between the atoms. The lone oxygen atom goes off and finds another lone oxygen atom that has just been snipped, and the two form a bond and float off into the atmosphere together as a molecule of oxygen (O_2). The scissors then go to work on the hydrogen atoms. Since a hydrogen atom is nothing but one proton and one electron, only one snip is needed. The loose electron can go over and replace the missing electron in the chlorophyll molecule and the proton can go get on that shuttle bus.

Now we are ready to go back and discuss the shuttle bus that was heading to the pumping station. Let's see what happens next.

At the station, the electrons and protons are stuffed into the pump. The electrons provide a surge of energy to propel the protons up and out the top of the pump. When the electrons come out the other side they have given off a lot of their energy and are tired. They need to be re-charged to be of any further use. They get picked up by another shuttle bus. (We'll come back to the protons in just a minute.)

This next shuttle takes the tired electrons to another photosystem. The electrons get charged

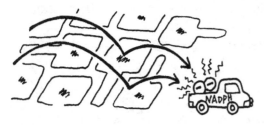

up again and then they are put into a fancy shuttle called NADPH. This letter group isn't very pronounceable. The closest word might be NAPA, an auto parts dealer in North America that has a fleet of blue and white pick-up trucks with big yellow hats on their roofs. So we've drawn the NADPH shuttle as a pick-up truck. The truck will take these energized electrons over to a sugar factory.

Now back to those protons that were pushed out the top of the pump. We need to zoom out for a second and look at where this assembly line is located. It lies right in the middle of the thylakoid membrane. The tops of all the little machines are on the inside (**lumen**) of the thylakoid, and the bottoms are outside of the thylakoid, in the fluid-filled space of the chloroplast (the **stroma**).

The protons collect in the lumen of the thylakoid. The pumps keep pumping them in. Soon there are so many that they are looking for a way to escape. There is more "personal space" available out in the stroma, so that is where they want to go. This is where the generator comes in.

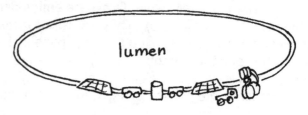

lumen

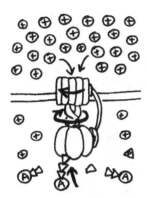

The correct name for the generator is ***ATP synthase***. "Synth" means "to make." This machine doesn't make ATP from scratch, though. It just pops the third phosphate back on. (ATP that is missing the third phosphate is called ADP, with the D being an abbreviation for "di," meaning "two.")

The protons upstairs in the lumen would like to get down where it is not so crowded and the only escape route is through this machine. The protons don't mind going through it, and on the way down their positive charge is used to turn the rotor of the machine. The bottom part of the rotor has spaces that were designed for ADP to be held in place while a phosphate is snapped back on. So all the ADPs in the area are re-charged back into ATPs.

This first part of photosynthesis has as its only goal the recharging of ATPs and the filling of NADPH shuttle buses with high-energy electrons. The next part of the process is the formation of sugar molecules. This process does not need light because it is powered by these little bio-batteries. (But since the batteries need light to be re-charged, even this Light Independent process is still ultimately dependent on light.)

Let's imagine our little NADPH shuttle buses and ATP molecules pulling into the parking lot of a sugar factory. (We were tempted to call it a candy factory, since candy is made from sugar, but then you would have been disappointed when the man who came out to greet you was not Willy Wonka.) The sign above the door says, "Welcome to the Calvin Cycle." The manager comes to the door to greet us and introduces himself as Professor Melvin Calvin. (Okay, he's not as cool as Willy Wonka, but he did receive a Nobel Prize in 1961, so try to be impressed.) When asked if he invented or built

this factory that bears his name, he humbly admits that he simply discovered it. It was already built and in operation when he arrived. He just figured out how it worked. However, his friends were so impressed with his discoveries that they decided to name the factory after him.

Professor Calvin invites us inside to watch the factory in operation. The assembly line is a large circle. Fastened to the conveyor belt are compartments with black balls inside them. We learn that these black balls are carbon atoms. The Professor laughs as he comments how strange it is that sugar is made of carbon atoms—the same kind of carbon atoms that are found in the gasoline we put into our cars. He thinks of this factory as a fuel factory more than a sugar factory.

There is an air hose hanging from the ceiling in one place. The professor explains that the hose brings in a constant supply of air from the outside. The air contains something very necessary for this sugar-making process: carbon dioxide molecules. The compartments right below the air hose contain 5 carbon atoms. We notice that one of the carbons in each 5-carbon chain has a phosphate attached to it. Apparently,

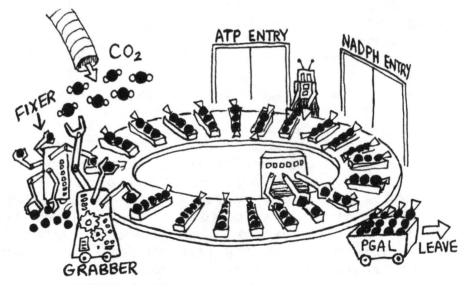

phosphates show up others places, too, not just on ATP. Professor Calvin says that phosphates are very common in the world of biological chemistry.

As we watch, a little robotic machine reaches up and grabs a carbon dioxide molecule. It snips off the two oxygens and then tries to stuff the carbon into a compartment that already has five carbons in it.

"This is what I can't understand," says the Professor. "The compartments can only hold five carbons, but the robot is programmed to try to add a sixth carbon. It never works. As soon as the circle begins to rotate, the six carbons fall out of the compartment! Luckily, the next robot down the line picks them all up and then puts sets of three carbons into compartments. I've thought about fixing that first robot so it doesn't keep trying to overload the compartments, but even without repairs, the assembly line manages to crank out an amazing number of sugar units, so I decided not to mess with it. Since the second robot fixes the first one's mistake, I call this part of the operation 'carbon fixing.'"

The 3-carbon arrangement works out very well, and as we watch the circular conveyor rotate, the carbons stay in groups of three for the rest of the ride. After the carbons leave the "fixer" robot, one carbon in each group of three has a phosphate attached to it. Professor Calvin then warns us that the next two steps won't make a lot of sense to us. At the next station, some ATPs are waiting and ready. They pop off their third phosphate and give it to a 3-carbon group. Now the group has two phosphates—one at each end. At the next station, we see some NADPH trucks ready to unload their passengers of high-energy electrons. Oddly enough, after being given a high-energy electron, the carbon groups then lose the phosphate they just gained! What was the point of receiving a phosphate if you are just going to get rid of it right away? The Professor tells us that there is more to this process than meets the eye. The end result of this cycle is that the 3-carbon groups are energized and ready to become part of a 6-carbon sugar molecule. These ready-to-go, 3-carbon molecules are called PGALs. (You can say "pea-gals" if you want to. That makes it easier to remember, too.)

This is the end of the cycle, but we notice that some of these 3-carbon groups stay on the belt, ready to go around the loop again. We are confused.

"It's simple math," says the Professor. "This process always begins with 5-carbon groups. The lowest number of 3-carbon groups that can be turned into 5-carbon groups without any left over is five groups. $5 \times 3 = 3 \times 5$. Five of these PGALs must be recycled around again, to form three more 5-carbon units. One out of every six PGALs is taken off the conveyor belt. Seems very inefficient to me, but I've decided not to tamper with the system."

⇐ 5 out of 6 PGALs will go around again.

We ask if the factory runs 24 hours a day or whether it shuts down at night.

"We can only operate if we have an adequate supply of ATPs and NADPH electrons. They come from the solar farm down the street. On sunny days there's plenty of energy. At night the solar farm can't operate. After the sun goes down, we eventually run out of ATPs and NADPH electrons and have to shut down. We do have some emergency back-up systems, though. If it gets really hot and dry and our plant has to close its air vents (to prevent water loss) we can store some of the incoming carbon dioxide by mixing it with chemical preservatives. But we'd much rather have a steady supply of carbon dioxide coming in through our air hose."

We have one last question for the Professor. We wonder what happens to those PGALs that leave the conveyor belt.

"Those are like half-sugars. This factory doesn't have to worry about final assembly. The PGALs get dumped out into the stroma where floating robots pick them up. The robots are programmed to take two PGALs and put them together to form a 6-carbon molecule called **glucose**. Glucose is a type of sugar. I guess calling this a sugar factory is a tiny bit inaccurate, since we don't do the final assembly. But all the hard work gets done here. The final assembly is such a 'snap' that this hard-working factory gets credit for the sugar-building process."

GLUCCOSE: $C_6H_{12}O_6$

We thank the professor for the tour. What a strange but fascinating place! As we are leaving, he adds one last comment.

"I forgot to warn you—not everyone calls our products PGALs. If you hear someone talking about G3Ps, don't get confused. They're talking about PGALs."

We promise to remember his warning and not get upset about molecules having more than one name. We know someone who gets called "Robert" by his parents, "Bob" by his classmates, and "Blinky" by his best friend. (We're too polite to ask the best friend where the nickname "Blinky" came from.)

ONE FINAL NOTE: We have greatly simplified the Calvin Cycle. We've focused on just the carbon atoms, since they form the "backbone" of the glucose molecule. Glucose also has oxygen and hydrogen atoms attached to it. In the picture above, the darkest atoms are the carbons, the tiny ones are the hydrogens and the medium gray ones are the oxygens. The carbons almost form a ring, but not quite. One oxygen completes the ring, with one carbon stuck off to the side.

ACTIVITY 1: WATCH ANIMATIONS OF ATP SYNTHASE

Go to YouTube.com/TheBasementWorkshop and click on the Botany playlist. You will find some awesome computer animations showing the ATP synthase machine in action. There are also a few other photosynthesis-related videos. (Watch any other videos listed for this chapter that you have not already watched.)

ACTIVITY 2: MATCHING

Match the cell part on the left with its function on the right.

1) nucleus ___
2) endoplasmic reticulum ___
3) Golgi bodies ___
4) leucoplasts ___
5) chloroplasts ___
6) vacuole ___
7) mitochondria ___
8) ribosomes ___
9) cytoplasm ___
10) cytoskeleton ___

A) makes energy
B) does packaging and shipping
C) jelly-like fluid
D) an empty area
E) network of fibers
F) stores starches and fats
G) uses light, water and CO_2 to make sugar
H) assembles proteins
I) assembles, transports, gives shape
J) contains DNA instructions

ACTIVITY 3: MORE MATCHING

Can you match the cell part with the factory part or factory worker that it is most similar to?

1) nucleus ___
2) Golgi bodies ___
3) vacuole ___
4) mitochondria ___
5) ribosomes ___
6) leucoplasts ___
7) endoplasmic reticulum ___
8) cytoskeleton ___

A) workers on the assembly line
B) foreman (boss)
C) empty courtyard in middle of factory
D) storage tanks
E) sidewalks, roads
F) shipping department
G) generator supplying electricity
H) assembly line

ACTIVITY 4: ANSWER THESE QUESTIONS

1) In your own words, what does the chlorophyll molecule do? _____
_____

2) What two molecules provide energy for the Calvin Cycle? _____

3) What biological "machine" puts the third phosphate back onto ADP? _____

4) What cellular process is the "opposite" of photosynthesis? _____

5) What type of energy is used to excite the electron in the center of the chlorophyll? _____

6) We know that plants need CO_2. In what phase of photosynthesis is it used? _____

7) Carbon fixation is when a plant takes _____ molecules from the air and uses the
_____ atoms to make sugar molecules.

8) After ATP has its third phosphate popped off, it is no longer called ATP. It is now called _____.

9) Where does final assembly of glucose occur? (the formation of a 6-carbon sugar from two 3-carbon PGALs) _____

10) Out of every 6 PGALs made, how many have to ride around again? ____

11) What scientist received a Nobel Prize for his research on photosynthesis? _____

12) How many carbons are in a glucose molecule? _____

13) Where is the Light Dependent Phase assembly line located?
    a) stroma of chloroplasts   b) thylakoid lumen   c) thylakoid membrane   d) cytoplasm of cell

14) Where does the Calvin Cycle occur?
    a) the stroma of the chloroplasts   b) the lumen of the thylakoids   c) the thylakoid membrane

15) What type of particle goes down through the ATP synthase "generator" machine? _____

LESSON 2: PLANT CLASSIFICATION

LEVEL ONE

Day 1

Now you have it firmly in your mind that a plant is an organism that uses the process of photosynthesis. However, there's one more little technicality about qualifying as a plant. You have to have more than one cell. That may sound obvious, but did you know that there are lots of one-celled organisms that use photosynthesis? For example, some kinds of bacteria use photosynthesis. There are also some types of one-celled protozoa that use photosynthesis, such as the euglena and the volvox. So to be a plant, you can't be a bacteria or a protozoa. You must be made of many cells.

The plant "kingdom" is huge. There are millions of different types of plants. Scientists who study plants (**botanists**) like to sort them into categories (classify them). Without a way to put plants into categories, botanists would feel like their field of science was incredibly disorganized. They'd feel the way you'd feel if you woke up one morning to discover that someone had gathered up all the items in your house, then randomly distributed them into storage areas. If you opened a dresser drawer you'd find a random assortment of objects—a flashlight, a spoon, a marble, a couple of toys, a pencil, a book, a battery, a plate, a toothbrush and maybe a sock. Open a closet and you'd find a tennis racket, a stack of books, a pair of jeans, a radio, a flower pot, a guitar, a toy car, a stuffed animal... you get the idea. Now if you wanted to get dressed and needed a shirt and a pair of pants, where would you look for them? How long would it take to find a particular toy or book? Way too long! That's why we organize our houses, putting all the similar objects together. If you want a frying pan, you know to go to the kitchen. If you want to play tennis, you know your racket will be in the garage with the sports gear. Botanists feel the same way about organizing plants into categories. (Okay, so they're science geeks.) Here is the way botanists organize the plant kingdom.

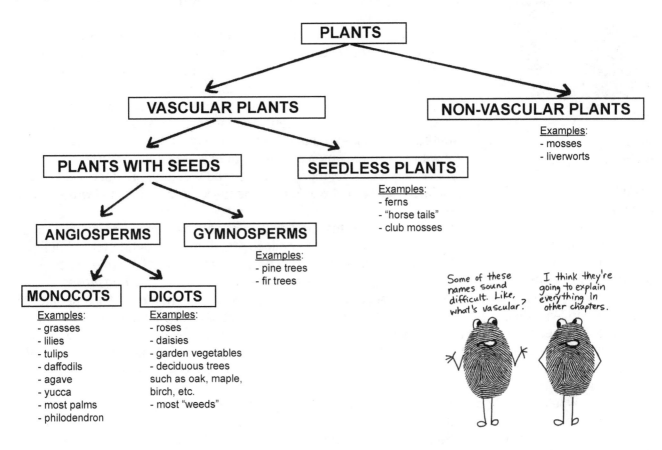

You can look back at this chart whenever you get confused by terms like "vascular" or "gymnosperm."

One of the first scientists to tackle the problem of classification was a man named Carl Linnaeus. Carl grew up in Sweden in the early 1700s and had loved plants since he was a small child. When he was learning to talk he wanted to know all the names of the plants in his father's garden. Carl's father loved plants, too. In fact, he changed the family's last name from Ingermarrson, which means "farmer's son," to Linnaeus, in honor of a large linden tree which grew near their house. When Carl was seventeen, he left home to begin his university studies. Back in those days, university students often had people called "patrons" who gave them money while they were in school. Carl was very good at getting patrons who were interested in supporting his studies. Unfortunately, however, as soon as he found a better patron he dropped the previous one. He made many friends and many enemies this way. Both the friends and the enemies will come back into the story later on.

Even with patrons, Carl never had a lot of money and was always worrying about how to make ends meet. His fretting about money came out in a humorous way one day when he said this: "My hair stands on end and lice bite at its roots when I look at the prices in this catalog!"

Carl was a very good scientist, though. He made many discoveries about the life cycles of plants, especially the importance of flowers. Until then, no one knew that flowers have male and female parts. Even before he had graduated from the university, Carl was being asked to give lectures on plants. Before he was 30 years old, he had published several books on plants.

The title page from a 1760 edition of Carl's book *Systema Naturae*.

Back in Carl's time, botanists and naturalists were expected to go on long journeys to collect specimens for their studies. Carl went to Lapland (Finland) and hated every bit of the trip. He complained about bad weather, bad food, bad travel conditions and (worst of all)... bugs! He hated bugs. During this trip someone told Carl about a very interesting place in Lapland that he really should see. Carl agreed it would be a fantastic addition to his itinerary (list of places he went). The only problem was that this area was 300 miles inland, which meant several more weeks of bad weather, bad food, bad travel conditions, and bugs. So Carl just imagined what it would have been like to go there and wrote about it in his journal, faking the details!

At some point in his studies, Carl realized that botanists needed a system of naming plants, a system that would be recognized all over the world. Carl noticed that some plants had very simple, common names like "white oak," and other plants were known by complicated Latin names such as (just try to say this in one breath) *physakis amno ramosissime ramis angulosis glabris foliss dentoserratis*. Carl suggested that each plant should have a two-word Latin name, just like people have first and last names. Latin was best for this because it was already used by scientists all over the world, and because it was a "dead" language (no one actually spoke it as their real language) so it wouldn't change over time. This method of naming plants (and animals) would be called **binomial nomenclature**, which is a fancy way of saying "the two-name naming system" (bi=two, nom=name, nomen=name, clature=call).

Carl would think up a name for a group of plants (what we now call the **genus**), then make up a name for each specific member of that group (what we now call **species**). For example, the group of trees we know as oaks have the genus name *Quercus (kwer-kus)*. The white oak is *Quercus alba*, the gray oak is *Quercus grisea,* and the leather oak is *Quercus durata*. The group of plants we call

18

the honeysuckles are the *Lonicera (lon-i-sare-uh)*. The yellow honeysuckle is the *Lonicera implexa* and the sweet honeysuckle is the *Lonicera japonica*. (Notice that the names are written in italics and only the genus is capitalized.)

Now those friends and enemies come back into the story. Carl had to come up with a lot of new plant names, and often he would use the names of people he knew. Someone once said that you could make a list of Carl's friends and enemies by looking at a list of plants he had named. Plants that were attractive or useful bore the names of people Carl admired. Plants that were prickly or ugly were used as a way to get just a tiny bit of revenge on folks he hadn't gotten along with. For instance, Carl named a species of unpleasant weeds *Siegesbeckia,* after Johann Siegesbeck, the director of a Russian botanical garden who had given Carl a hard time about his books—he thought Carl had talked too much about the "love life" of flowers. The "black-eyed Susan" (a flower with a dark center and yellow petals) was named after a real person named Susan, a woman Carl admired. The sheep laurel, with its beautiful bunches of red or purple flowers, was named *Kalmia augustifolia*, after Peter Kalm, one of Carl's botanical students. The *Lonicera* (honeysuckle) was named after Adam Lonicer, a German doctor of the 1500s who studied plants and used herbal medicines.

Eventually, Carl's naming system was adopted by all scientists everywhere in the world. It became more and more complex as more people started adding their ideas to it. Today, there are seven basic levels in the naming system: ***kingdom, phylum, class, order, family, genus, species***. However, often extra subdivisions and sub-categories are added. And, as we warned you, not all scientists use the same divisions. For example, here are two ways to list the full classification of the white oak. You could use either one and be correct:

Kingdom: Plants (or "Plantae")
Division: Angiosperms
Sub-division: Dicots
Sub-division: Rosids
Order: Fagales
Family: Fagaceae
Genus: *Quercus*
Species: *alba*

Kingdom: Plants
Subkingdom: Tracheobionta (vascular plants)
Superdivision: Spermatophyta (seed plants)
Division: Magnoliophyta (flowering plants)
Class: Magnoliopsida (dicots)
Order: Fagales
Family: Fagaceae
Genus: *Quercus*
Species: *alba*

Can it get any more confusing?!

Yep! Another name for classification is "**taxonomy**."

As if these difficult words weren't enough, other reference sites add the categories "Euphyllophyta" and "Fabids" to these lists! As we said, there isn't a single "correct" way to classify plants. You'll get a slightly different list from each book or website you consult. However, it is still a good idea to know the basic seven categories: kingdom, phylum, class, order, family, genus, species. These words come up often in many branches of science and it's good to be familiar with them.

ACTIVITY 1: LEARN THE CLASSIFICATION SONG

The sound track for this song can be accessed by going to **www.ellenjmchenry.com** and then clicking on the MUSIC tab.

Kingdom, phylum, *(clap, clap),* **class, order,** *(clap, clap),* **family,** *(clap, clap),* **genus, species,** *(clap, clap).*
Kingdom, phylum, *(clap, clap),* **class, order,** *(clap, clap),* **family,** *(clap, clap),* **genus, species,** *(clap, clap).*
Kingdom, phylum, class, order, family, genus, species!
Kingdom, phylum, class, order, family, genus, species!
REPEAT

ACTIVITY 2: PLANTS NAMED AFTER PEOPLE

Some plants were named after people—either the scientist who discovered the plant, or a friend or family member of the scientist. See if you can guess the last name of the person for whom these oak were named. (We'll only do a few of these because they're pretty much no-brainers!)

1) *Quercus muehlenbergii* _____
2) *Quercus engelmannii* _____
3) *Quercus michauxii* _____
4) *Quercus kelloggii* _____

ACTIVITY 3: USE YOUR "WORD DETECTIVE" SKILLS

See if you can match the scientific names with the common names. All you need to do is use "word detective" skills. Think of words you know that look or sound like the scientific names. Start with the matches that are easiest.

1) *Daucus carota* _____
2) *Solanum tuberosum* _____
3) *Pinus cembra* _____
4) *Acer saccharum* _____
5) *Juglans nigra* _____
6) *Citrus sinensis* _____
7) *Sophara japonica* _____
8) *Primula vulgaris* _____
9) *Papaver orientale* _____
10) *Paulownia imperialis* _____

A) Oriental poppy
B) Cembrian pine
C) Carrot
D) Empress tree
E) Primrose
F) Orange
G) Potato
H) Sugar maple
I) Black walnut
J) Pagoda tree

ACTIVITY 4: HAVE SOME FUN WITH SCIENTIFIC LATIN

What? Fun with Latin?! Sure, why not?
Use some made-up Latin words to classify yourself. Use this guide:

Kingdom: country
Phylum: state
Class: county
Order: city/town

Family: neighborhood or street
Genus: last name
Species: first name

Use some classic Latin endings such as -us -um -ae -ica -ii -ius
Example: *Americanus Pennsylvanicus Alleghenus Pittsburghae Avalonica Smithus Jamesii*
(We know him as Jim Smith from Pittsburgh, PA.)

Your (silly) Latin scientific name: _____

_____

Now make up one for someone else: _____

_____

LEVEL TWO

You won't catch me crying over anything botanical!

Me neither.

Not everyone immediately adopted Linnaeus' new naming system. Some botanists resisted change, even if it was for the better. That's just how some people are. A botanist named Johann Dillenius accused Linnaeus of "throwing all botany into confusion." However, when Dillenius went to see Linnaeus and let Linnaeus explain the advantages of this new system, Dillenius realized how ingenious this system was. In fact, he got so emotional over it that he almost cried (or so the story goes). One by one, botanists came to see how superior this new system was and eventually they all began using it.

The work of Carl Linnaeus was only the beginning. Since Carl's time, many organized minds have added to the classification system. As far as we know, all *known* plants and animals on Earth have been named and classified. (However, there are some disagreements among scientists about certain species or sub-species because they don't fit perfectly into this system.) As soon as any new plant or animal is discovered, it is compared to all similar organisms so it can be put into a kingdom, phylum, class, order, family and genus. Then the discoverer gets to choose a species name for it. All these words must be in Latin and must have correct endings, such as "ius," "ium," "ae," or "ii." (The ending "ii" means "of." So *jamesii* would mean "of James.")

Kingdom is the most general category. There are basically five kingdoms: plants, animals, fungi, monerans (bacteria), and protists (single-celled protozoa). Sometimes scientists like to get all fancy with the names of the kingdoms and use Latin endings, making the animal kingdom *Animalia* and the plant kingdom *Plantae*. Within each kingdom are large groups called **phyla** (one phylum, two phyla). Now just to make everyone's life difficult, botanists decided that they'd rather called the phyla **divisions**. So don't be confused when you see the word "division." Just think "phyla." (That way the classification song will still make sense for the plant kingdom.)

The major plant divisions include **bryophytes** (mosses and some algae), **pteridophytes** (ferns) (and that initial "p" is silent), **coniferophytes** (conifers), and **anthophytes** (flowering plants). Now, you may want to know why we showed you that chart on page 17 if it doesn't match up with these divisions. Well... that chart is still valid because science books still use those categories when talking about the plant kingdom. The world of science terminology is sometimes confusing because it has evolved over hundreds of years. And to make things worse, scientists sometimes disagree about terminology or categories. The chart on page 17 is still very helpful, even though it doesn't give Latin names of divisions. It gives you a good overall sense of how botanists think about the plant kingdom.

The classes, orders, and families of plants are the least well-known terms among non-botanists. (You can always look them up on the Internet.) You can probably guess that certain types of plants are grouped together, such as grasses, cacti, squashes, or garden flowers. Hobby gardeners probably know more genus and species names (such as *Quercus alba* for the white oak) than they do classes, orders or families.

Every scientific name, no matter how boring it sounds, has a story behind how it got its name. Some of these stories are short and not too interesting. Others have quite a bit of history behind them. Here are some of the more interesting stories:

The weeping willow is *Salix babylonica*. All willows are *Salix*, but the weeping willow is *babylonica* as a reference to Psalm 137 in the Bible, where it says, "By the waters of Babylon we sat down and wept. We hung our harps on the willow trees there." The Israelites were taken captive by the Babylonians in 582 B.C. and forced to live out the rest of their lives in Babylon, far from their homeland.

The *Phlox drummondii* was named after Thomas Drummond, a Scottish botanist who came to America in 1831 to study and collect plants. Poor Thomas had a really bad time in America. He tried to survive a northwest winter alone in the wilderness and almost didn't make it. He was attacked by grizzly bears and then almost starved to death, spending weeks chewing on nothing but an old deerskin. Later, he survived a cholera epidemic, lost the use of his arms for two months, and had boils (sores) all over his body that were so severe he couldn't lie down. He went south to Texas and almost starved to death again while stranded on Galveston Island. He finally died during a voyage to Cuba. Whenever he found a new plant, he would send specimens back home to botanists he knew in Britain. The last plant Thomas sent over before he died was a species of white phlox, and his friends decided it should be named in his honor. (The world "phlox" is Greek for "flame," named for its fiery red color.)

The nasturtium (*na-stur-shum*) comes from the Latin word "nasus" meaning "nose," and "tortus" meaning "twisted." When you smell a nasturtium you wrinkle (twist) your nose because of the strong smell. The scientific name for nasturtium is *Tropaeolum*, from the Greek word "tropaion" meaning "trophy." The leaves of the nasturtium reminded Linnaeus of Greek shields. In ancient Greece, the soldiers would hang the shields and helmets of the defeated enemies on tree trunks. When Linnaeus saw a nasturtium vine growing up the side of a tree, the leaves and flowers reminded him of ancient Greek shields and helmets hung on trees.

The marigold comes from the phrase "Mary's gold" and was the official flower of the Virgin Mary in medieval times. Church altars were decorated with marigolds almost year-round. Now for the ironic twist--we go from the heavenly to the earthly. The scientific name for the marigold is *Tagetes patula*, and Linnaeus is to blame for this one. Tages was the grandson of the Roman god, Jupiter. Tages was a god of the underworld who came up out of the dirt in a field one day and taught humans the fine art of fortune-telling by examining the intestines of animals. No kidding. The Romans and Greeks would kill an animal and look at its guts before making major decisions. Was this Linneaus' idea of a joke? Or maybe he thought marigolds smelled as bad as animal intestines? No one knows. (*Patula* just means "spreading." Marigolds do spread out quickly and grow to be quite large.)

The scientific name for the butterfly bush is *Buddleia davidii*, named after Rev. Adam Buddle of Essex, England, and Père (Father) Armand David, a French Jesuit missionary to China. Rev. Buddle was just a nice amateur botanist whom Linneaus apparently liked (and who was an expert on mosses, not bushes), but Père David was another one of those crazy, adventuresome botanists who braved countless hardships in order to collect plants. David recorded in his diary that "although it was inconvenient," he was so afraid of the local wolves that he kept his donkey with him in his tent at night. He also said it took great courage to eat the local food. David was lucky, however, and lived long enough to return to France. Some of his Jesuit friends were not so lucky—they were tortured and killed by the natives. Père David managed to send thousands of Chinese plants back to Europe, many of which are common sights now in both Europe and North America.

This spectacular water lily is *Victoria amazonica*, although the name has been changed several times. When it was first brought to England from the Amazon, a flower was presented to Queen Victoria and she was told the flower would be named *Victoria regina* ("Victoria the queen") in her honor. But, oops—a bit later they found out that someone had already discovered it and named it ten years earlier. Now what do you tell the queen? Then they did even more research and discovered that the two plants were not identical, so they could still keep the name of the queen, but by then they thought they really should make some reference to the place the flower came from—the Amazon. However, at that time anything associated with the Amazon was considered to be uncivilized, so putting the queen's name next to the word "amazon" would have been unseemly. So the solution they came up with was to go ahead and change the name of the plant to *Victoria amazonica* but just keep the true name a secret until after the queen died.

The sunflower's botanical name is *Helianthus*, from the Greek words "helios," meaning "sun," and "anthos" meaning "flower." There's a reason for this name: these flowers turn so that they are always facing the sun! The Greek myth associated with this plant is that of Clytie, the mortal who was in love with the Titan god Helios, who had been raised to the sky and turned into the sun. Helios never even noticed poor Clytie. (But don't feel too bad for her; when she found out that Helios loved her sister, she buried her sister alive!) The sunflower is native to America, not Europe, so the ancient Greeks never saw this plant. How this myth became attached to this flower is a mystery.

ACTIVITY 1: MATCH THE PLANT NAME WITH ITS ORIGIN ✓

1) Clematis H

2) Impatiens ____

3) Chrysanthemum I

4) Foxglove A

5) Geranium C

6) Daisy F

7) Candytuft I

8) Gladiolus B

9) Columbine G

10) Forsythia E

A) The seeds of this plant pop out as if they are in a hurry.

B) The leaves of this plant look like a Roman gladiator's sword.

C) The name of this flower comes from the Greek word "geranos," meaning "crane" (the bird) because its seed pod looks like the beak of a crane.

D) This plant produces long, thin flowers that resemble fingers.

E) Named after William Forsyth, a rascal of a botanist who sold the British government a secret plant medicine which turned out to be nothing but cow dung, lime, sand, soapsuds and urine.

F) Centuries ago, this plant was said to be the "day's eye" because its flowers opened in the morning and closed at night.

G) If held upside down, this flower looks a bit like a ring of doves. The Latin word for dove is "columba."

H) This name is from the Greek word "klema" meaning "twig."

I) This name comes from two Greek words: "chrysos" meaning "gold," and "anthos" meaning "flower."

J) This name comes from the place of the plant's origin: Candia (the island of Crete)

23

ACTIVITY 2: WATCH A VERY NICE BUT VERY SHORT BIOGRAPHY OF LINNAEUS ✓

There's a very nice 4-minute summary of the life and work of Linnaeus posted on the Botany playlist at www.YouTube.com/TheBasementWorkshop.

ACTIVITY 3: PLANTS WITH PLACE NAMES ✓

Some plants are named after places where they grow, or the place where they were first discovered. See if you can identify the place name in each of these plant names.

1) A flower named *Callistephus chinensis*: _____China_____
2) A flower named *Arum italicum*: _____
3) A wildflower named *Tradescantia virginiana*: _____
4) A tree named *Azadirachta indica*: _____
5) A decorative flowering plant named *Dianella tasmanica*: _____
6) A grass named *Raddia brasiliensis*: _____

ACTIVITY 4: "ALL IN THE FAMILY" ✓

Have you ever heard someone talk about plants or animals being "related" to each other? You might have heard something like, "Spiders are related to crabs." What does this mean?

The more classification categories two organisms share, the more they are considered to be "related." For example, look at the classification (taxonomy) of these three plants. Their taxonomy is listed starting with the kingdom and going all the way down to genus and species.

POTATO: Plants, Angiosperms, Dicots, Asterids, Solanes, Solanaceae, *Solanum, tuberosum*
TOMATO: Plants, Angiosperms, Dicots, Asterids, Solanes, Solanaceae, *Solanum, lycopersicum*
SWEET POTATO: Plants, Angiosperms, Dicots, Asterids, Solanes, Convolvulaceae, *Ipomoea, batatas*

Which is more related to a potato—a tomato or a sweet potato? If you look at a potato and a sweet potato they seem very related. But if you look at their classification (taxonomy) you will see that the lists for the potato and the tomato are almost identical except for the species. The sweet potato list is different right after "Solanes." The sweet potato isn't even in the same family with the potato, but the tomato is!

Here are some members of the (very large) Prunus family:

CHERRY: Plants, Angiosperms, Dicots, Rosids, Rosales, Rosaceae, *Prunus, serotina*
PLUM: Plants, Angiosperms, Dicots, Rosids, Rosales, Rosaceae, *Prunus, domestica*
PEACH: Plants, Angiosperms, Dicots, Rosids, Rosales, Rosaceae, *Prunus, persica*
APRICOT: Plants, Angiosperms, Dicots, Rosids, Rosales, Rosaceae, *Prunus, armeniaca*

The members of this family all share a common trait when it comes to forming seeds. Can you think of what it might be? (Hint: Compare their seeds with those of apples, pears or bananas.)

If you have Internet access, try to find the answers to these questions. (Wikipedia is very helpful.)

1) Which is more "related" to a zucchini--an acorn squash or a cucumber? _____
2) Which is more "related" to a carrot--a tomato or a yam? _____
3) Which is more "related" to an oak tree--a maple tree or a chestnut tree? _____

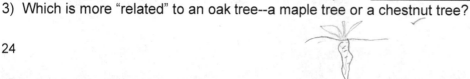

LESSON 3: NON-VASCULAR PLANTS

LEVEL ONE

Now let's tackle one of those categories on page 17: the ***non-vascular*** plants. These plants *don't* have whatever "vascular" is. The word vascular comes from the Latin word "vascularis," meaning a vessel or duct that has some kind of fluid flowing through it. So vascular plants have vessels running through them and non-vascular plants don't.

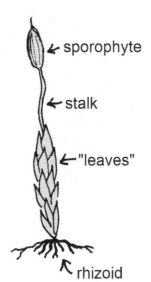

Non-vascular plants are basically ***mosses*** and make up the division called ***bryophytes*** *(bry-o-fites)*. The word bryophyte comes from two Greek words: "bryon," meaning "moss," and "phyton" meaning "plant." (A related type of plant, the **liverwort**, is usually put into this category also. If you want to know more about liverworts, read level 2.) This lesson is on moss, that soft green stuff you find growing around the roots of trees or between bricks on your shady patio. Mosses are a bit strange and deserve their own category because they don't have seeds and they don't have proper roots or stems or leaves. (But they are still plants because they use photosynthesis.) If we want to talk about the parts of a moss plant, we can't really talk about their leaves because technically they don't have leaves. But they do have green things that look like leaves and these green things do carry on photosynthesis, so we'll just use the word "leaves" but with quote marks around it, indicating that we all know that mosses don't *really* have leaves. For roots, we'll say "rhizoids." The rhizoids' job is to anchor the moss to the ground. They don't take up water like the roots of vascular plants do. (We'll talk about that sporophyte on the next page. Sorry to leave you in suspense for a few minutes...)

A vascular system is a system of "pipes" that allows plants to pump water to all parts of the plant, no matter how tall or wide the plant grows. Non-vascular plants don't have this system. The only way the parts of a non-vascular plant can get water is to absorb it right into their cells when it rains or when dew falls. For this reason, non-vascular plants must stay very small and must be in places where it stays damp. Where have you seen mosses growing? If they are in your lawn, they certainly aren't out where the sun shines a lot. They'll be in shady spots such as around the bases of large trees Some mosses can tolerate a bit of sun, but very few can survive all-day sun.

Cells that are not on the outside surface get their water by a process called ***osmosis***. This is a strange-sounding name for a simple idea. Osmosis is when a lot of something moves to a place where there is less of it. In a crowded building this might mean people moving from crowded rooms to empty rooms. Once all the rooms are equally filled, people will stop moving. In plants, osmosis means water molecules moving from cells that have lots of water to cells that have less water.

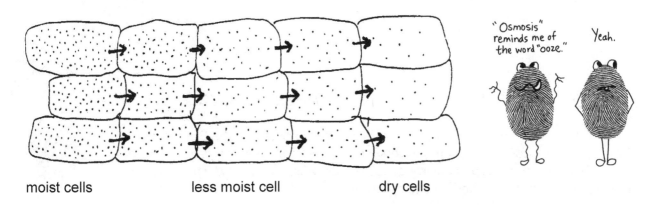

moist cells   less moist cell   dry cells

Mosses have a very strange life cycle. Like many forms of life, they produce male and female cells. However, they also produce spores like mushrooms do. They alternate back and forth between producing spores and producing male and female cells. This cycle is called **alternation of generations**.

The moss plant (technically called the **gametophyte** [gah-MEE-toe-fite] stage) grows a stalk out the top, and at the top of that stalk a **sporophyte** appears. The sporophyte produces—spores, of course. The sporophyte bursts open and all the spores float down and land somewhere in the nearby vicinity. It's best for the moss if they land just a little bit away, but not too much. If they land too close, the bed of moss won't grow larger, but if they land too far away, it might be out in an area that isn't suitable for moss to grow (too sunny, for example). When the spores land, they grow into a green mat-like thing that then starts to produce little male and female parts. The male parts produce sperm and the female parts produce eggs, just like in animals. Then the egg and sperm must join together to form a **zygote**. (The word "zygote" comes from the Greek word "zygotos," meaning "joined together.")

The egg can't move at all. It just sits there and waits for the sperm. The sperm can swim a very short distance, but they need water to swim in. When it rains, the sperm get picked up by the water droplets and splashed around, hopefully landing near enough to the eggs that they are only a short swim away. The sperm then swim down the venters and join with the eggs, creating a zygote that will be able to grow into a new moss plant. Then that new moss plant grows a sporophyte that produces spores. Then the spores grow into a plant that produces male and female cells, which form a zygote which grows into a moss plant, which produces a sporophyte...

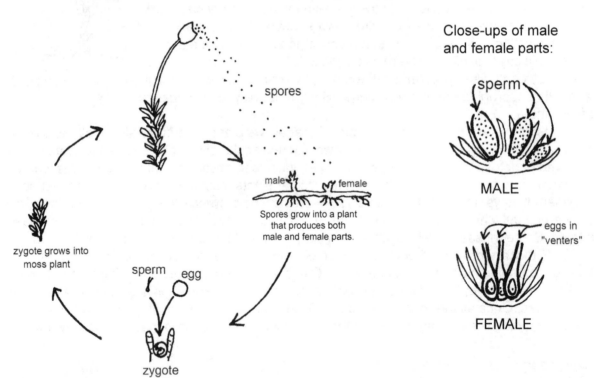

Close-ups of male and female parts:

sperm

MALE

eggs in "venters"

FEMALE

spores

male   female

Spores grow into a plant
that produces both
male and female parts.

zygote grows into
moss plant

sperm   egg

zygote

Sorry for this chapter being a bit boring— but at least it's short!

<u>ACTIVITY</u>: WATCH AN ANIMATION OF THE MOSS LIFE CYCLE

An animation of the information on this page is posted on the Botany playlist at www.YouTube.com/TheBasementWorkshop. There will be some new words we haven't learned here, but don't worry about it—just enjoy the show. The pictures are very helpful in understanding this cycle.

"Mosses" by Ernst Haeckel, 1904

"Liverworts" by Ernst Haeckel, 1904

LEVEL TWO

Another main type of bryophyte is the *liverwort*. The ending "-wort" comes from medieval times in Europe when it meant "healing herb." (You'll see the word "wort" in many plant names.) It was once thought that the liverwort was a healing herb that could help your liver. Perhaps medieval people saw some resemblance between the shape of the liverwort and the shape of a liver. Or maybe not. No one knows.

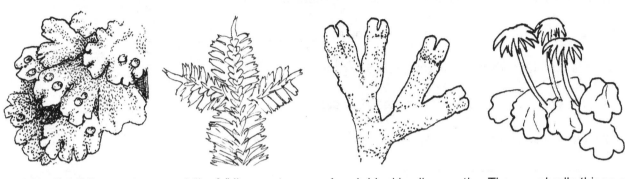

A "thallose" liverwort with gemma cups　　A "leafy" liverwort　　A weird-looking liverwort!　　These umbrella things are male and female parts

Liverworts are found all over the world, even at the edges of deserts and arctic tundras, but they can't survive in the heart of the deserts and tundras because there isn't enough water. Like mosses, liverworts have non-vascular systems that depend on osmosis. They need to be close to the ground and be kept moist as much as possible. The liverworts that live in extreme climates must have special adaptations that allow them to be able to survive. (You'll learn about adaptations in lesson 7.) These adaptations (perhaps extra-skinny "leaves" that keep moisture in, or sporophytes that can survive drought) are not present in most mosses.

Like the mosses, the liverworts have *alternation of generations*. (It's similar enough to mosses that it's not worth drawing another diagram.) They produce sporophytes that then produce a *protonema* that looks like either a mass of stringy green fibers, or they make a tiny, flat green thing called a *thallus*. (The word thallus comes from the Greek word "thallos" meaning "young shoot or twig.") The thallus produces male and female parts that produce sperm and eggs that join together whenever there is enough rain to allow the sperm to swim. You can see in the drawing above (on the far right) that in some liverworts the male and female parts look like fancy umbrellas.

Liverworts also have a way of reproducing without the male and female cells. They can form a type of bud called a *gemma* (the "g" is soft, like in the word "gem"). A gemma can be a single cell or a group of cells that break off from the main plant and are then capable of growing into a whole new plant. These gemma are often found in gemma cups, little cup-like things on the tops of the liverwort "leaves." You can see some gemma cups in the first drawing above (on the left). The little gemma cells sit in the cups and wait for it to rain. Then the raindrops splash the gemma out onto other surfaces, away from the "parent" plant, where the gemma can grow into an "adult" plant.

ACTIVITY 1: WATCH SOME SHORT VIDEOS OF LIVERWORTS (WOW—HOW EXCITING!)

There are some spectacular videos of liverworts and gemma cups on the Botany playlist at www.YouTube.com/TheBasementWorkshop.

ACTIVITY 2: REVIEW SOME OF THE WORDS WE JUST LEARNED

Answer these 10 questions. Then go down below to the STUPID PLANT JOKE and write the letters that correspond to each number. (Hey, it's better than having quiz or test, so don't complain!)

1) When a sperm fertilizes an egg, the result is a ___ ___ ___ ___ ___ ___
                  25   21 8

2) The process by which the cells in a moss plant receive water: ___ ___ ___ ___ ___ ___ ___
                        3   11

3) The part at the top of the stalk on a moss plant: ___ ___ ___ ___ ___ ___ ___ ___
           4   9   28   31

4) Mosses and liverworts are members of this group: ___ ___ ___ ___ ___ ___ ___ ___ ___
        23   27   30

5) This flat, green thing produces male and female parts: ___ ___ ___ ___ ___ ___
            5   17

6) A regular moss plant, the type we are used to seeing, is technically called this stage:

___ ___ ___ ___ ___ ___ ___ ___ ___
  18   29   19

7) This type of cell is NOT a reproductive cell, but nevertheless it can split off from a liverwort and

grow into a new liverwort: ___ ___ ___ ___ ___
       16   1

8) The medieval word for "healing herb" is ___ ___ ___ ___
        10   24

9) Mosses and liverworts do NOT have this system: ___ ___ ___ ___ ___ ___ ___
      7   22 15

10) The life cycle of mosses and liverworts is called ___ ___ ___ ___ ___ ___ ___
          13   12   2

___ ___ ___ ___ ___ ___ ___ ___ ___
26   14   6   20

A STUPID PLANT JOKE

What do you call it when a ___ ___ ___ ___ and a ___ ___ ___ ___ ___ ___ ___ ___ ___ have an
                        1 2 3 4   5 6 7 8 9 10 11 12 13

___ ___ ___ ___ ___ ___ ___ ___ ? ___ ___ ___ ___ ___ - ___ ___ ___ ___ ___ !
14 15 16 17 18 19 20 21   22   23 24 25 26   27 28 29 30 31

ACTIVITY 3: WATCH A 30-MINUTE DOCUMENTARY ON BRYOPHYTE SCIENTISTS

Some scientists spend their whole life studying mosses and liverworts. Meet some Belgian botanists who have cataloged hundreds of species of European bryophytes and listen to them explain why it is so important both to study them and to conserve (protect) them. The video is posted on the Botany playlist.

NOTE: Half of the film is in French, but there are subtitles written in English.

LESSON 4: THE VASCULAR SYSTEM

LEVEL ONE

Without water, most plants die fairly quickly. A plant must have a way to absorb water and distribute it to all its cells. Osmosis works very well for mosses and liverworts because they are small and live in areas with plenty of moisture. The cells in the center of a moss plant are still close enough to water to be able to absorb it by osmosis. Water flows right in and among all the cells.

This system doesn't work so well for vascular plants. Most vascular plants are much larger than mosses. Osmosis may work well enough for tiny plants, but not for larger ones. Also, the outside layer of cells in most vascular plants is covered with a waxy substance that protects the cells from drying out. This protection is necessary, but it does rule out relying on osmosis as the primary way to get water to the cells. (Compare regular paper to waxed paper. If you put a drop of water on regular paper, it soaks in. If you put a drop of water on waxed paper, the droplet will sit there, unable to penetrate the paper. Non-vascular plants are like the regular paper and vascular plants are like the waxed paper.) So vascular plants need a way to deliver water to all their cells.

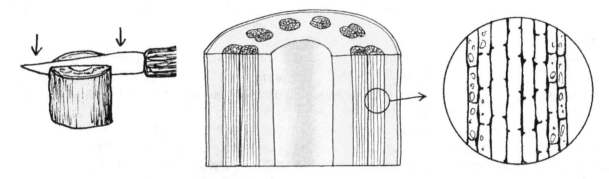

If we cut the stem of a vascular plant and look at it under magnification, we will see bundles of vessels—little "pipes" running the length of the stem. (If you've ever eaten celery, you've met these little bundles; they may have gotten stuck between your teeth or on the back of your throat.)

There are two kinds of bundles: *xylem* (*ZI-lem*) and *phloem* (*FLO-em*). The xylem tubes carry water (in which minerals are dissolved) from the roots up to the leaves. Phloem tubes carry sugary water up or down, depending on the plant's current needs.

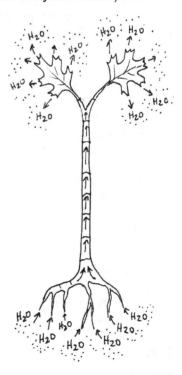

In animals, fluids are circulated around the body by the heart, or by other muscles. Plants don't have muscles. How, then, can an oak tree move water from its roots all the way up to the highest leaves? It uses a process called *transpiration*.

Transpiration happens in the xylem tubes, and starts out in the leaves, where a plant does something akin to exhaling. When you exhale (breathe out), your breath contains some water vapor. You can see this water vapor in your breath if you exhale on a very cold day. Plants breath out, too, but you can't see their breath, even on a cold day. Plants are constantly releasing water vapor through microscopic holes in their leaves. As the water evaporates out from the leaves, the cells inside the leaves start to dry out. Water from tiny xylem tubes flows out to replenish the cells. As the water in the tiny tubes begins flowing out into the leaf, the tiny tubes begin drawing water out of the larger tubes they are attached to. When these larger tubes start to get dry, water from even larger tubes begin flowing into them. This process keeps going, with water being drawn from deeper inside the plant. Eventually this process reaches all the way down to the roots. When the root cells begin to get dry, they start taking in water from the dirt around them. The roots can't suck in water like you can from a straw. Their ability to take in water is the result of what is happening in the plant above them.

Transpiration depends on the electrical attraction between water molecules. Each water molecule has a positive side and a negative side. The positives and negatives attract and hold the water molecules together. You might want to imagine the water molecules as elephants in a line, trunks holding tails. When the first elephant moves, the others have to follow along. In plants, the first water molecules in the line are the ones evaporating from the leaves. All the other water molecules then follow, one after another, like the elephants. It's amazing to think that this electrical attraction is strong enough to overcome gravity!

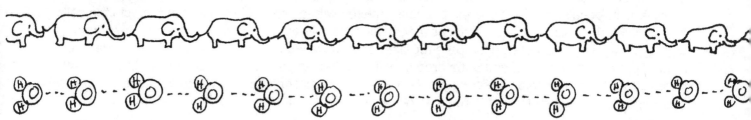

The water molecules can travel fairly quickly. The fastest transpiration speed ever recorded was about 75 centimeters per minute. That's about as fast as the minute hand on a clock sweeps around the dial.

The xylem tubes are used to transport water and minerals up from the roots into all the stems and leaves. The phloem tubes don't use transpiration. The use a form of osmosis where a lot of something goes to places where there is less of it. In this case, the "something" is sugary sap produced by the plant. The sap flows to places where there is less of it—places where it is needed.

Scientists have had trouble studying the phloem because if you try to open up the tubes to study them, they stop working. Then someone had a brilliant idea. Little insects called aphids feed on sap. They have specialized mouth parts designed to drill into a plant stem and tap into the phloem tubes. The aphids stick their mouth parts into the phloem tubes, then just hang there letting the sap flow in and fill them up. The phloem tubes don't stop working for the aphids—they keep right on flowing. The brilliant idea was to let an aphid stick its mouth into the phloem, then cut its body and head off, leaving just the mouth part stuck into the phloem. (Now this would be cruel to do to a higher animal, but remember that an aphid is just a little bug and doesn't have a proper brain. It's just a bug!) By using this little "window" into the phloem, scientists could then perform experiments.

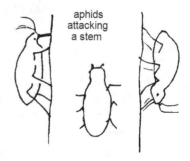

aphids attacking a stem

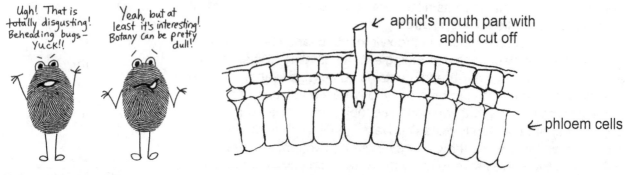

Ugh! That is totally disgusting! Beheading bugs— Yuck!!

Yeah, but at least it's interesting! Botany can be pretty dull!!

← aphid's mouth part with aphid cut off

← phloem cells

Okay, we'll go back to boring. Go back to page 17 and take a look at the chart again. We need to discuss those two bottom categories: the **monocots** and **dicots**. One of the differences between these two groups of plants is the arrangement of xylem and phloem tubes in their stems. (There are other differences, too, but we'll come to those later.) Before we go on, let's talk about these weird names. You may already know that "mono" means "one" and "di" means "two." But what is a "cot"? Sorry to make things more complicated, but "cot" is actually a shortened version of this word: **cotyledon** (cot-ell-EE-don). Their full names are monocotyledon and dicotyledon. You can see why they usually get shortened to monocot and dicot. So what is a cotyledon? The cotyledons are the first little "leaves" that come out of the seed when it begins to grow. Sometimes cotyledons are called "seed leaves" because they aren't proper green leaves. They don't do photosynthesis. (We'll take a closer look at cotyledons in a later chapter.) It's very easy to identify monocots and dicots when they sprout. You just count the seed leaves. Monocots have one, dicots have two. That's one of the easiest parts of botany.

So who really cares how many seed leaves a plant has? One, two, three... what difference does it make? The number of seed leaves isn't the most important difference between these two groups—it's just the most obvious one. The real importance for gardeners and botanists is that these two groups have chemical differences. These differences allow us to make chemicals that kill dicots while leaving monocots unharmed. Grasses are monocots and most weeds happen to be dicots. Presto--you can spray your lawn with dicot killer and kill the weeds without harming the grass! (This is not an official endorsement of lawn chemicals, just a piece of scientific information.)

Now back to the subject of xylem and phloem. In monocots, the xylem and phloem are arranged in bundles that are scattered fairly randomly throughout the stem. In dicots, the bundles are arranged in a very particular pattern, in a circle around the center.

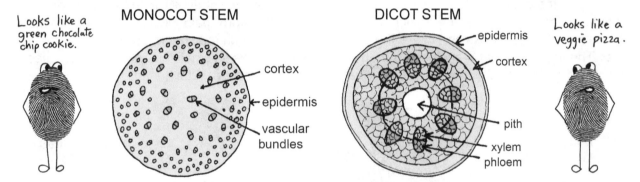

Xylem and phloem aren't really blue and red; they are clear. We used colors just to make them easier to see.

The center of a dicot stem is called the **pith**. (In some dicots, the center of the pith area can be hollow—a dandelion stem, for example.) In a monocot, the pith is pretty much all the stuff around the vascular bundles. The very outer layer of both a monocot and a dicot stem is called the **epidermis** ("epi" means "outside" and "dermis" means "skin'). Right inside the epidermis is the **cortex**.

Notice how in the dicot the bundles are arranged so that all the phloem tubes are on the outside and all the xylem tubes are facing the inside. (Just in case you are wondering, the area around the vascular bundles in the dicot does have a name, but we didn't bother you with it. Want to know it anyway? Okay--it's called the **parenchyma**. That's why we didn't bother you with it.) In trees, the phloem produces the bark and the xylem becomes wood. (You can remember which is which if you know that xylophones are made of wood.)

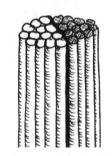

A vascular bundle with the xylem tubes on one side and the phloem tubes on the other.

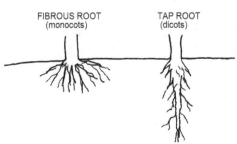

FIBROUS ROOT (monocots)   TAP ROOT (dicots)

NOTE: Not all tap roots are as long (or as thick) as this one.

Since the roots are part of the vascular system, and we happen to be discussing the vascular system right now, this would be a good time to mention another difference between monocots and dicots. Monocots have **fibrous roots** and dicots have **tap roots**. If you look at the picture on the left you'll immediately understand the difference between the two. Monocots have roots that stay near the surface and spread out. Dicots have a long central root with some much smaller roots branching off. Not all fibrous roots and tap roots look just like these. There are lots of variations, but the idea is the same. The fibrous roots are shallow and the tap roots run deep.

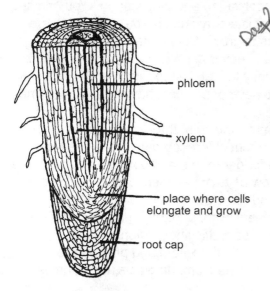

phloem

xylem

place where cells elongate and grow

root cap

Since roots are part of the vascular system, they have xylem and phloem, just like stems and leaves do. Xylem and phloem tubes run down the center of every root, even the very tiny ones (**root hairs**). The end of the root has a "cap" on it that protects the xylem and phloem as the root pushes through the soil. The space between the xylem and phloem and the root cap is called the **area of elongation**. This is the area where the most growth occurs. The cells in this area are doing some major mitosis!

The roots are the bottom end of the vascular system. At the top end of the vascular system are the veins running through the leaves. You've seen these veins and you've probably noticed how the veins get smaller as they go out to the edges of the leaves. What you probably don't know is that you can tell whether a plant is a monocot or dicot by looking at the pattern of the veins. Monocots have parallel veins that all run in the same direction. Dicots have "palmate" veins that branch off . You can see the word "palm" inside the word "palmate." Palmate means that it looks sort of like the palm of your hand, with the fingers branching out from the center. The tiny veins that branch out from the main veins can be so small that you can't even see them. We'll be looking at some microscopic veins in the next lesson. Stay tuned...

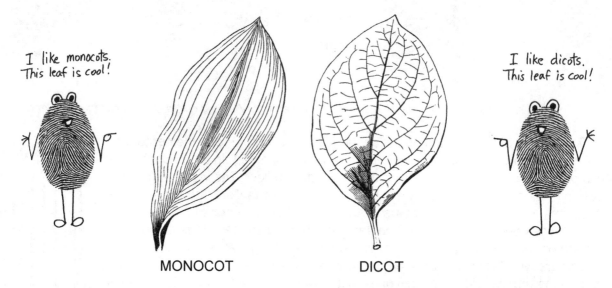

I like monocots. This leaf is cool!

I like dicots. This leaf is cool!

MONOCOT   DICOT

If you took a careful look at the chart on page 17, you might be wondering if we are going to talk about the other branch of vascular plants: the seedless plants (which are mainly ferns). We seemed to have skipped right over them and moved to the bottom of the chart very quickly. (If you didn't notice this, you might want to take a quick look at page 17 right now.)

Most of what we'll learn about ferns is at the beginning of chapter 6. But let's take a quick look at the vascular system of ferns since they are indeed part of the "vascular plants" category. It would be unfair to skip over them completely.

Ferns have actual roots, stems and leaves, like all vascular plants do. However, ferns are in their own category because they do not produce seeds. They are neither monocots nor dicots. They have neither fibrous roots nor tap roots. Let's look at a cross section of a fern stem and compare it to the monocot and dicot cross sections we looked at on page 29.

On the left is a section from a fern plant. Fern roots are usually called rhizomes. They run along under the ground and have many fronds (leaves) sprouting up from them. If we make a cut and then look at that cut end (center picture), we'll see some tiny ovals. If we put one of those ovals under a microscope, you'll see that the oval is a vascular bundle and has xylem and phloem cells. The xylem and phloem are not arranged like the monocot or the dicot. The fern has its own arrangement.

If we cut a fern stem and look at the sliced end, it will look something like this:

It has the same parts as the monocots and dicots, but they are arranged in a different pattern. The vascular bundle looks more like a xylem banana with phloem pockets at either end. (To see an astounding color photograph of what this looks like, go to: **http://www.sciencephoto.com/ media/17206/enlarge**. You'll see a micrograph—a photograph taken with a microscope.)

Not all fern stems are this shape. If you search for images of cross sections of fern stems, you'll see that they don't all look just like this one. The basic shape and pattern will be similar, though—much more like this picture than like the monocot and dicot pictures on page 29.

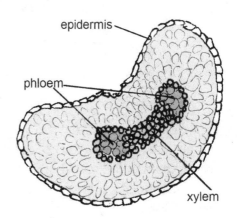

ACTIVITY 1: A SHORT VIDEO ABOUT TRANSPIRATION

There is a very short video about transpiration posted on the Botany playlist.

ACTIVITY 2: AN ONLINE GAME ABOUT ROOTS

Here is an interactive game you can play online. It's just a quick game that won't take any more than 10 minutes or so. You identify fibrous and tap roots, then guess if they are edible or not. There is extra information about the edible roots. (You will need Adobe Flash Player, but it will install automatically if you don't have it. Just make sure you uncheck the boxes about installing the ad-ons.)
    http://www.harcourtschool.com/activity/root/rootfac.html

Another way to access this game is through SQOOL TUBE.

ACTIVITY 3: USE LEAF PATTERNS TO IDENTIFY MONOCOTS AND DICOTS

Look at the patterns on these leaves and guess which are monocots and which are dicots. Write "M" for monocot or "D" for dicot. (Remember, monocots have parallel veins.)

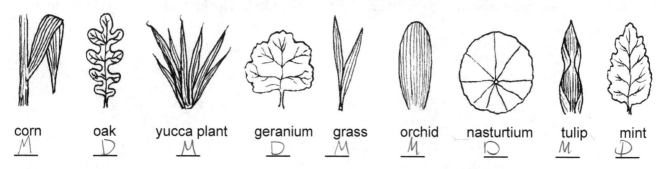

corn M   oak D   yucca plant M   geranium D   grass M   orchid M   nasturtium D   tulip M   mint D

ACTIVITY 4: FILL IN THE GAPS

Catastrophe Cathy was asked to write some paragraphs about vascular plants. Unfortunately, she used edible writing paper and then left the page outside. Some hungry caterpillars came along and decided to have a snack. Can you fill in the words that the caterpillars ate?

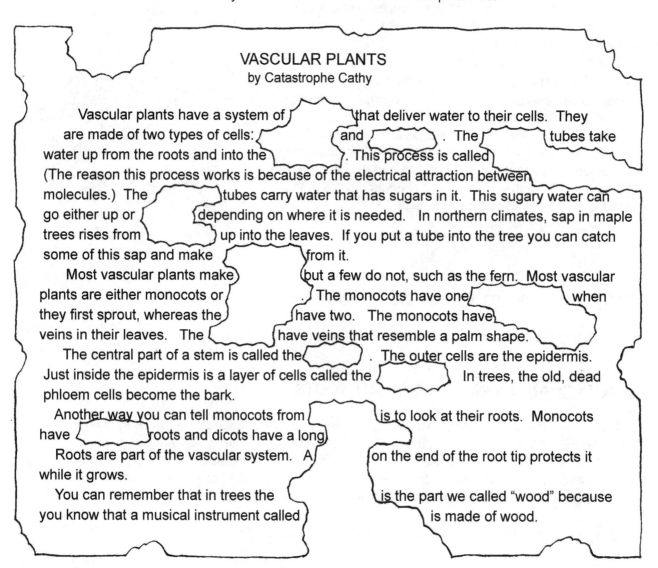

VASCULAR PLANTS
by Catastrophe Cathy

Vascular plants have a system of ⬚ that deliver water to their cells. They are made of two types of cells: ⬚ and ⬚. The ⬚ tubes take water up from the roots and into the ⬚. This process is called ⬚ (The reason this process works is because of the electrical attraction between ⬚ molecules.) The ⬚ tubes carry water that has sugars in it. This sugary water can go either up or ⬚ depending on where it is needed. In northern climates, sap in maple trees rises from ⬚ up into the leaves. If you put a tube into the tree you can catch some of this sap and make ⬚ from it.

Most vascular plants make ⬚ but a few do not, such as the fern. Most vascular plants are either monocots or ⬚. The monocots have one ⬚ when they first sprout, whereas the ⬚ have two. The monocots have ⬚ veins in their leaves. The ⬚ have veins that resemble a palm shape.

The central part of a stem is called the ⬚. The outer cells are the epidermis. Just inside the epidermis is a layer of cells called the ⬚ In trees, the old, dead phloem cells become the bark.

Another way you can tell monocots from ⬚ is to look at their roots. Monocots have ⬚ roots and dicots have a long ⬚

Roots are part of the vascular system. A ⬚ on the end of the root tip protects it while it grows.

You can remember that in trees the ⬚ is the part we called "wood" because you know that a musical instrument called ⬚ is made of wood.

LEVEL TWO

Roots seem to know which way is down and stems know to grow upward. This used to mystify botanists. They knew it was true but hadn't a clue why. A botany text from 1858 says, "What makes the root grow downwards into the ground, and the stem turn upwards, we no more know than why newly-hatched ducklings take to the water at once." Botanists would still be wondering about this if it were not for advancements in the field of chemistry during the 1900s. It turns out that chemicals are the key to plant growth.

Plant cells make chemicals called **hormones**. You probably recognize the word "hormone" and have undoubtedly heard it used in sentences that also contain words like "teenager" and "puberty." But hormones occur in both plants and animals and they do lots of other jobs besides controlling reproduction. In animals, hormones regulate most bodily functions, including blood pressure, appetite, body temperature and the sleep cycle. In plants, hormones control the formation of all the parts, the ripening of fruit, the amount of light a plant needs, what it does in each season of the year, how long it lives, and many other things.

A hormone called **auxin** (*ox-in*) is responsible for the growth of roots and stems. Auxin stimulates cells to grow faster and longer. Botanists have done all kinds of experiments to determine just how much auxin it takes to influence growth. They discovered that it only takes a very tiny amount, and at high levels this growth hormone is actually poisonous to plants. Yes, their own hormone can be used to poison them! And dicots are much more susceptible to this hormone poisoning than monocots are. Since most plants that we consider to be weeds in our lawns are dicots, and grass is a monocot, this natural plant hormone can actually be used as a weed-killer for lawns.

Is "auxin" plural for "aux"?   Ha, ha. Very funny.

Part of the DNA code inside a plant cell is instructions for how to make auxin. The amount of auxin a cell produces is related to the amount of light it receives. The lower the level of light, the more auxin will be produced, stimulating growth. This is because the plant needs light. If the plant is in an area where the light is coming from only one side, it will eventually "lean" out into the light so that it can absorb as much light as possible. The cells on the dark side of the stem receive less light so they produce more auxin, which makes the cells grow longer. The cells on the light side produce less auxin and there is less growth. This uneven cell growth results in the stem tipping to one side.

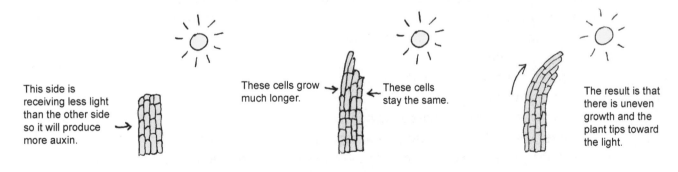

This side is receiving less light than the other side so it will produce more auxin.

These cells grow much longer.

These cells stay the same.

The result is that there is uneven growth and the plant tips toward the light.

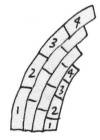

If we take a close-up view of this process and simplify it down to only four cells, it would look something like this drawing. Each row has the same number of cells, but they are longer on the left side. Since the cells are basically connected and can't slide apart very much, this results in a bend in the stem.

Here's an interesting question—what if there isn't very much light on either side? Do both sides produce more auxin and therefore more growth? Well, if you've ever seen seedlings grown indoors where they don't get enough light, you know the answer. The little plants get very tall but very thin. The stems are so thin that they can hardly bear the weight of their own leaves. Too much auxin produces too much cell elongation. The cells grow too long, making the stem too tall and thin. (Plants like this usually don't survive.)

I am exhibiting DONOTROPISM — the tendency to go towards donuts!

The same kind of thing goes on in the roots, only the cells don't react to light, but rather to gravity. Gravity causes the changes in the hormone levels, instead of light. In reduced gravity situations, such as on a space station, roots grow in all directions. When a plant reacts to its environment, it's called *tropism*. The word "tropo" means "to turn or change." The response to light is called *phototropism* ("photo" means "light"), and the response to gravity is called either *gravitropism* or *geotropism* ("geo" means "earth").

ACTIVITY 1: A SHORT VIDEO THAT TALKS ABOUT TROPISMS AND AUXIN

Watch a brief video that talks about tropisms and auxin. You will hear the narrator talk about positive geotropism (growing toward gravity) and negative geotropism (growing away from gravity). You will also hear the term "apical dominance." This means that the tip of the central stalk determines how the plant will grow. The video is posted on the Botany playlist.

ACTIVITY 2: AN ONLINE INTERACTIVE DEMONSTRATION OF AUXINS (FOR KIDS)

Here's more discussion about auxins and a demonstration of how they control plant growth.
http://www.kscience.co.uk/animations/auxin.htm

ACTIVITY 3: A TRUE/FALSE QUIZ

Write T for true, or F for false.
1) ____ In the word "monocot" the word "cot" is short for "cotyledon."
2) ____ The word "cotyledon" is the correct name for the root cap on the tip of the root.
3) ____ In dicots, the vascular bundles are scattered randomly throughout the stem.
4) ____ The beginning of transpiration is when leaves "exhale" water.
5) ____ Transpiration only works because water molecules are attracted to each other.
6) ____ Roots aren't really part of the vascular system because they are in the soil.
7) ____ Water goes up the stem through xylem cells.
8) ____ Auxin is a plant hormone.
9) ____ Hormones control growth in plants.
10) ____ Monocots have parallel veins.
11) ____ The outer layer of a stem is called the pith.
12) ____ The first little "seed leaves" a baby plant sprouts are called the cotyledons.
13) ____ In dicots, the phloem cells are closer to the outside than the xylem cells are.
14) ____ Monocots have deep tap roots that keep them anchored in the soil.
15) ____ Too much auxin can kill a plant.
16) ____ A low level of light stops the production of auxin.
17) ____ Geotropism is a plant's reaction to the pH of the soil.
18) ____ Both monocot and dicot stems have a cortex.
19) ____ A dicot leaf has palmate veins.
20) ____ Grass would be a good example of a dicot.

LESSON 5: LEAVES and TREES

LEVEL ONE

This lesson might also be called "more about the vascular system." We are going to study leaves, which are part of the vascular system, and trees, whose trunks and bark are also a part of the vascular system. Let's look at leaves first.

There are names for the parts of a leaf:

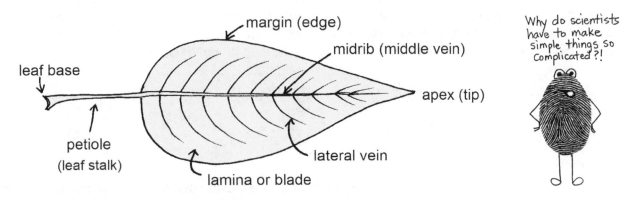

Some of you may be thinking the same thought that our friend is. Why do scientists always have to make things more difficult by using hard words? It's because science requires precision not just with experiments, but with words, too. Some of the words on the leaf diagram appear in other branches of science, not just botany. For instance, the word "lateral" pops up in many branches of science, and no matter where you see it, it always means "side," or something having to do with sides. "Apex" always means "tip," and the word "lamina" always refers to something flat.

Leaves come in a great variety of shapes, and botanists have come up with names for all of them. (That's great news, eh?) Every leaf can be classified as one of these:

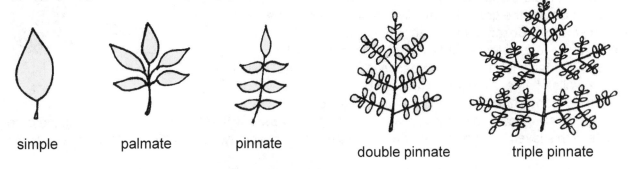

Look carefully at the patterns of the double and triple pinnate leaves. Can you see how the same pattern is repeated? In the triple pinnate leaf, the tiny branches and the intermediate branches have the same pattern as the whole leaf.

There are a great variety of simple leaf shapes and some of these shapes don't look so simple. The lobed type doesn't look simple, but it's not palmate or pinnate, so it's classified as simple.

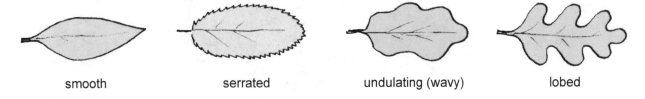

Serrated things have very sharp little bumps along the edges. You might have a serrated knife in your kitchen. Serrated knives are good for cutting breads or meats. Why do leaves have serrated edges? We can only guess—we don't know for sure.

NOTE: The natural world doesn't always make classification easy. Plants don't know that they are supposed to conform to these categories. For example, what type of leaf is this on the right? It looks both lobed AND serrated.

Botanists also like to look at the way the leaves are attached to the stem. Pairs of leaves that come off the stem at the same place are called **opposite**. When the leaves alternate sides, they are called **alternate**. There are also **whorled** patterns where the leaves come out in bunches at certain points. Sometimes the leaves make a **spiral** pattern as they go up the stem.

opposite   alternate   whorled   spiral

Now it's time to do some microscope work. We'll be looking at a super-close up view of a leaf that has been cut in half. Leaves are so thin you might think they only have one layer of cells, but they actually have four distinct layers. This will take a little imagination because we are going to show you a two-dimensional slice of a three-dimensional object. Some of the cell layers might look a little strange because of flattening it to two dimensions.

The top of the leaf is covered with a waxy protective layer called the **cuticle**. (This doesn't count as one of the four layers.) The first real layer is the **upper epidermis**. Under that there's the **palisade** layer. A palisade is an old-fashioned military fort with walls made of logs stuck into the ground vertically (up and down). The person who first looked at these leaf cells decided that this second layer resembled a palisade fort because the cells are long and tall and thin with no spaces in between, just like the walls of a palisade fort. The cells of the palisade layer have many chloroplasts and do a lot of the leaf's photosynthesis. Under the palisade layer is the **spongy mesophyll** (*MEZ-o-fill*). Notice all the empty spaces in this layer. This is the layer that looks the strangest in two dimensions. There are cells that

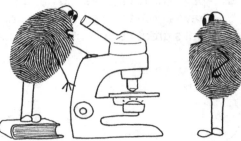

I can't reach the focus knob.

Hurry up! I want a turn!

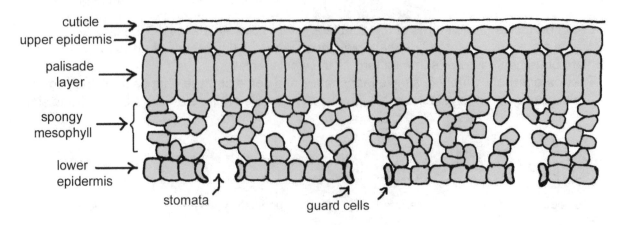

cuticle
upper epidermis
palisade layer
spongy mesophyll
lower epidermis
stomata
guard cells

40

look like they are hanging in mid-air. But remember that there are cells in front and behind that are attached to these cells. The empty air spaces in the spongy mesophyll layer are where the carbon dioxide and water vapor can come into contact with the cells that need them.

The fourth layer is the **lower epidermis**. In this bottom layer are holes called **stomata**. Around the edges of the holes are special cells called **guard cells**. The guard cells can make the holes larger or smaller depending on whether the cells in the spongy mesophyll layer are wet or dry. If the leaf starts to dry out, the holes can close, keeping water vapor trapped inside the leaf. (It's sort of like keeping the bathroom door closed so your warm steam doesn't get out. When you open the door, the bathroom dries out quickly.) The guard cells look very strange in the cross-section view on page 36. You can't determine their real shape. Let's switch to a top view.

This picture shows how the guard cells change their shape to open or close the hole. This system works automatically because it is the moisture level of the leaf that makes them work. If the leaf is moist, so are the guard cells. When the guard cells are full of water they curve outward, keeping the hole open. When the leaf dries out, the guard cells lose moisture and shrivel shut, closing the hole.

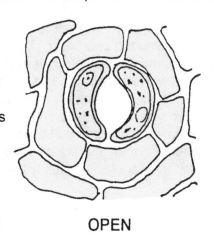

OPEN

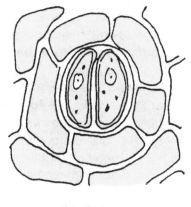

CLOSED

As we learned in lesson one, it's the chlorophyll in their cells that make plants green. So what happens when leaves turn red and yellow? In the autumn, the northern climates get less sunlight. Not only does the sun go down earlier, but it also comes up later. The plants start getting less than 12 hours of sunlight per day. There is less light for photosynthesis, so the plants can't produce as much chlorophyll. As the amount of chlorophyll goes down, you start to be able to see other chemicals that were there in the leaves all along but were "masked" by the green chlorophyll. Two of these chemicals are **xanthophyll** (*ZAN-tho-fill*) and **carotene**. (In Greek, "xantho" means "yellow," and "phyll" means "leaf.") The xanthophylls create the brilliant yellows in fall leaves. The carotenes provide the bright oranges and reds. These chemicals are in the leaves all year—we just can't see them. They help catch energy from light, just like chlorophyll does, but they catch different wavelengths of light. (This is where physics meets botany.) They also seem to help protect the chlorophyll. Chlorophyll does most of the work, but xanthophyll and carotene are important helpers.

These chemicals are found in other places, too, not just leaves. The orange color of carrots comes from a high level of carotene. In fact, as a general rule, anywhere you find orange in the natural world, it's probably carotene. Egg yolks are yellow because of the carotene the hens ate. The hens' bodies processed the carotene from their food and used it to color the yolks. Humans have a spot at the back of their eye that is yellow because it contains carotene. This spot helps to protect the eye by absorbing harmful light waves. (Carrots also have vitamin A, which is necessary for eyes to work properly.)

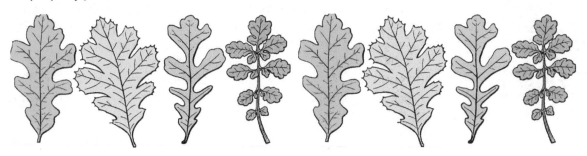

Now let's switch over to a different part of the vascular system and talk about stems again. Stems that are relatively small and soft are called **herbaceous** (*er-BAY-shuss*) stems. Plants such as flowers and garden vegetables have herbaceous stems. Larger, sturdier plants, such as bushes and trees, need stems that can support their weight, so their stems must grow wider and become tougher. Stems that are hard and thick are called **woody.** Tree trunks are actually very large stems.

Let's take a look at the anatomy of a tree trunk. Bark is actually dead phloem cells that are getting pushed out away from the tree (sort of like shedding or molting in animals). The tree is constantly growing new phloem cells under the bark so the old bark needs to fall off to allow the trunk to expand and grow. Each species of tree has its own type of bark. Experts can look at a piece of bark and tell you what kind of tree it came from.

Right underneath the bark is a layer of phloem. (Remember the phloem? It carries fluids both up and down.) Inside the phloem is a layer called the **cambium**. This is a very thin but extremely important layer. **From the cambium layer come all the new xylem and phloem cells.** The inner side of the cambium is constantly growing new xylem cells. The part of the tree trunk that we think of as "wood" is actually layers of dead xylem cells that have accumulated over the years. The older xylem cells eventually become clogged and stop transporting water very well. Each year the cambium grows a new ring of xylem. The xylem rings can be used to tell the age of a tree. The smallest ring at the center was originally the pith when the tree was a baby plant. Start with that tiny pith ring, then count outward until you reach the bark (well, actually the cambium layer just inside the bark) and you'll know the age of the tree.

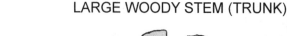

HERBACEOUS STEM

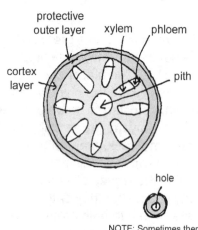

protective outer layer — xylem — phloem

cortex layer — pith

hole

NOTE: Sometimes there is a hole in the middle of the stem, with the pith around it.

LARGE WOODY STEM (TRUNK)

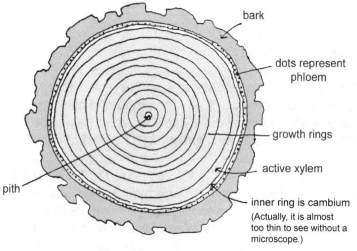

bark

dots represent phloem

growth rings

active xylem

inner ring is cambium
(Actually, it is almost too thin to see without a microscope.)

pith

The Renaissance artist and scientist Leonardo da Vinci was the first person (in recorded Western history) to figure out that you can tell the age of a tree by counting its rings. He also figured out that the relative sizes of the rings correspond to the weather conditions of each year. A very wet, rainy spring produces very large rings. A dry spring produces thinner rings. In this way, a tree leaves a record of weather conditions during its lifetime.

In 1904 it was discovered that you can match tree ring patterns in lumber and figure out the age of wooden archaeological artifacts. This branch of science is called **dendrochronology** ("dendro" is "tree," "chrono" is "time.").

ACTIVITY 1: "THE ALIEN PLANT" DRAWING ACTIVITY

Just for fun, let's imagine that a space expedition has just returned from an alien planet. They tried to bring back a really bizarre plant specimen they found there, but unfortunately the specimen got crushed so badly in the baggage compartment that it was almost unrecognizable by the time they got back to Earth. Fortunately, one of the astronauts had taken a botany course recently and could accurately describe the plant in its prime condition. Use the astronaut's description to draw what the plant would have looked like.

"The plant consisted of one main stalk with three compound palmate leaves. One of the compound palmate leaves was at the top of the stalk and the other two were opposite each other at the middle of the stalk. Each compound palmate leaf was made up of three laminas. The top lamina was perfectly round, had undulating edges and was blue. The second lamina was diamond-shaped with serrated edges and it was green. The third lamina was oval with lobed edges and was purple. All three petioles were red and so was the stalk. All the midribs and veins were black. The roots of this strange plant were fibrous, like monocots here on Earth."

ACTIVITY 2: DETERMINE THE AGE OF THIS TREE

Try to determine the age of this tree by counting the rings. How old was the tree when a very wet summer occured? (For an online activity about dendrochronology, go to: **http://www.pbs.org/ wgbh/nova/vikings/treering2.html**)

ACTIVITY 3: THE BOTANY SONG (The tune is the same as the song "Oats, peas, beans and barley grow.")

Oats, peas, beans and barley grow,
My botany teacher told me so,
She made me learn some plant info,
Some day I may need it, you never know!

Photosynthesis is how
Plants make sugar, remember now:
Light and water and CO_2
Make sugar and water and O_2.

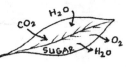

It's chlorophyll that makes them green,
But some turn colors by Halloween;
The days get short, then can be seen
Xanthophyll and carotene.

Water goes up through xylem cells;
They also carry minerals.
Through the phloem the sugar goes down
And up and down and up and down.

Oats and barley are monocots,
Just one seed leaf is all they gots
Parallel veins and fibrous roots
Are their outstanding attributes.

Dicots all have two seed leaves;
Our dicots here are beans and peas.
With long tap roots and palmate veins
They take in water when it rains.

(If this curriculm came to you as a digital download, or if you ordered it via The Basement Workshop webstore, you should have the audio tracks that go with this song. If this booklet was purchased through Amazon or at a bookstore, you will need to download the audio files at www.ellenjmchenry.com, click on MUSIC tab.)

ACTIVITY 4: LOOK AT A CROSS SECTION OF A REAL LEAF

Use an Internet image search with key words "leaf cross section" (might want to add the word "photograph"), to find some images of real leaves that have been cross-sectioned. Also try "pine leaf cross section." If you don't want to search the Internet, there are a few pictures available as part of the free downloadable file labeled: "Color supplements for the 'Botany in 8 Lessons' curriculum" at **www.ellenjmchenry.com**. (Click on "Free downloads," then on "Plants.")

If there is any pink or red or blue in the picture, the botanist has used a stain on the leaf to stain certain cells or parts of cells so they are more visible.

ACTIVITY 5: DRAW A TWIG (and learn about tree growth while you draw)

Twigs may not be the most fascinating things on the planet, but they're more interesting than you'd think. Get a pencil and a piece of paper and sketch along with the drawing lesson posted on the Botany playlist: "Draw a Twig." (You might also find this labeled drawing helpful: **http://www.bio. miami.edu/dana/226/226F09_7.html**)

LEVEL TWO

So you've digested all the information in level one and are ready for more? Okay, great! Let's learn a little bit more about leaves and trees.

There are many more names for leaf shapes. Have you ever seen any leaves that look like the ones in this picture? You've probably seen quite a few of these shapes but didn't know they had names. Do we expect you to remember all these names? Of course not. But it's interesting to know they exist and if you ever need to know their names you can always look them up on the Internet by entering the key words "leaf shapes."

There are several weapon-related words here. You probably recognized the word "lance" in the word "lanceolate." Hastate comes from the Latin "hasta" meaning "spear," and "sagittate" comes from the Latin "sagittatus" meaning "arrowhead." Cordate comes from the Latin word "cord" meaning "heart" (related to our English word "cardiac"). Obcordate means "opposite of cordate." See how it's the same shape only upside down? The deltoid is named after the Greek letter delta ("D"), which looks like a triangle. The lyrate leaf is supposed to look like a lyre (harp). Runcinate leaves have their lobes turned backwards like an old-fashioned working tool called a "plane," which in Latin is "runcina." Acicular *(ah-SICK-u-lar)* is from the Latin "acus" meaning "needle."

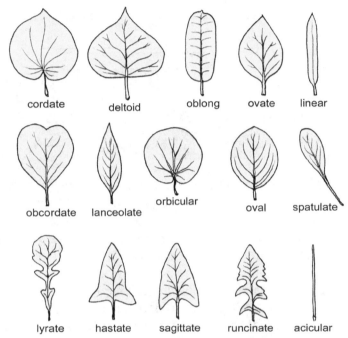

cordate   deltoid   oblong   ovate   linear

obcordate   lanceolate   orbicular   oval   spatulate

lyrate   hastate   sagittate   runcinate   acicular

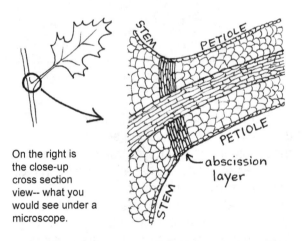

On the right is the close-up cross section view-- what you would see under a microscope.

In northern climates the leaves of **deciduous** *(de-SID-ju-us)* trees fall off before winter sets in. ("Deciduous" is the fancy Latin way to say "falling off.") The "why" of this phenomenon is that winter is not only cold but also dry. Leaves are the primary source of water evaporation. If the tree kept its leaves during the winter, it would dry out. (Pine trees can keep their leaves [needles are really leaves!] because the needles are so small and thin that they don't let much water evaporate.)

Severe cold is a problem, too. The water in the leaves would freeze and the tree would be stuck with dead leaves hanging all over it. Better to just get rid of the leaves and grow new ones in the spring!

The "how" is accomplished by a special layer of cells at the base of the petiole. When the leaf first grew, this layer of cells was also grown, in preparation for the eventual fate of the leaf (falling off). This layer of cells is called the **abscission layer** *(ab-SIJZ-un)*. This word is related to the words "incision" and "scissors," and it means "cutting off." When the number of daylight hours decreases to a certain point, the tree starts producing a hormone that tells the abscission cells to start swelling. As they swell, they not only push the leaf away from the branch, but they also form a protective layer that will seal the branch after the leaf falls off, to protect it from disease or insect damage.

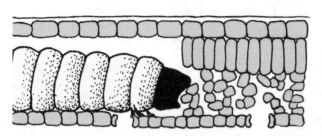

Here's something really interesting to look for next time you are on a nature hike. See if you can find a *leaf miner.* You know what miners are—people who tunnel into the earth to find coal or diamonds or metal ores. A leaf miner is a very small insect that spends the larval stage of its life tunneling between the upper and lower epidermis layers of a leaf. Remember, you can only see these layers with a microscope, so we're talking really small larvae! The adult insect pricks the top of a leaf and lays its eggs inside, under the epidermis layer. When the larvae hatch, they start eating and don't stop until they are ready to break out of the leaf and begin their adult life as moths or beetles or flies. (Even as adults, these guys are pretty small. A leaf miner moth has a wing span smaller than the width of a pencil. A leaf miner fly could fit inside this letter "O.") The larva chomps away at spongy mesophyll and palisade, leaving an empty tunnel behind it.

As the larva grows, so does the size of the tunnel. If you hold the leaf up to the light, you can see a trail of poop that the larva left behind as it ate its way through the leaf. If you are lucky, you might even find the larva still in the tunnel. The larva spends less than a week in the leaf, so you'll have to find it during that time. When the larva is ready to turn into an adult, it eats through the epidermis layer and escapes. Next time you go on a hike, be on the look-out for leaf miners.

Leaf miners make squiggly patterns that are fascinating to look at.

Now for a bit of chemistry. Another natural pigment that plants make (in addition to chlorophyll, xanthophyll and carotene) is *anthocyanin* (AN-tho-SIE-uh-nin). That one sounds poisonous, doesn't it? If someone told you there was anthocyanin in your food you might not eat it! But anthocyanin is just a harmless natural pigment that makes the reds, blues, and purples in the plant kingdom. ("Antho" means "flower" and "cyan" means "blue.")

Anthocyanin has a special quality that the other pigments don't have. It can change color. For a one-plant demonstration of what anthocyanin can do, check out the hydrangea. This bush produces large flowers that are sometimes red, sometimes white, and sometimes blue. This mystified ancient peoples—it was almost magical to them. We now know that soil chemistry is responsible for this amazing phenomenon. Acidic soil causes the hydrangea to make blue flowers, neutral soil produces cream-colored flowers, and alkaline soil (the opposite of acidic) produces pink or purple flowers.

Anthocyanin isn't just in flowers; it can be found in any part of a plant: roots, stems, leaves, flowers and fruits. It's the red in beets and apples, the blue in blueberries, and the purple in purple cabbages. In leaves, it acts as sort of a sunscreen, absorbing the sun's harmful rays.

Before we end this lesson, let's take a closer look at tree trunks.

The outer part is called the **sapwood**. It tends to be very soft and wet. This is the part of the trunk that contains the living xylem and phloem cells. Sapwood is host to many insects and their larvae. Woodpeckers instinctively know this and drill into the sapwood to feed on the insects.

The inner core of xylem inside a tree trunk is made of cells that are pretty much non-functional. These inner cells have become clogged and are no longer the main transport tubes. The main transport action occurs away from the center, closer to the bark. The inner core is called the **heartwood**. It may be of little use to the tree (except to help give it strength) but it is this part of a tree that is most useful to us. The heartwood is what we call "wood."

The quality of the heartwood is slightly different in each species of tree. Woodworkers know this well, and have discovered which types of wood are best for certain things.
- Oak is extremely hard and is great for things like floors and tables.
- Pine is very soft and nails go in easily. This makes it a good choice for building houses.
- Ash is used to make baseball bats and boat oars.
- Persimmon is sometimes used for golf clubs.
- Maple and birch are great for kitchen cutting boards.
- Walnut and cherry make beautiful (and very expensive) furniture.
- Cedar is rot-resistant and is used for shingles, siding, and outdoor furniture.
- Spruce and willow are used to make violins.
- Balsa is unbelievably lightweight and is perfect for making model airplanes.

Over the centuries, people have found uses not only for the xylem, but also for the fluids that flow through the phloem in the sapwood. Here are just a few examples:
- Maple syrup is made from the rising spring sap of sugar maple trees.
- Certain pine trees make a substance that can be used to make turpentine, a solvent used with oil paints. Turpentine can also be used to make rosin (*roz-in*), which is rubbed onto the bows of stringed instruments such as violins and cellos.
- The sumac tree produces tannin, a chemical used to tan animal hides and make leather.
- The juice of willow tree has been used as a natural source of aspirin.

We learned how to tell the age of a tree by counting its xylem rings. Here's a method for determining the age of a pine tree: count the "whorls" on the trunk and branches. A whorl is a place where several twigs or branches are attached. Many kinds of pine trees grow one "leader" and a set of whorls each year. Begin counting back along the branch, one year for each whorl. After you have counted the whorls, add four years to that number because a pine tree is usually four years old before it puts out its first whorl.

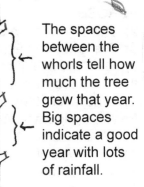

The spaces between the whorls tell how much the tree grew that year. Big spaces indicate a good year with lots of rainfall.

ACTIVITY 1: REVIEW CROSSWORD PUZZLE

ACROSS:

2) This pigment is responsible for the orange color in carrots.

6) The holes on the underside of a leaf

7) This type of leaf has edges that go in and out even more than an undulating leaf.

11) The layer at the base of the petiole that detaches the leaf from the twig when autumn comes

12) This means a bunch of leaves going out from the same point on a stem.

14) This type of leaf can be single, double, or triple.

17) This pigment is yellow.

20) This layer's name means "outer skin."

21) This word means "tip."

I know all the answers, but I'm not telling! I'll just sit here and watch you work...

22) These tubes carry water and sugars (sap) up and down, up and down.
24) These cells surround the stomata.
25) This is the correct name for the leaf stalk.
26) These tubes transport water from the roots up to the leaves.

DOWN
1) This type of tree drops its leaves before winter.
3) This pigment can make a plant either blue or red.
4) The waxy layer on top of a leaf
5) This layer in a tree trunk grows new xylem and phloem cells.
6) This means the leaf has sharp points along the edges.
8) The science of using tree rings to date an old wooden artifact
9) This is a fancy word for "edge."
10) This means "heart-shaped."
13) This leaf shape is named after the Greek letter "delta."
14) This type of leaf resembles the shape of your palm.
15) This kind of stem is hard and can grow into a trunk.
16) This layer resembles an old-fashioned fort.
18) This type of stem is soft and can't grow to be very large.
19) This is the middle layer in a leaf. (It is often described as "spongy.")
23) This is the correct name for a leaf (not including the petiole).

ACTIVITY 2: PHOTOS AND VIDEOS OF LEAF MINERS

Use an Internet search engine set on "images" to search for "leaf miners." Then use the key words "leaf miner larva" to see close-up pictures of these tiny tunneling larvae.

There are some videos of leaf miners posted on the Botany playlist on the YouTube.com/TheBasementWorkshop channel. One of the videos shows a very large leaf miner inside the leaf of a boxwood tree. The other videos show more typical tiny miners.

ACTIVITY 3: TREE VIDEOS ✓

There are several videos posted on the Botany playlist that give more information about tree rings. There are also videos about the tallest tree in the world and the oldest tree in the world.

ACTIVITY 4:   TREE IDENTIFICATION FOR THE DIGITAL GENERATION
Yes, there's an app for that!

If you are into apps, check out a new free app called Leafsnap. You take a picture of a tree leaf (put it against a light-colored background) and the app will tell you what kind of tree it came from. It will also give you lots of extra information about the tree, just in case you are interested.

If you don't use apps, you can still be digital. Try using this online tree identification guide by the Arbor Day Foundation:
http://www.arborday.org/trees/whatTree/

NOTE: These resources were designed for North America. If you don't live in North America, try searching the Internet using key words "online tree identification guide," plus the area where you live.

ACTIVITY 5: DRAW A WINTER TREE

Did you know that trees are mathematical? The pattern that their branches make closely resembles a pattern that mathematicians call a *fractal*. A fractal is a shape or pattern that repeats itself over and over again, getting smaller and smaller. These designs on the right are not real trees—they are computer-generated fractals. Can you see how the same shape is repeated at the end of each branch?

No shape in nature is perfect. Part of the beauty of nature comes from its imperfections. Real trees have odd bends and twists that mathematical fractals don't have. However, knowing about fractal patterns can help you to analyze tree shapes. (The shape of a tree can be used as an identification clue, too.) Some trees have a strong central "leader" that goes straight to the top, and branch leaders that go straight out to the sides. Other tree trunks fork right away, turning into branches that also fork right away. Some trees make lots of branches, others are sparse. Some have straight branches, others have branches with lots of little quirky bends.

Look at these real tree shapes below and see if you can identify their pattern.

Draw at least two tree silhouettes in the space below. Don't copy any of the trees shown above! Make up your own based on the idea of fractal patterns. Think of a basic shape, and keep it firmly in your mind as you add branches to your tree. The shapes of the smaller branches should reflect the shape of the larger branches.

LESSON 6: PLANT REPRODUCTION

LEVEL ONE

Like every living thing on earth, plants need to make more of themselves. Biological structures wear out over time and need to be replaced with new ones. We've already looked at how non-vascular plants reproduce (mosses and liverworts) so now it's time to look at vascular plants.

If you look back at the chart on page 17, you will see that vascular plants are divided into two main categories: plants that produce seeds and plants that don't produce seeds. The vascular plants that do not make seeds are basically the ferns. There are a few other smaller categories such as "horse tails" and club mosses, but if you just remember the ferns, that's fine. So let's take a look at how ferns make more ferns.

The leaves of ferns are called *fronds*, and brand new leaves that have not yet totally uncoiled are called *fiddleheads* because they look like the scroll-shaped end of a violin. Technically, the entire frond is a leaf. What looks like a stem is actually the fern's equivalent of a petiole. (Botanists call it a stipe.) The stem of a fern plant runs under the ground and is called a *rhizome*. Ferns also have roots, like all other vascular plants. The roots grow out from the bottom of the rhizome.

Ferns produce spores, just like mosses do. At certain times of the year, the backside of some fern fronds will be covered with little dots called *sori*. Sori is the plural form, meaning more than one of them. Just one is called a *sorus*. Sorus is a Greek word meaning a "bunch or heap." If you look at a sorus under a magnifier it does indeed look like a heap of little dots.

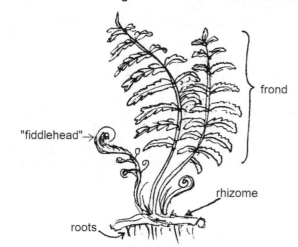

This is how one sorus looks under a magnifier.

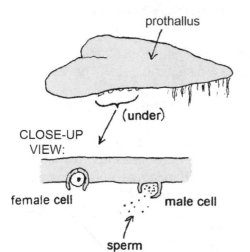

The individual bumps on a sorus are called *sporangia*. Inside each sporangium are many microscopic *spores*. The sporangia break open when they are "ripe" and release their spores into the air. When the spores fall to the ground they grow into a heart-shaped thing called a *prothallus* (very similar to a moss thallus). The prothallus then produces male and female structures that make sperm and eggs.

When it rains, the sperm can swim through the water to reach the eggs. When egg and sperm join, they will make a baby fern plant that grows up as a frond.

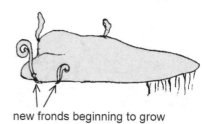

new fronds beginning to grow

The fern displays the same **alternation of generations** pattern that the mosses do. The fronds produce spores that produce a prothallus that makes male and female cells, which grow into a sporophyte that produces spores. Each part of the cycle has certain advantages. The advantage of making spores is that the plant can make millions of them, increasing the odds that the plant will successfully reproduce, with some of the offspring perhaps at quite a distance from the parent plant. The advantage of having a prothallus that makes male and female cells is that the female cells can be fertilized by male cells from another plant, thus increasing the variety of its DNA. If a fern's egg cells were always fertilized by its own male cells, the baby plants would always be clones of the parent—identical in every way. If every single plant in a species is identical, the species is more vulnerable to extinction. Some ferns might have DNA that make them more able to survive drought or to survive an attack by a fungus. By swapping male cells, stronger plants can "share" their DNA with weaker plants, so to speak, thus strengthening the species as a whole.

← FERN SPERM

O ↖
FERN SPORE

Sometimes a fern prothallus will produce only female parts so that it can't possibly fertilize itself. Then, when it rains, the female parts produce a chemical that attracts male cells. If there is enough water, male cells from neighboring ferns will be able to swim over and literally "follow the scent" to find the female cells. (This sounds like something Carl Linnaeus got in trouble for talking about!)

Ferns also have a "Plan B." Relying completely on spores and on male cells finding female cells would limit ferns in their ability to survive. The weather isn't always cooperative, after all. Periods of rainfall might not come when the fern's life cycle needs them. Ferns, like most plants, can do something called **vegetative reproduction**. The vegetative parts of a plant are the ones that are not involved in these complicated reproductive processes. The vegetative parts are the leaves, stems, and roots. Vegetative reproduction means that new plants can grow from leaves, stems and roots. (Gardeners will often take "cuttings" from plants—pieces of leaves, stems or roots—and then replant them.) Fern rhizomes will grow longer and longer under the ground, putting up new fronds along the way. If you cut off a section of rhizome and replant it somewhere else, you'll have a new fern plant. Technically, you can also cut off a frond, plant it, and it will grow a rhizome. But this method is tricky and doesn't always work, even for professional gardeners.

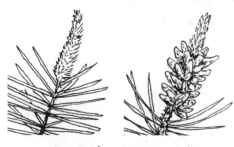

Are you going to demonstrate how to snip off a cutting?

Actually, I was going to give that fern sperm a haircut!

Plants that make seeds are the plants you are most familiar with. They fill our yards and gardens. Look back to page 17 again and you will see that seed-bearing plants are divided into two categories: the **gymnosperms** and the **angiosperms**. ("Sperm" just means "seed.") Let's look at the gymnosperms first.

The gymnosperms are mostly pine trees and fir trees. The word "gymno" is Greek for "naked." (Greeks ran naked in their gymnasiums.) Yes, that little seed inside a pine cone doesn't have any fruit covering it! It's shocking but true. The seed is botanically naked.

The reproductive structure of a gymnosperm is called a **cone**. No great surprise there—you already knew that. What you may not know is that cones can be male or female. What you think of as a pine cone is actually a female cone. Male cones are smaller than female cones and they are usually more fuzzy. They appear just for a few weeks at certain times of the year. The male cones produce **pollen**. Each tiny grain of pollen contains two sperm cells. The pollen grains are so small you need a magnifier to see them.

male cones

The male cones release their pollen into the air. The pollen grains of pine trees have two little "balloons" attached to them that help them float upward in currents of air. Being airborne as long as possible is an advantage for the pollen. It increases the odds of finding female cones. Even so, many pollen grains don't make it very far. That's why a tree has to release millions of pollen grains. (If you are allergic to pollen, this isn't good news!) Most of the pollen ends up on the ground, on other plants, or all over your car—places where it won't do any good. But a small portion of the pollen will land on the developing female cones.

The pollen grains that land on the female cones become trapped in a sticky substance at the base of each scale. Each scale contains two female parts, called **ovules.** Inside the ovules are **eggs.** After a pollen grain gets stuck on the end of an ovule, it starts growing a tube. This tube keeps growing until it

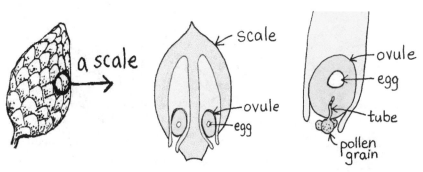

reaches the egg. Pine tree sperm can't swim like fern sperm can, so the pollen tube has to take them directly to the egg. Only one of the two sperm can enter the egg. Like it or not, the natural world is very competitive. The winner enters the egg and the loser disintegrates and disappears. (The story is a bit happier for angiosperms, though. There is a runner-up prize for the other sperm.)

When the sperm and egg join together, a **zygote** is formed. A zygote is a single cell. As this single cell begins to divide and develop, we no longer call it a zygote, but an **embryo**. The ovule around the embryo turns into a hard protective covering but remains attached to the "seed wing." It is now officially a seed. When the seeds are ready, the female cone opens up and the seeds drop out. This whole process, from when the pollen grains first stick to the scale until the day the mature cone opens up and sheds the finished seeds, takes two years. Green pine cones are female cones that are only one year old. They will need another season to finish their growth.

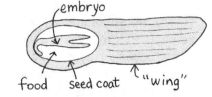

The seeds don't have to start growing immediately. They can sit and wait, sometimes for a very long time. The most extreme case of pine seeds waiting to grow is a species of pine tree that requires a forest fire to open its female cones. The cones will wait for years and years until there is a fire. The fire will destroy the parent tree, but it will also force the female cones to open and release the seeds. Since all the trees in the area were destroyed by the fire, the new seedlings will have plenty of wide open space in which to grow!

Day 2 And now... the angiosperms.

Wait! Can we stop for a few minutes? I need a break.

Yeah. I took a sneak peek at the next page. I might need a coffee.

Okay, it's intermission time. Get a snack, take a walk, maybe check out some of the fern videos on the Botany playlist. When you get back, we'll begin our study of flowers.

The word "angio" comes from Greek and means "vessel or container." The seeds of angiosperms are surrounded by a special container called the **ovary** (not to be confused with the **ovule**). The ovary eventually develops into a fruit, so it would also be correct to say that the covering around an angiosperm seed is a **fruit**.

Angiosperms are also called "flowering plants." Flowers come in all sizes and shapes, so we'll have to show you an "average" flower. This isn't any particular type of flower, it's just an imaginary, average flower.

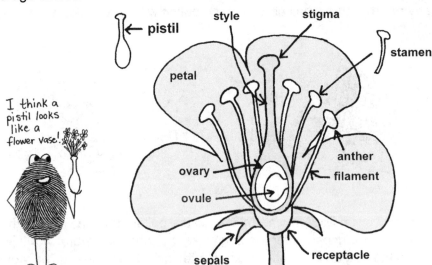

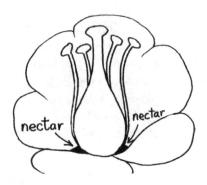
I think a pistil looks like a flower vase!

Many flowers look very different from our "average flower."

The **sepals**, right underneath the flower, are usually green, and their job is to protect the flower while it is developing. When the flower was just a bud, the sepals were the coverings around the bud. After the flower opens, the sepals' job is done, but they stay underneath the flower and just sit there looking pretty. The bump that the sepals come out of is called the **receptacle**. It doesn't look very important in this picture, but in some cases (apples, for instance) the receptacle will become part of the fruit.

The **petals** of the flower are often brightly colored in order to attract insects. Many flowers need insects to transfer the pollen from the male parts to the female parts. The **stamen** is the male part of the flower. This is easy to remember because the word "men" is part of the word "stamen." The little part on top of the stamen is called the **anther** and the skinny "stick" it sits on is called the **filament**. The anther is covered with pollen grains.

The female part of the flower is called the **pistil**. (Don't confuse this word with the word "pistol," meaning a gun.) Some botanists prefer to use the word **carpel** instead of pistil. You can use either word. The **style** is the long "neck" of the pistil and the **stigma** is the knobby part at the top. The bottom of the pistil is the **ovary** containing the **ovules**, which contain the **eggs**.

The process of transferring pollen from the anthers to the stigma is called **pollination**. Insects (or small birds or bats) are attracted by the look and smell of the flower. They know that those colors and odors will lead them to a source of food—a sugary liquid called **nectar**. (Some insects, bees in particular, also gather the pollen itself, not just the nectar.) The word nectar probably comes from two very ancient words: "nec," meaning "death"—as in the word "necropolis"—and "tar," meaning "to overcome." In mythology, "nec-tar" was the drink of the gods. (Undoubtedly, it didn't take too long for people to realize that drinking nectar would not make them immortal like the gods!)

The places where a plant produces nectar are called **nectaries**. (It sounds like a blend of the words "nectar" and "factory.") Many nectaries are located at the base of the pistil. When an insect or bird explores a flower, they are often trying to find the nectaries. (Though, as we mentioned, some insects come for both

You can see a lump of pollen on this bee's back leg.

nectar and pollen.) For insects just interested in nectar, the pistil and the stamen are objects that get in the way. They have to brush past them in order to get down to the nectar.

Whether they've come to collect pollen or not, the insects get pollen grains stuck all over their legs and abdomen. If they happen to bump against the stigma, some of the pollen grains will fall onto it. However, it's unlikely that these pollen grains will fertilize the flower's eggs. This is because most flowers have a timing device that prevents the stamen and the pistil from being ready at the same time. The goal for the flower is to swap DNA with another flower of the same species. You'll remember that it is an advantage for a living organism to exchange DNA with other members of its species. This guarantees genetic variety in the offspring, which is necessary for the survival of the species as a whole. Therefore, the ideal outcome is for that insect or bird to fly to another flower, hopefully one that has a pistil containing eggs that are ready to be fertilized, and rub some pollen onto its stigma.

An angiosperm pollen grain contains two cells: a "generative" cell that will make (generate) two sperm, and a tube cell that will make a tube. After it lands on a suitable stigma, the pollen grain releases the tube cell and it starts to grow. (We saw this happen with gymnosperms, too.) The tube cell grows down through the stigma, and into the ovary, heading for the bottom of the ovule. (The tube cell doesn't have eyes or a brain so how does it know where to go? Botanists are fairly sure that those two cells next to the egg cell give off chemical signals that guide the tube cell in the direction it needs to go.) As the tube cell grows, the generative cell is carried along with it. Toward the end of its journey, the generative cell splits in half, making two sperm.

What happens next is what makes angiosperms different from gymnosperms. Remember that in gymnosperms, only one sperm gets to fertilize the egg. There is a winner and a loser. In angiosperms, both sperm get to join with a female cell— no losers here! Since both sperm get to fertilize something, this process is called **double fertilization.**

As you can see, the ovule looks crowded. There are seven "sisters" in it. Only one of them is the actual egg cell. The two cells next to the egg cell are the ones that guide the pollen tube to the ovule. The three cells at the top are more mysterious. Botanists are not really sure what they do. They seem to be non-essential because as the embryo starts to grow, they just disappear. The two dots in the center turn out to be very important. They are called the **polar nuclei.** The two attached nuclei sit there all alone, with no organelles and no membrane. So do we count them as a cell? (Or two cells?) Botanists can't even answer that. They just call them "the polar nuclei" and leave it at that.

corn seed

So in come the sperm. One sperm joins with the egg to form a zygote, which will grow into an embryo. The other sperm joins with those two polar nuclei in the center and they create one of the strangest combinations in biology—a cell that isn't really a cell and has one-and-a-half times the amount of DNA found in a normal cell. This strange "megacell" will become the seed's **endosperm**, a food source for the embryo. (Endosperm is a good food source for people, too. You eat endosperm all the time: beans, corn, wheat, rice, and nuts.)

pollen grain

pollen tube

ovary
ovule
future endosperm

egg

sperm

There is a very good video about this posted on the Botany playlist. You might want to take a break from reading and watch the video!

As the endosperm and the plant embryo develop, the ovule will harden and form a **seed coat**. Some flowers start out with multiple ovules, so they will end up with multiple seeds. (Our "average" flower picture had only one ovule, so it would make only one seed.) While the ovules are turning into seeds, the ovary will change, too. In some plants, such as berries, tomatoes and grapes, the ovary becomes a soft fruit, while in other plants, such as apples and pears, the ovary enlarges but stays inside the fruit. The part of the pear we eat is actually the receptacle, much enlarged and a lot more tasty than it was when the pear was still a flower. The anatomy of the fruit depends partly on where the ovary was located in the flower. In this picture of a pear, you can see the sepals on the opposite end from the stem. The ovary was under the flower. Now think of a tomato. The sepals are right on the stem. This means that the ovary sat above the sepals and inside the flower.

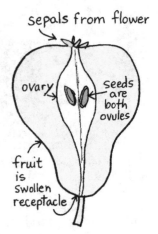

Some of the foods we call fruits really are fruits, such as apples, pears, melons and oranges. Vegetables such as squash, beans, and tomatoes are classified as vegetables by non-botanists, but technically they are fruits. They are not sweet, so we don't think of them as fruits. Nuts are also fruits, as are many inedible seed cases (like burrs) that you might meet on a walk through a field or forest. If it contains seeds, it's a fruit.

A vegetable comes from a plant part that is not involved in reproduction: leaves, stems and roots. True vegetables include spinach, lettuce, and cabbage (leaves), asparagus and celery (stems), and carrots and beets (roots). Potatoes might seem like roots because they grow out from the roots and don't contain seeds, but they are classified as **tubers**. The "eyes" on tubers will sprout and form a new plant, so they must be considered a reproductive structure. **Bulbs**, such as onions and garlic, are also vegetative reproductive structures. So we can cross those foods off the list of true vegetables, also. To be a true vegetable you have to be a plain old leaf, stem or root.

During our discussion of ferns, we learned that vegetative reproduction is when a plant grows a new plant from one of its vegetative parts, such as leaves, stems or roots. Angiosperms are masters of vegetative reproduction. In fact, some angiosperms rely primary on this form of reproduction. Strawberry plants, for example, send out stems called **runners**. When the tip of the runner hits the soil it begins to grow leaves and roots. Runners will take over your strawberry patch a lot faster than plants grown from the strawberry seeds. This method of reproduction works very well as a short-term strategy for rapid reproduction. The plants produced by vegetative reproduction are exact clones of the parent plant, however. In the long run, the plant will need to reproduce using seeds in order to exchange DNA with other plants and produce a healthier species.

We can't leave this section until we see what happens to those little plant embryos inside the fertilized seeds that we talked about on the last page. The sperm fertilized the egg, turning it into a zygote. Then the zygote grew into an embryo surrounded by endosperm.

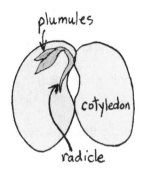

plumules

cotyledon

radicle

This picture shows the inside of a bean seed. Beans are ideal seeds to examine because they are large and have a very visible embryo. You can often see little tiny leaves called **plumules**. The part that will turn into the root is called the **radicle**. (You can think of a radish, which is a root.) The two halves of the endosperm become the cotyledons. They are filled with starch (the stuff pasta and potatoes are made out of), and will provide food energy for the embryo.

When a seed begins to grow, we call this **germination**. Water soaks into the seed and makes it swell, splitting apart the hard seed coat. Sometimes the seed coat falls off very quickly but other times it gets stuck halfway open and remains clipped to the cotyledons for several days. The cotyledons will eventually grow enough that the seed coat will pop off. As the plant grows and puts out leaves, the cotyledons will start to shrivel and will eventually fall off.

The radicle grows downward and becomes the roots. If the plant is a monocot the radicle will develop into fibrous roots. If the plant is a dicot, the radicle will become a tap root. The plant will grow larger and larger until one day it begins to flower. Then we're back to the beginning of the cycle again, with the formation of a seed.

true leaves

cot.   cot.

radicle

ACTIVITY 1: WATCH SOME VIDEOS OF THE THINGS YOU JUST READ ABOUT

Go to the Botany playlist on YouTube.com/TheBasementWorkshop and click on some of the videos listed for chapter 6. There are computer animations, time lapse videos, and mini-lectures.

ACTIVITY 2: BOTANICAL FOOD SORTING: TRUE FRUIT OR TRUE VEGETABLE?

Classify the following foods as either true fruits or true vegetables. If you don't know enough about the food to be able to decide which it is, you can do some research by either examining a real one or by using the Internet. (Remember, to be a vegetable you have to be a leaf, stem or root.)

tomato, spinach, lettuce, carrots, peas, beans, pumpkin, corn, kale, cabbage, broccoli, beets, zucchini, asparagus, cucumber, celery, parsley, peppers, eggplant, rhubarb, olive, avocado

TRUE FRUIT: _____

_____

_____

TRUE VEGETABLE: _____

_____

_____

ACTIVITY 3: FIND SOME PLANT EMBRYOS IN YOUR KITCHEN

Poke around in your cupboards or refrigerator and see if you can find one or more of these: beans of any kind (even in a can), peas, corn, peanuts. Very carefully pry or cut one of these seeds half. For dried seeds, it's best to soak them until they are soft. Don't try to cut anything hard and round with a sharp knife! It might roll over suddenly causing the knife to slip and cut your finger. Get adult help if you are using a sharp blade.

Make a sketch of what you see inside. Try to do three different seeds and draw them below, one per box. Write what type of seed it is and label the parts (cotyledons, plumules, radicle).

ACTIVITY 4: RECORD THE GROWTH OF A BABY PLANT

Do you have a photo album that shows sequential pictures of you when you were a baby—a newborn picture, then pictures at one month, two months, three months, etc.? In this activity, you can make a baby photo album for a plant. Plants grow more quickly than humans, though, so you will need to record growth day by day, not month by month. Put a seed in a wet paper towel and wait until it germinates. Sketch a picture of what it looks like when it has just begun sprouting. Then draw a picture every other day or so, showing what it looks like as it puts out seed leaves, roots, and finally real leaves. You won't need any dirt for this. The plant will grow for quite a while sitting in a wet paper towel. Don't forget to write how old the plant is in each picture.

ACTIVITY 5: ANOTHER STUPID PLANT JOKE

Yes, another terrible pun for you to solve. Fill in the answers to these questions, then write the letters in the numbered spaces below. Enjoy the joke.

1) This is formed when an egg and sperm join. __ __ __ __ __
                              3   37 17

2) The male part of a flower is called the __ __ __ __ __ __ .
             12   21

3) The very top of the male part of the flower is called the __ __ __ __ __ __ .
            24   30 2

4) The female part of a flower is called the __ __ __ __ __ __ .
            5   22

5) This word means "vessel or container." __ __ __ __ __
               39 25

6) This flower part is between the stigma and the ovary. __ __ __ __ __
           51 33   44

7) This is what a flower will eventually develop into. __ __ __ __ __
           36   18   47

8) When a zygote begins to grow, it is then called an __ __ __ __ __ .
           35   10   15

9) The outside of the ovule will do this when a seed is formed. __ __ __ __ __ __
           43   4   46

10) This vascular plant does not produce seeds. __ __ __ __
          23   14

11) This is the skinny "stick" that holds up the anther. __ __ __ __ __ __ __ __
           13   20   41

12) Flowers are a way for plants to "__ __ __ __ __" DNA with others of their species.
    16 28   38

13) The thickened underground stem of a fern is called a __ __ __ __ __ __ __ .
           48   40   49

14) This is at the base of the flower and sometimes becomes part of the fruit.

__ __ __ __ __ __
 29   9   7 45   26

15) This is the primarily pollinator of pine trees. __ __ __ __ __ __
          27 8   1   6

16) When a fern looks like a flat leaf we call it a __ __ __ __ __ __ __ .
          50   42 34   32

17) When two sperm are needed, we call it __ __ __ __ __ __ fertilization.
      19 11   31

__ __ __   __ __ __   __ __ __   __ __ __ __ __
1 2 3   4 5 6   7 8 9   10 11 12 13 14 15

__ __ __ __ __ __ __   __ __ __ __   __ __ __   __ __ __ __ ?
16 17 18 19 20 21 22 23 24 25 26 27 28 29 30 31 32 33

__ __   __ __ __ __ __ __   __ __ __ __ __ __ __ !
34 35 36 37 38 39 40 41 42 43 44 45 46 47 48 49 50 51

ACTIVITY 6: TIME TO REVIEW!

How much can you remember from the first five lessons? Can you remember the answers to the these questions? (The questions are taken from just the level one sections, not level two.)

1) What molecule can capture energy from sunlight? _____

2) What is the process where plants and animals burn glucose molecule to release energy for their cells to use? _____

3) Can you fill in these blanks? 6 ____ + 12 _____ + light → ___ glucose + 6 ____ + 6 ____

4) What is it called when a cell divides, making a duplicate of itself? _____

5) Which organelle contains DNA? _____

6) The plant kingdom is divided into plants that are _____ and plants that are non-_____.

7) The plants that make seeds are divided into two groups: _____ and _____

8) A flowering plant that has vascular bundles scattered randomly through the stem is a _____.

9) Name a non-vascular plant: _____

10) Non-vascular plants rely on _____ to get water to all their cells.

11) A sporophyte is a structure that makes _____.

12) The answer to number (11) gives rise to a thallus that makes _____ and _____ parts.

13) There are two types of tubes in vascular plants: _____ and _____.

14) The center of a dicot stem is called the _____.

15) The texture of a dicot stem can be either _____ or _____.

16) The roots of a monocot are _____ .

17) The veins of a monocot leaf look _____.

18) The heartwood of a tree is made of dead _____.

19) The bark of a tree is made of dead _____.

20) The sapwood of a tree contains these tubes that take sugar up and down: _____

21) This thin layer of cells produces both types of vascular tube cells. _____

22) A fern's underground stem is called a _____.

23) The correct name for the stalk of a leaf is the _____.

24) This Latin word means "tip." _____

25) The holes in the bottom of a leaf are called _____.

26) This layer of cells in a leaf looks like an old-fashioned log fort: _____ layer

27) Which one of these is NOT an edible pigment you would find in a plant?

   a) carotene   b) chlorophyll   c) cyanide   d) anthocyanin   e) xanthophyll

28) Which one of these does NOT describe the shape of a leaf?

   a) undulating   b) photosynthesizing   c) serrated   d) pinnate   e) palmate   f) simple

29) What type of cell regulates the amount of air and water that come in and out of a leaf? _____

30) The study of tree rings as a way to date wooden artifacts is called _____.

LEVEL TWO

We began our section on gymnosperms by saying that this group is *mainly* conifer trees. Conifers include pines, firs, hemlocks, spruces, junipers, larches, cedars, and cypress trees. If someone showed you pictures of the trees in this list and asked you to classify them, you would probably guess that they were gymnosperms because you'd see cones hanging from their branches. There are some weird gymnosperms, however, that are hard to classify. Here are a few of these odd members of the gymnosperm family.

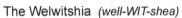

The Welwitshia *(well-WIT-shea)*
This plant grows in the deserts of Namibia and Angola. It can only germinate when there is a lot of rainfall, but once it gets its roots established, it is an incredible survivor. Some plants are estimated to be over 1000 years old. They can grow to be several meters in diameter but consist of only two leaves. Those two leaves grow very long and they split and get tattered so it looks like there are more than two leaves. Each plant is either male or female. This one is a female.

The Sago palm
This plant looks like it should be in the same family with coconut palms and date palms. True palms are angiosperms, however, so this cone-bearing plant can't be a palm tree even though it looks like one. The sago was originally from Japan, but can now be found all over the world. The most important thing to know about the sago palm is that it is **poisonous** to both humans and animals. Pets will get very sick if they chew on the leaves.

The Ephedra
You'd never guess that this tall, grass-like plant was a gymnosperm! The Ephedra can be found in dry parts of Asia, Europe, and North and South America. It has been used for medicinal purposes for thousands of years. The drug "Sudafed" is made from the same chemical that is found in the Ephedra. It is a stimulant, but acts as a decongestant by shrinking the blood vessels in the nose and sinuses.

The other odd gymnosperm worth mentioning is the ginkgo tree. Actually, no one is sure if it *is* a gymnosperm. It's such a strange plant that it isn't "related" to any other plant on Earth! Its full name is: Gingkophyta, Gingkoopsida, Gingkoales, Gingkoaceae, *Gingko biloba*

The "*biloba*" part was given by Linnaeus, because the leaves can often look "bi-lobed." Botanists have argued for years how the Gingko should be classified. The male plant makes cones, but the female plant does not. It makes ovules that look like fruits, but they can't be "true" fruits because they aren't inside an ovary. Don't eat those fruits—they contain butyric acid, the substance that gives rotten (rancid) butter its bad smell. (The word "butter" comes from "butyric.") Some people say that ginkgo fruits smell like vomit.

Despite the bad smell of the fruits, the tree is still edible and is one of the most common plants used in herbal medicine. The Gingko is very resistant to insect damage and plant diseases and can live for a very long time. China has Gingko trees that are thousands of years old.

Enough about gymnosperms for now—is there anything more to say about angiosperms? A lot more! (But perhaps that's not good news.) Let's start with something sweet and delicious and talk a bit more about fruits.

We've learned that all fruits contains seeds. Can we turn that around and say that all seeds have fruits? No. Gymnosperms have seeds that are "naked" and are not protected by a fruit. Only angiosperms make fruits around their seeds. In fact, we can state categorically that *all* angiosperms make fruits. Sounds like a silly, pointless statement, but if we start thinking of angiosperms that don't grow in our gardens and orchards, that statement will seem impossible in many cases. For example, a dandelion is an angiosperm. Where is its fruit? What about maple trees, daisies, grasses, and weeds? Do they make fruits?

In botanical terms, all seed coverings are fruits, no matter what they look like. Those burrs that stick to your pants when you hike through the woods, "helicopters" that fall from maple trees, milkweed pods, pea pods, acorns, peanut shells—they are all botanical fruits. Fruits that are dry and hard are called **dry fruits**. Fruits that are wet are not called wet fruits, though. They are given a fancier name that sounds like a word a chef would use to describe a fruit: **succulent**. *(SUK-yu-lent)*

DRY FRUITS   SUCCULENT FRUITS

In dry fruits, the shells and pods and wings are the fruits. Strange as it may seem, pods are fruits even if we find them inedible. Hard shells around nuts are botanical fruits because they are the mature ovaries of those plants.

But that's not enough classification to satisfy botanists. Oh, no. There are lots of other categories that fruits can be placed into. **Simple fruits** are fruits that formed from an ovary that had a single pistil. Simple fruits include the beans, nuts, grains, apples, tomatoes, melons, olives, and "stone fruits" (that *Prunus* family we met in lesson 2: cherries, peaches, and plums). **Multiple fruits** formed from a cluster of flowers, not just one flower. As the individual fruits matured, they merged (grew together) to form what looks like a single fruit. Examples of multiple fruits include pineapples, figs, mulberries and bread fruits. Halfway between the simple fruits and the multiple fruits are the **aggregate fruits**. *(AG-reh-gate)* They formed from a single flower but that flower had more than one pistil. Examples of aggregate fruits are strawberries, blackberries, raspberries and boysenberries (none of which are true berries!).

SIMPLE FRUITS   AGGREGATE FRUITS   MULTIPLE FRUITS

It should not surprise us that botanists don't consider strawberries and raspberries to be berries, because, after all, these are the same folks who tell us that dandelion seeds and peanut shells are fruits. Botanists define **berries** as "succulent fruits produced by a single ovary." Examples of botanical berries include grapes, tomatoes, chili peppers, kiwis, eggplants, avocados, bananas, coffee beans, persimmons, pomegranates, currants, and... gooseberries, blueberries and cranberries. (At least there were a few berries in the list!) There is also a category for "sort-of-berries." These

semi-berries (which they call **hesperidium**) have a thick rind and a very juicy interior. You can guess from that description that citrus fruits are in this category. Other hesperidium include cucumbers, melons and squash.

Fruit classification can get even more complicated than this. To further classify fruits we have to start using names like indehiscent, accessory, achene, caryopsis, legume, cypsela, drupe, loment, samara, schizocarp, silique, and utricle. And to make matters worse, the categories overlap, so it can get really confusing. Let's take a look at just one of these categories—**the legumes**. You'll meet this word again at some point in the near future, especially if you are watching for it.

The **legume family** is sometimes called the bean family and includes beans, peas, lentils, soy beans, carob beans, clover, alfalfa, and peanuts. Besides providing nutritious, dry, simple fruits, this family has another important characteristic. The roots of these plants are very special. They have a "friendship" (the correct word is **symbiosis**) with a certain type of bacteria. The legumes allow the bacteria to live in little colonies in their roots. The colonies look like little round bumps or "nodules." The bacteria are happy to have a nice place to live and the legume plants are happy because the bacteria provide something they need: nitrogen.

Have you ever head the phrase, "Water, water everywhere, but not a drop to drink"? A plant might think, "Nitrogen, nitrogen everywhere, but not one molecule is usable!" The air around them is mostly nitrogen. Plants need nitrogen to make many of their molecules, but the problem is that they can't use nitrogen in its gaseous form. So they are surrounded by nitrogen but can't use a single molecule of it. Plants can only use nitrogen if it is part of a molecule that contains hydrogen atoms, such as **ammonia**, NH_3.

The bacteria, on the other hand, <u>can</u> use the nitrogen in the air. The bacteria take nitrogen atoms from the air and attach them to hydrogen atoms, creating just what the plant needs: ammonia molecules. This process of taking nitrogen out of the air and turning it into ammonia is called **nitrogen fixing**. This type of bacteria is often referred to as **nitrogen-fixing bacteria**, and their colonies are called **nitrogen-fixing nodules**.

So these lucky legumes have little ammonia factories in their roots, providing them with a convenient and constant source of nitrogen. The bacteria don't harm the plants at all—they help them. So it works out very well. Other plants benefit, too, because after the legume plants die, the little nitrogen nodules stay in the soil and continue to release their nitrogen. Thousands of years ago, farmers discovered that legumes were good for the soil. They didn't know about nitrogen, but they knew that legume plants could restore soil in a way that other plants could not. So they rotated their crops from year to year, making sure that each field was planted with legumes once in a while. **Crop rotation** is still practiced today. Farmers who can't rotate their crops for some reason usually put nitrogen fertilizer on their fields. (Fertilizers can provide nitrogen to the soil faster and in greater quantities than legumes can.)

One of the more interesting and fun aspects of botany is observing the many methods plants use for seed dispersal. Dispersing something means spreading it around, or sending it away from you. All living things are designed to want to spread out and fill as much of their environment as possible. It's like all the plants in the world are competing for world domination. There are many battles for territory, but it's rare that one species is actually successful in taking over. However, that doesn't stop them from trying...

The goal for a seed is to get to a place that is a bit away from the parent plant, but no so far away that the environment is no longer suitable. There are four main modes of travel that seeds use: wind, water, animals, and "explosions."

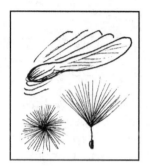

Wind is the most common mode of travel for seeds. Many seeds are small, and even if they don't have wind-catching devices, a strong gust of wind can pick them up and scatter them. Some seeds, however, have special designs that allow them to stay airborne for a while. One of the most well-known designs is the "helicopter" seed of the maple tree. These seeds spin and twirl as they fall off the tree, delighting children and fascinating botanists. Another popular design is the dandelion "parachute"—a piece of "fluff" so light that the tiny seed can stay airborne for many minutes. Thistles, bulrushes, and many roadside weeds make fluffy fruits, too.

Water is used by plants that live in or near water. Trees such as the willow and the silver birch grow along the edges of rivers and streams. They produce seeds that are very small and light and float well. Foxglove and harebell flowers are also found along streams and use this same strategy. Trees found on tropical beaches often make seeds with woody, waterproof coatings that can enable them to survive a long voyage in salty water. The coconut and the "sea bean" are the most well-known seeds in this category. The sea bean holds the record for the largest seed in the world; it can grow to be as large as a beach ball! (18 inches or 40-50 centimeters in diameter)

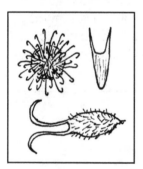

Animals can provide transportation for some types of seeds. This can happen in several ways. Sometimes the animals have no idea they are transporting seeds. Some seeds cases are covered with miniature hooks that will get stuck in the fur of an animal that brushes past. Later, the animal will clean itself and the seeds will fall to the ground. Other seeds prefer to travel inside an animal. Many animals eat berries and small fruits. The next day... well, you know what happens. Also, animals can literally carry seeds from one place to another. Squirrels pick up seeds, carry them to other locations, then bury them in the ground. How convenient is that?!

Now we'll end this section with a bang and discuss plants that use miniature explosions to jettison their seeds away from them. Usually, these plants make pods that are rigged to explode as the pods dry out. The geometry of the pod makes it dry unevenly, creating mechanical tension. The sun comes out and begins to dry the pods and then—POP!—the seeds go flying. Geraniums, lupines, wisteria and gorse bushes use this method of seed dispersal, as do many other plants whose names are a bit too Latin to bother you with. (There are some great videos of exploding seeds on the Botany playlist at YouTube.com/TheBasementWorkshop.)

If you are ready to quit reading, you may stop. If you have just a little more patience left and can stand to hear one fascinating little detail about double fertilization, you can acquire a piece of trivia that most people don't know.

We learned that mosses and ferns have a life cycle called "alternation of generations." The generations look very different. The sporophyte generation of a fern is a leaf-like frond, and the **gametophyte** generation (the one that produces male and female cells) is a flat, heart-shaped prothallus lying on the ground. The difference is obvious—it's easy to seem them alternate.

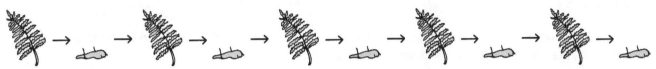

Scientists have discovered that *all* plants have this same pattern of alternation of generations. No one knew that seed plants had alternating generations until the invention of the electron microscope in the middle of the 20th century. With microscopes that were a thousand times more powerful than anything they had ever used, botanists could examine the process of plant reproduction like never before. They discovered that the anthers and the ovules don't actually produce pollen and eggs directly. They produce spores first.

The anthers produce tiny spores (**microspores**), and the ovules make large spores (**megaspores**). The microspores turn into pollen grains and the megaspores turn into eggs and other female cells. So the alternation of generations happens at a microscopic level where we can't see it. If someone asked you to name a plant whose life cycle included the alternation of generations, you could name any plant in the world and you'd be right.

Spores occur in other organisms, too, not just in plants. Fungi are the most notable spore-producing organisms. If reproduction can be accomplished using either spores or seeds, then what is the difference, and why would a plant make both? The easiest way to compare them is with a chart:

SPORE	SEED
Microscopic	Can be seen without a microscope (usually)
Made of one cell (usually)	Made of many cells
Was not created by union of male and female cells	Was created by the union of male and female cells
Does not contain an embryo	Contains an embryo
Contains no food	Has stored food for the embryo
Produced in great quantities, usually millions	Plants make as few as one, as many as hundreds
Needs conditions to be just right to start growing	Can tolerate less-than-ideal conditions because of the resources stored in the endosperm
Can survive very harsh conditions for a very long time	Fairly hardy, but cannot survive as long as spores can

Spores are designed for quantity, seeds are designed for quality. Spores are made without any exchange of DNA, seeds are the result of a DNA exchange. The DNA of a spore is identical to that of the parent plant. The DNA of a seed is a unique combination of the DNA from two parent plants. It takes both spores and seeds to keep the plant kingdom thriving year after year.

ACTIVITY 1: "ODD ONE OUT"

One word in each list doesn't belong. It's up to you to figure out which one and why.

Example 1: maple, chestnut, daisy, oak
Answer: The daisy does not belong because it is a small herbaceous flower and the others are trees.

Example 2: stem, flower, root, leaf
Answer: The flower does not belong. The other three parts are vegetative but the flower is part of the reproductive system.

Got the idea? Great. We'll start with some words from this chapter, then we'll throw in some words from previous chapters. Review is always good!

1) anther, pollen, stigma, stamen _____

2) tomato, cherry, almond, blueberry _____

3) spinach, tomato, celery, carrot _____

4) walnut, peanut, acorn, pecan _____

5) ovary, stigma, style, filament _____

6) cabbage, celery, asparagus, rhubarb _____

7) apple, cherry, plum, apricot _____

8) apple, pineapple, zucchini, tomato _____

9) alfalfa, dandelion, clover, pea _____

10) carrot, beet, turnip, potato _____

11) cranberry, blueberry, strawberry, gooseberry _____

12) date palm, sago palm, coconut palm, fan palm _____

13) xylem, phloem, cambium, bark _____

14) geranium, grass, lily, corn _____

15) whorled, serrated, alternate, opposite _____

16) gemma, rhizome, fiddlehead, frond _____

17) chordate, pinnate, deltoid, lamina _____

18) moss, fern, pine tree, daisy _____

19) chloroplast, chlorophyll, nucleus, vacuole _____

20) hydrogen, carbon, magnesium, sodium _____

ACTIVITY 2: WATCH SOME AMAZING SEEDS IN ACTION

There are several videos of exploding seed pods in the Botany playlist. (Don't be expecting dynamite, though. Remember, these are tiny seed pods!) There is also a video showing some of the most amazing airborne seeds in the world.

LESSON 7: PLANT ADAPTATIONS

LEVEL ONE

Life is seldom ideal. We all live with situations that are difficult for us in some way. Some people face severe problems such as not being able to find enough food or clean water, living in extremely hot or cold climates, or having to deal with a chronic illness. Others of us live with milder limitations having to do with our age, our size, our family situation, the neighborhood where we live, the work our parents do, the personalities of our siblings, and so on.

We don't think of plants as having the same problems that we do, but to a large extent, they really do. They can experience malnutrition, extreme temperatures, unfriendly neighbors, competition for territory, "parents" who overshadow them, "siblings" who are more or less successful than they are, chronic and acute illnesses, and problems due to aging. Obviously, they can't think about their problems like we can. All of their responses come not from their brains (which they don't have) but from their pre-programmed DNA that allows them to adapt and survive.

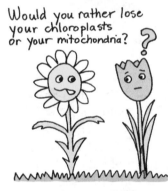

Let's take a look at two of the most basic problems a plant might face. We could introduce these problems as a silly "Would You Rather...?" question. In the "Would You Rather...?" game, players are forced to choose between two bad options. For example, "Would you rather be trapped in outer space or at the bottom of the ocean?" No matter which you choose, the outcome will not be good. You must choose what you feel to be "the lesser of two evils," and then explain your choice. The game is intended to encourage interesting discussions and hopefully bring some laughter along the way. If plants were playing this game, one of them could ask this question: "Would you rather have almost no water at all, or so much water that you are drowning in it?"

Assuming that a plant had a brain and could think about this question, it would ponder the consequences of each option. Not having enough water would mean that as transpiration occurred, there would be no way to replace the water lost through the leaves. The plant would dry out and probably die. Being immersed in water would mean that the stomata (holes) in the leaves would be filled with liquid water, preventing the plant from "breathing," causing the plant to die. Too much water might also encourage the growth of harmful bacteria. So which option is worse? It's like choosing between dying of thirst and drowning. Two bad options!

Some plants would definitely choose the "too little water" option. In fact, they live out that scenario every day and mange to survive. Desert plants have special adaptations that allow them to live in places that get less than 10 inches (25 cm) of rain a year. In deserts, rain is often seasonal, and months can go by with no rain at all. How is it possible for a plant to survive that long without water? Garden plants start wilting if they don't get rain every week.

A normal plant growing in a place with adequate rainfall has a constant flow of water going in through its roots, up through its stems, and out through its leaves. (Remember, the beginning of this process is actually the "out through the leaves" part. The loss of water in the leaves causes water to flow up through the stems, and finally come in through the roots.) If there is not a constant source of water available, this mode of living doesn't work. What changes would have to be made to a plant's anatomy in order to prepare it for life in a desert?

LEAVES: This is where the water loss problem starts. That pesky transpiration process is constantly allowing water molecules to go flying off into the atmosphere. Can this be prevented? Could we just get rid of the leaves? Maybe, but leaves are where photosynthesis occurs, so the plants would starve without photosynthesis. If a plant did not have leaves, it would have to have photosynthesis occurring somewhere else. Or maybe we could just reduce the size of the leaves instead of getting rid of them altogether. Smaller leaves would mean less water loss.

STEMS: What changes could be made to the stems? Could photosynthesis occur here? Could the stems be adapted for water storage instead of simply holding tubes for water transport? If so, the stems might have to become very large at times.

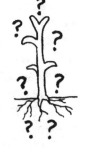

ROOTS: Is there any way to make roots more efficient at gathering water? Should the roots go deeper? Or would it be better to keep them shallow and near the surface so that they can quickly soak up rain when it comes? Would having more tiny root hairs help?

I didn't know cacti made flowers.

Yeah, and they make fruit, too!

The most famous of all desert plants is the cactus, of course. Cactus plants look like they have no leaves. Technically, their sharp spines are actually leaves, but these leaves are so thin that they lose almost no water at all. We saw a similar adaptation in pine trees. Pine needles are actually very thin leaves. However, since pine needles are green, it is easier to think of them as leaves. Cactus spines just don't seem like leaves, but botanists assure us that spines are indeed highly adapted leaves.

What could possibly be the purpose of a leaf that can hardly do photosynthesis and doesn't initiate transpiration? What are cactus spines good for? The main thing they do is hurt like crazy if you get them in your skin. Sharp spines help to protect cacti from thirsty desert animals who might want to quench their thirst with a big bite of juicy cactus stem. Some botanists think the spines might also help to collect water at night. Little droplets of dew form on the spines. These droplets run down the spines toward the stems, then they flow down the stems, ending up at the base of the plant where the roots near the surface can absorb the moisture quickly before the sun comes up.

The body of a cactus is technically a stem. Most cacti are green (or at least green-ish), which tells you that these bulky stems contain chlorophyll. Wherever there is chlorophyll, photosynthesis is occurring. Cacti must use adapted forms of photosynthesis, however. Regular photosynthesis requires a constant supply of water and carbon dioxide from the air. The "downside" of not having regular leaves is that you can't use regular photosynthesis. The types of photosynthesis desert plants use are called "C4" and "CAM." (Regular photosynthesis is known as "C3" since it produces 3-carbon sugars. C4 produces 4-carbon sugars. "CAM" is an abbreviation for a gruesomely complicated word that even scientists don't like to use because it's too long. They just say "CAM.")

Cactus stems have the ability to store a lot of water—enough water to keep the cactus alive during dry seasons that last for many months. The body of a cactus usually looks like it is made of "pleats" that go in and out. This shape allows for easy expansion and contraction without any disruption of the roots at the base of the plant. The root system of a cactus is often very shallow and extends outward from the plant quite a distance. When rain comes, the cactus has thousands of root hairs waiting and ready right near the surface. Large cacti can take in over 100 gallons (400 liters) during a single rain storm.

A few types of cacti have very long tap roots in addition to lots of surface roots. The long central tap root can be twice as long as the body (stem) of the cactus. This deep root can store a lot of water.

Cactus stems have a structure that other plants do not have: bumps called **areoles**. Botanists guess that areoles are most closely related to the branches of regular plants. It is from the areoles that both spines and flowers grow.

One last important cactus survival strategy is to grow slowly. Cacti don't need to be in any hurry. Growth takes energy. A plant's energy comes from sugars made during photosynthesis. Desert plants are already at a disadvantage when it comes to photosynthesis because they have to keep their stomata shut all day to prevent loss of moisture. Growing slowly reduces the need for sugar.

The bumps are areoles.

This beautiful succulent is called aeonium.

Cacti are not the only type of plants that can survive in dry climates. Plants called **succulents** are similar to cacti in many ways, though they have actual leaves, not spines. The leaves of succulent plants feel thick and "juicy." The stems are often very thick and can store water. Some succulents have stems and leaves that are filled with a gooey substance called **mucilage** (*MEW-sell-ahj*). The mucilage acts like a sponge and holds water. A common succulent plant that many people recognize is the aloe vera plant. Some people call it the "burn plant" because you can break open the leaves and use the mucilage to soothe burned skin. The mucilage may feel slimy and weird, but it does make your skin feel better.

Succulent leaves feel like they are covered in a waxy substance. This is because they *are* covered in a waxy substance. We met this waxy substance back in lesson five when saw the cross section of a leaf. The thin top layer was called the cuticle. All leaves have at least a tiny bit of cuticle, but succulent leaves have a lot of it. Cuticle is fairly waterproof, so it keeps moisture from getting out of (or going into) the leaf.

Another characteristic of succulent leaves is a reduced number of stomata. Those little stomata holes are where air and moisture get in and out of a leaf, so if you have fewer holes you have less of a problem with water molecules escaping. Succulents have fewer stomata than regular plants. Also, succulents tend to close their stomata during the day when the sun is hot and evaporation (and therefore dehydration) will occur quickly. They open their stomata at night, when the air is cooler and evaporation is less of a problem.

This is a photo of a real stoma.

I decided to upgrade to stomata.

These stomata tricks are pretty slick, but there's a downside to them. The reduced number of stomata and the daytime closings also mean that a succulent leaf can't take in as much carbon dioxide as a normal leaf can. Like cacti, succulents need to use those alternative forms of photosynthesis: "C4" and "CAM." In these forms of photosynthesis, carbon dioxide is brought in at night and the carbons are snipped off and stored in the form of an acid. (You could think of it like canning food, perhaps?) The succulent cells have to be very efficient with their carbon atoms because there is a limited supply of carbon dioxide.

One last succulent survival trick worth mentioning is hair. Some plants grow hairs on their leaves or stems in order to provide some extra protection from the wind and sun. The hairs act like a layer of insulation, slowing down the rate of evaporation.   On cold desert nights, dew can condense on the hairs and perhaps a small trickle of water will reach the roots by morning.

A really thick layer of hairs probably also functions as a way to deter insects from biting into the plant. The insect can't get its mouthparts close enough to the stem because the hairs get in the way. This feature can be seen on plants in temperate (not so hot) areas of the world, not just in super dry climates. You might have some plants with hairy stems and leaves growing right near you. Sunflowers, for instance, have very hairy stems. The plant called "Lamb's Ear" has leaves so fuzzy they feel like animal ears, not plant leaves.

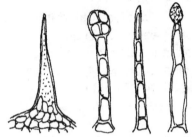

Some trichome cells are long and skinny. The round tips make smelly oils.

Plant hairs are not made from the same stuff that animal hairs are. Animal hair is made of "dead" protein molecules. Plant hairs are made of living plant cells. Plant hairs are properly called **trichomes**, and they are extensions of epidermis cells. (Remember the upper and lower epidermis cells from the leaf cross section?) These specialized epidermis cells can grow to be very long and thin. Some have specialized cells at the tip that can secrete strong-smelling substances. The strong smell of most herbs (such as mint) come from smelly oils produced by gland cells on the tips of trichomes.

Day 2

Let's turn now to the other terrible option for plants: drowning in water. Too much water will kill most plants, but there are some plants that are adapted for living in water all the time. What adaptations would a plant need to have in order to survive being in water all the time? Would the stomata be a problem? Would water still flow up the xylem tubes? Would the roots need to be in dirt?

There are many types of aquatic plants and their adaptations are just what they need for their specific environment. Some plants have their roots submerged in water all the time while their leaves stay out of the water. Other plants have roots and stems under the water and leaves that float on the surface. The most extreme water plants live completely submerged all the time.

What adaptations would a plant need to have in order to be able to live submerged in water all the time? Would it need stomata or cuticle? What about roots? Would it be able to make flowers?

A manatee eating seagrass. (USGS photo)

Seagrasses spend their entire life under the water. They look and act very much like regular grass. They even have those pesky rhizomes that let them use vegetative reproduction to spread very quickly. This is annoying in your garden when the grass starts taking over your strawberry patch, but along seashores this ability to spread quickly is a very good thing. Seagrasses are a very important part of shoreline ecosystems. Seagrasses reproduce using flowers and seeds, too. The pollen is carried by water instead of wind.

Seagrass leaves have neither cuticle nor stomata. It's pointless to try to keep water in or out when you are surrounded by it all the time! The cells in the leaves are okay with being saturated with water all the time and the cells have micro-adaptations that let them take carbon dioxide right from the water. Like all leaves, seagrass leaves need sunlight for photosynthesis. This means that seagrasses can only grow in relatively shallow water. If the water becomes cloudy because of pollution, the deeper seagrasses will start to die out. Dying grass might not sound like a big deal, but seagrasses occupy a very important place in many aquatic ecosystems. Seagrass beds are filled with all kinds of animal life. If the grasses disappear, so do the animals.

Seagrasses have another adaptation that helps them to survive in the water. They have

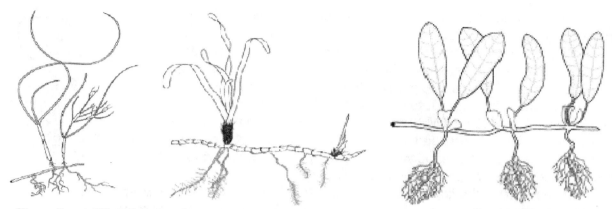

These three different types of seagrasses all have leaves that flex and bend with the water currents.

microscopic air sacs in their leaves and stems that act like little floaties, keeping the leaves upright in the water. (If you take seagrass out of the water, it droops over your hand like a wet noodle. The leaves don't have stiff central veins like regular grass blades do. Seagrasses need to be able to bend and flex and "go with the flow" in the water. If their leaves were stiff, they'd get torn apart by the motion of the water.) The tiny air sacs in the leaves and stems provide just the right amount of buoyancy so that the leaves stay upright in the water, reaching toward the sunlight.

Water plants are surrounded by water, so transpiration is not necessary. Cells can get whatever they need by osmosis. (Remember, osmosis is when molecules go right through the cell's membrane.) The carbon dioxide, water, and nutrients are abundant all around the cells, so xylem tubes aren't really necessary. In most water plants, the vascular bundles are very much reduced, and in some cases they are almost absent.

A slightly less drastic situation is when a plant is only partly submerged in water. The bottom half of the plant stays in the water while the top part is allowed to touch the air. A great example of a plant adapted to this situation is the water lily. Let's take a close-up look at a lily that holds the world record for the largest leaf in the plant kingdom: the Amazon lily.

Found in the Amazon River in South America, this lily can grow leaves that are up to 8 feet (2.5 meters) across. These giant leaves are almost perfectly round and look like floating plates. They are quite stable and can support the weight of small birds and animals. Their strength is due to a network of strong veins on the underside of the leaf. Their ability to float is due to small air pockets inside the veins. In addition to being strong, these veins can also be deadly—they are covered in sharp spines. Fish learn very quickly that nibbling lily veins is a bad idea!

The bottom sides of the lily leaves have two other features that are worth mentioning. Like seagrasses, they have no stomata and no cuticle. Unlike seagrasses, these undersides have lots of red pigment in them. The red pigment molecules help to catch wavelengths of light that are missed by the green chlorophyll pigments on top.

The top side of a lily leaf is nothing like the bottom side. It's green, is covered with waxy cuticle, and contains stomata. The top side is adapted to living in air, the bottom side to water.

The life cycle of the Amazon water lily sounds like something from a fantasy story. Its flowers bloom for only two days. The first night it blooms, the flower is female. It's white and smells like fragrant perfume, an odor that scarab beetles find irresistible. Once the flower has attracted beetles, it closes up, trapping the beetles inside. During the night, the flower changes its gender from female to male, and its color from white to pink. It also stops making perfume. When the flower opens up at the end of the second day, the beetles are freed from their flowery prison but are covered with pollen grains. The flower no longer smells good, so they fly off to find another white lily flower, carrying the pink pollen grains with them.

Once fertilized, the flower closes and falls to the bottom of the river where it forms a seed. The seed does not begin to grow until the next year. Lily seeds usually germinate right as the Amazon River is reaching its annual flood stage, with the water rising several inches a day. The newly sprouted water lily stem must grow at an unbelievably fast rate in order to keep its "head" above the rising water. The stem is capable of growing up to 20 feet (7 meters) tall in just a few weeks. When the waters stop rising, the lily starts growing giant leaves (lily pads).

It's then a battle of lily versus lily, with each plant attempting to dominate its area. (Sibling rivalry happens even among plants!) Once a giant leaf has spread itself out over the water, any plant underneath it will die from lack of sunlight. A side benefit of this situation is that algae are also prevented from growing. This is why water lilies (usually varieties other than Amazon) are planted in outdoor water gardens. People would rather look at lily leaves than algae "scum."

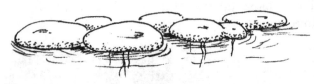

One of the smallest aquatic plants on earth is called "duckweed" or "water lentils." Duckweed looks like tiny green dots floating on the surface of a lake or pond. They are bright green and look very clean. True to its name, ducks love duckweed. Other water birds eat it too, as well as people in some parts of the world. It's a great source of protein, even better than soybeans, and it produces more starch per acre than corn! It's possible that duckweed could be turned into ethanol fuel, just like corn is. Some day our cars might run on fuel made from duckweed!

A duckweed plant consists of just a tiny leaf, with no visible stems or roots. (In some species, the leaves have very small root hairs dangling from the underside.) If duckweed doesn't have stems or roots can it still be classified as a plant? We decided way back at the beginning of lesson one that there are only two requirements for being a plant: 1) you must do photosynthesis, and 2) you must be made of more than one cell. Duckweed qualifies on both counts. In fact, it's even classified as an angiosperm since it occasionally produces flowers—the tiniest flowers in the plant kingdom, no larger than the width of a piece of thread!

duckweed
flowers
↓
. . . . . .

It's kind of funny to think of cars and ducks both being powered by duckweed!

Yeah. Um... Those stomata are creeping me out. Can you get rid of them before the next chapter?

ACTIVITY 1: SIT LIKE A LUMP ON YOUR CHAIR OR COUCH AND WATCH VIDEOS

This activity should not be too difficult. Log on to www.YouTube.com/TheBasementWorkshop and enjoy the videos about desert plants and water lilies.

ACTIVITY 2: PLANT PUZZLE

Fill in the missing words in the clues, then transfer the letters to the numbered slots underneath the pictures. Assuming you've filled in the clues correctly, you'll find out the names of the succulent plants in the pictures. (We're counting cacti as succulents. Sometimes the word succulent is used as a more general term, with cacti being a subcategory.)

1) Succulents have fewer ___ ___ ___ ___ ___ ___ ___ and more ___ ___ ___ ___ ___ ___ ___ .
   68 18 94   1   31   11   22 65 45 36
They also have gooey stuff called ___ ___ ___ ___ ___ ___ ___ in their stems and leaves.
                                    52 54 9 32 84 2

2) Cacti have bumps called ___ ___ ___ ___ ___ ___ ___ on their ___ ___ ___ ___ ___ .
                            59 38   74   95   5

3) Desert plants must use two other forms of photosynthesis: "___4" and "___ ___ ___ ."
                                                                90   53 39

4) The water plant called ___ ___ ___ ___ ___ ___ ___ ___ looks like tiny green dots. Even though
                          71 28 66   48 57
it does not have stems or roots, it is still a ___ ___ ___ ___ ___ because it does photosynthesis and
is made of more than one cell.   86   3   10

5) Duckweed is very nutritious. Like soy, it is a good source of ___ ___ ___ ___ ___ ___ ___ and
like corn, it is a good source of ___ ___ ___ ___ ___ ___ .   47 7 19   96 20
                                   67   49 41 62 56

6) Like all plants, when a duckweed flower is pollinated, a Z ___ ___ ___ ___ ___ is formed.
                                                            35 46 70   24

7) This type of animal loves to eat seagrass: ___ ___ ___ ___ ___ ___ .
                                               72 16 55

8) Plant hairs are called ___ ___ ___ ___ ___ ___ ___ ___ ___ and originate from the
                          50 87 13 63 33
___ ___ ___ ___ ___ ___ ___ ___ layer.
21   93   34 78   42

9) The ___ ___ ___ ___ ___ ___ side of an Amazon lily ___ ___ ___ is the color ___ ___ ___ and
       37 15   97 81   25 8   79 61
has sharp ___ ___ ___ ___ ___ ___ on the veins.
          88   60 26

10) When water evaporates out through the leaves, causing an upward flow of water from the roots,
this is called ___ ___ ___ ___ ___ ___ ___ ___ ___ ___ ___ ___ .
               73 69 27   40 29 77 76   64 14

11) The aloe plant is sometimes used to treat this type of injury: ___ ___ ___ ___
                                                                    6   92 58

12) S ___ ___ ___ ___ ___ ___ ___ plants have very B ___ ___ ___ ___ stems. This lets
    91 23 43   80   75   30 44 51
them store water so they can S ___ ___ ___ ___ ___ in desert climates.
                             17   82 4   89

13) This word root means "naked" in Greek: ___ ___ ___ ___
                                            83 98   12

73

‾ ‾ ‾ ‾ ‾
1 2 3 4 5

‾ ‾ ‾ ‾ ‾ cactus
6 7 8 9 10

‾ ‾ ‾ ‾ ‾ ‾ plant
11 12 13 14 15 16

‾ ‾ ‾ ‾ ‾ plant
17 18 19 20 21

‾ ‾ ‾ plant
22 23 24

‾ ‾ ‾ ‾ ‾ ‾ cactus
25 26 27 28 29 30

‾ ‾ ‾ ‾ plant
31 32 33 34

‾ ‾ ‾ ‾ ‾ plant
35 36 37 38 39

‾ ‾ ‾ ‾ ‾ ‾ ‾
40 41 42 43 44 45 46

‾ ‾ ‾ ‾
47 48 49 50

‾ ‾ ‾ ‾ ‾
51 52 53 54 55

‾ ‾ ‾   ‾ ‾ ‾
56 57 58 59 60 61

‾ ‾ ‾ ‾ ‾ ‾
62 63 64 65 66 67

‾ ‾ ‾ ‾ ‾ ‾ ‾
68 69 70 71 72 73 74

‾ ‾ ‾ ‾ ‾ ‾
75 76 77 78 79 80
cactus

‾ ‾ ‾ ‾ ‾
81 82 83 84 85
‾ ‾ ‾ ‾ cactus
86 87 88 89

‾ ‾ ‾ ‾ ‾ ‾ ‾ ‾ ‾
90 91 92 93 94 95 96 97 98
plant

74

LEVEL TWO

We now turn to the macabre (dark and spooky) side of plant adaptations—plants that eat animals, make poisons, and parasitize other plants. We'll meet several of the strangest plants on earth.

What would cause a plant to be carnivorous? ("Carn" means "flesh or meat," and "vor" means "eat.") Plants use photosynthesis to make all the food they need. They don't need an outside source of food energy. What else does a plant need besides carbon dioxide, water, and sunlight? Think about a chlorophyll molecule. Where does a plant get those nitrogen and magnesium molecules? As mitosis occurs and plants make new cells, they have to get the raw ingredients needed to manufacture more chlorophylls, plus many other types of molecules. Some of these molecules contain atoms such as sodium, phosphorus, potassium and calcium. Carbon dioxide and water only provide carbon, oxygen and hydrogen atoms.

Under normal conditions, plant take these minerals from the soil. Plants don't "eat" dirt, but they do take minerals out of it. If the soil doesn't contain enough minerals, the plants won't be able to grow there unless they have some alternate means of getting minerals. One alternative is to get the minerals from the bodies of animals (mainly insects and spiders).

The most famous of the carnivorous plants is the **Venus flytrap**. It's not uncommon to find these flytraps for sale in greenhouses in many parts of the world, but if you want to find a "wild" flytrap growing in its natural environment, you will have to go to the American state of North Carolina and find a bog within 60 miles of the city of Wilmington. Bogs are places that are wet and soggy all the time. The bogs where the flytraps grow have very little nitrogen and phosphorous in the soil. The flytraps are one of the few plants that thrive in these bogs. They get very little competition from other plants because of this lack of minerals in the soil. The flytraps appreciate not having any rivals in the area. In fact, Venus fly traps appreciate an occasional wildfire once in a while, too, just as a back-up to remove other plants from the area!

The leaf of a flytrap is the snappy trap on the end. The long flat part that looks like a leaf is actually the petiole. The petioles are the primary site of photosynthesis. As we mentioned in the opening paragraph, flytraps don't eat flies to get energy. They use photosynthesis just like all plants do. The flytrap is a flowering plant, as you can see in the picture. It's even a dicot. So in some ways, it's a very normal plant.

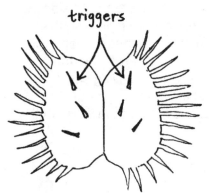

triggers

The hinged leaf on the end has two unique features that work together to catch flies. The first is a set of three trichomes ("hairs") on the inside of each lobe, which function as motion detectors. These triggers will cause the trap to close suddenly if one of the hairs is touched twice very quickly, or if two separate hairs are touched within 20 seconds. The second feature is the abilty of the two lobes to snap together in about 1/10 of a second.

Plants don't have muscles, so how is the flytrap able to do this? Scientists are still investigating, but it seems that the answer involves the sudden flow of water into and out of cells. Protons are a key to this rapid movement of water molecules. A sudden increase or decrease in the amount of water in a cell changes its shape. An overall change in shape can be seen in a flytrap leaf after it closes. While the leaf is open, the lobes curve outward; after closing they are bent inward.

Once the lobes have closed and the prey is trapped, digestive glands on the surface of the lobes begin to make digestive enzymes. Basically, the closed leaf becomes a stomach! The leaf stays tightly shut for about ten days. During this time the body of the prey is reduced to a puddle of molecules, with maybe some bits of outer shell left over. After the trap opens, the rain will wash away the remains of the meal. If the prey is too small and manages to escape, the trap will re-open in about 12 hours.

Almost as well-known as the flytraps are the **pitcher plants**. Their leaves are shaped in such a way that a "pitcher" is formed. Like water pitchers, these plant pitchers can collect and hold water. Pitcher plants attract their prey using colors, odors, and nectars. The unsuspecting bugs crawl along the slippery edge of the pitcher and inevitably slip and fall into the water pit below. If they manage to swim over to the edge of the pitcher and try to climb out, they find the walls of the pitcher extremely slippery or covered with downward-pointing hairs that prevent them from escaping. The bugs drown in the water and their bodies eventually dissolve with some help from digestive enzymes secreted by the plant cells.

The pitcher plants shown in the illustration above are the kind you find growing in the warm, humid parts of the American continents. A very different type of pitcher plant grows in Indonesia, south China, and northern Australia. The scientific name (the genus) for these pitchers is **Nepenthes**. This name can be traced back to a book written by Carl Linnaeus in 1737. It comes from Greek mythology (Homer's Odyssey), in a story where an Egyptian queen gives Helen a magic potion that causes her to forget all her sorrows. ("Ne" means "not," and "penthe" means "grief.") Carl Linneaus explains his choice of this name for this plant:

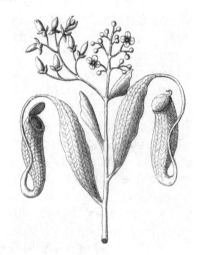

If this is not Helen's Nepenthes, it certainly will be for all botanists. What botanist would not be filled with admiration if, after a long journey, he should find this wonderful plant. In his astonishment past ills would be forgotten when beholding this admirable work of the Creator!

The Nepenthes does not have to rely on rain to fill its traps. It produces a thick fluid that makes escape impossible for the unlucky victims that fall into it. Even small lizards and mammals can drown in Nepenthes pitchers. However, a few species have managed to outwit the Nepenthes and are able to steal some of its food. Carpenter ants like to nest inside the tendrils from which the pitchers hang. The tendrils are hollow so this does not harm the plant. The ants able to swim in the pitcher fluid and will work together for hours to pull dead prey out of the trap. (Yes, the ants are carnivorous, too!) The plant actually benefits from this living situation because the ants clean up after themselves and leave the edges of the pitcher spotless. Pitchers inhabited by ants survive longer than those that are not.

In some parts of the world, the Nepenthes is called the "monkey cup." Monkeys and large apes are known to drink from these cups. (Ants? Yum, yum!)

"Cheers!"

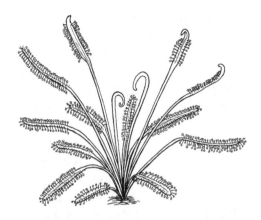

Another large family of carnivorous plants is the **sundews**. The sundews have trichomes on their leaves that produce droplets of clear sticky liquid. They look a bit like water droplets, as if dew droplets had formed on the tips of the trichomes. The droplets sparkle in the sun. (The "sun" part of the name could also come from the fact that the sundews are said to have flowers that turn towards the sun.)

The droplets produced by the sundew's trichomes are both sweet and sticky. Insects are lured in by the sweetness and trapped by the stickiness. After the insect is stuck, the trichomes begin to coil around it, trapping it even further. The motion can occur quickly, with the trichomes reacting in a matter of seconds. Within several minutes, the whole leaf can be completely curled up. Digestive glands on the leaves then release enzymes that dissolve the bodies of the insects, even their tough outer shell.

Other than their ability to trap and dissolve insects, the sundews (like all carnivorous plants) are normal flowering plants. They do photosynthesis and transpiration, they make flowers that get pollinated by insects (different species than the ones that get trapped) and make seeds that grow into new plants.

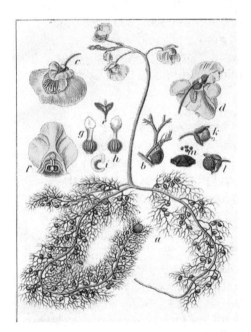

The things that look like roots are actually leaves. Both leaves and bladders remain under the water all the time. Only the flower sticks up out of the water. The plant does not need roots because the leaves are surrounded by water.

The last carnivorous plant on our list is the **bladderwort**. This plant has double adaptations. Not only is it carnivorous, it is also aquatic. In most bladderworts, the only part of the plant that sticks up above the water is the stem that has flowers on it. The flowers are shaped a bit like snapdragons and come in a wide variety of bright colors.

The bladders are tiny little sacs that grow among the underwater leaves. How tiny? On average, they are only about 1/4 inch (1/2 cm) in diamenter. The word bladder is a very general term that means a water-filled or air-filled bag. The correct name for the bladder in your body is the urinary bladder. The word bladder itself doesn't have any connection to urine. In the bladderwort, the bladders are pouches that act as high-speed traps. They catch aquatic animals small enough to fit inside the trap. Pond water is usually filled with semi-microscopic crustaceans (related to crabs) and insect larvae.

The bladders have a design that allows them to temporarily force their shape to curve inward, causing structural tension that is a bit like pulling back a spring. (Remember, plants don't have msucles, so this movement is caused by water and minerals flowing in and out of cells.) The trap has some trigger hairs around the opening. When a small animal bumps into the trigger hairs, the shape of the trap suddenly pops back to its normal open state, causing water to rush in. The animal is swept along with the mini-current and is sucked into the trap. The trap can snap shut in only 1/10,000 of a second!

As you might guess, there are digestive glands inside the trap that dissolve the animal's body. When digestion is finished, the trap can eject the remains and reset itself, pulling its shape inward again.

And now we switch from carnivory to... poisons!

(By the way, have you missed us?)

Some botanists think of a plant's ability to make toxins (poisons) as an adaptation because it helps the plant survive. Plants have very few ways to protect themselves from getting eaten. Remember, plants "want" to survive, too, just as much as animals do. Plant DNA is engineered to cause them to try to reproduce as much as possible, and to adapt the best they can in order to thrive in their environment. (In fact, in a past chapter, we accused them of being bent on world domination!)

Toxins are a very effective way for a plant to make itself less likely to be eaten. A plant's primary enemies are insects, so the toxins are really targeted at them, not at animals or humans. Since insects are very small, it takes only a small dose of the toxin to kill them. The dose that kills a bug won't do much damage at all to a large animal or a person. However, there are some plants that produce toxins strong enough to damage even a large mammal.

It would be very boring (or perhaps a little scary) for you to read a list of toxic plants, so we'll just look at two plants that played a part in Greek and Roman history.

Perhaps the most famous poisonous plant in history is the hemlock. The Greek philosopher Socrates was forced to drink a cup of poison hemlock as punishment for his "impiety" (meaning he was teaching young people to think for themselves instead of just accepting whatever the members of the ruling class told them). This hemlock plant is not related to the tree called the hemlock. They are entirely different. The scientific name (genus) for Socrates' hemlock is *Conium*. This word comes from the Greek word "konas," meaning "to whirl." Apparently, being dizzy (feeling like you are whirling) is one of the symptoms of a mild case of hemlock poisoning.

The scientific name of this plant, *Atropa belladonna*, sounds beautiful, but it's common names tell you all you need to know about it: "devil's berries," or "devil's herb." More recently, it has been called "deadly nightshade." It belongs to the same family of plants as the tomato and the potato (*solanaceae*, the "nightshades"). The name "belladonna" comes from Italian and means "beautiful woman." When the juices of this plant are used as eye drops, they cause the pupils to dilate. Ancient Italian women liked to have their pupils dilated when they met an attractive young man. They thought this made them look more beautiful. When ground up and mixed into a potion, this plant does more than dilate your pupils—it kills you. The wives of the Roman emperors Augustus and Claudius are known to have used this plant to poison their enemies. Before they died, the victims would have experienced not only dilated pupils but also mental confusion, rashes, headache, loss of balance, blurred vision, racing heart, sweating, hallucinations and convulsions. Not fun.

Interestingly enough, cows and rabbits can eat this plant and have no ill effects. For the rest of us, a handful of these berries can kill us. Since the berries look pretty and taste sweet, this is a danger for small children. Fortunately, treatment is available if you get to a medical facility quickly. A chemical produced by the African calabar bean plant can reverse the effects of the belladonna toxin. But don't take too much of this bean chemical, because in high doses this cure can be toxic, too. The calabar bean's toxin is considered to be one of the most potent in the plant kingdom.

A GENERAL GUIDELINE FOR AVOIDING POISONOUS BERRIES:

Don't eat any berries you find growing in the wild if they have a simple, round shape. Berries that are lumpy, like raspberries, are never poisonous. Some smooth berries are okay, but lots of them are toxic. Don't take chances—just stay away from smooth berries!

Our tour of the creepy side of botany ends with a look at plants that have become **parasites**. A parasite is any organism that must live in or on another organism. Many parasites end up harming their host to some degree, but not so much that they kill their host—or at least not until the parasite has had a chance to reproduce. We tend to have very negative feelings about parasites, but as we will see, some parasitic plants can be beneficial to the ecosystem they live in.

 The most well-known parasitic plant is the mistletoe, the plant that has been part of Christmas celebrations in western cultures for hundreds of years. A branch of mistletoe is hung at the top of a doorway or suspended from the ceiling. Couples who "happen" to cross each other's paths under the mistletoe are permitted a kiss. For each kiss, a berry is plucked off the branch. When the berries run out, so do the kisses.

You didn't know mistletoe was a parasite? Most people don't. The name "mistletoe" (originally "mistiltan") most likely comes from the Anglo-Saxon words "mistel" meaning "dung," and "tan" meaning "twig." So that makes the real name for this plant "dung-on-a-twig." The dung in question comes from birds. Birds eat the berries, and some of their dropping fall on tree branches. Mistletoe seeds happen to be very sticky, so they quickly adhere to the branch. When the seeds germinate, they can grow for a while in the bird dropping, as if it was dirt. As quickly as they can, though, the baby mistletoe plants start

A mistletoe starting to grow on a tree branch.

putting out special "roots" called **haustoria** *(hoe-STORE-ee-ah)*. The haustoria somehow grow their way through the tree's bark and get into the sapwood where the living xylem and phloem tubes are. They put their thin root-like tubes into the tree's xylem and phloem, as if putting a drinking straw into someone else's glass. The mistletoe slurps away, sucking water, minerals and sugars from the tree's vascular system. Thus, the mistletoe is permanently attached to a tree, instead of growing in the ground.

 The mistletoe is what botanists called a **hemiparasite** ("hemi" meaning "halfway"). The leaves can still do photosynthesis, so it is not completely reliant on the host tree. At first, the tree hardly notices the mistletoe and isn't especially bothered by it. If rainfall is adequate, there is enough water for both plants. However, as the mistletoe grows larger and larger, there is a greater possibility that the tree won't be able to keep up with the increasing demands the mistletoe places on it. Some trees do eventually die from mistletoe invasion, and, in general, gardeners see mistletoe as a threat. They usually prune off any tree branches that show mistletoe infestation.

Recently, researchers have discovered that in some places (Australia being a notable example) some species of mistletoe are quite a benefit to the natural environment. Though mistletoe berries are mildly poisonous to humans, birds love them. Areas with a lot of mistletoe will have a dense population of nesting birds. Also, the leaves and young shoots of mistletoe are a favorite snack for certain types of animals. Thus, areas with mistletoe tend to have more wildlife than areas without mistletoe. **Biodiversity** (the presence of many different forms of life instead of just a few) is considered to be a good thing. Ecologists all over the world are in agreement that it's healthy for an ecosystem to have lots of different species.

Other parasitic plants are what scientists call **obligate parasites**. The word "obligate" is related to the words "obliged" and "obligated." These paraites are completely dependent upon their host plant. In fact, these plants have lost the ability to do photosynthesis.

Hmm... well, how else can we classify them? They're not fungi, bacteria, animals or single-celled organisms. They make flowers with pistils and stamens—that's plant-like. Botanists guess that a long time ago these plants did do photosynthesis. Once they started feeding on other plants, their need for photosynthesis disappeared. The plant's cells somehow sensed this, and stopped making chlorophyll. This is just a guess, of course, as no one was there to witness this when it happened. It's just a theory. However, the possibility that this could have happened gives us license to go ahead and classify obligate parasitic plants as plants.

The most famous obligate parasite grows on the islands of Borneo and Sumatra. Its scientific name is *Rafflesia,* (and many people use this name), but it is also commonly called the "carrion flower." "Carrion" is a polite name for dead animals. Yes, this flower stinks like rotting animal carcasses. Why? Because any insect can pollinate a flower—it doesn't have to be cute little butterflies and bumblebees. In this case, the stinking flower draws flies. The flies are fooled into thinking that there is rotting meat inside the flower, and pollination is accomplished.

The *Rafflesia* holds the world record for being the largest flower in the world—which is kind of funny when you learn that the flower is the only part this plant really has. It has no leaves, no stems and no roots! The only other part the *Rafflesia* has is a network of haustoria. The haustoria are embedded in the veins of a vine plant, and are invisible from the outside. The only time you can be sure the *Rafflesia* plant is there is when it puts out a flower bud. Otherwise, you never see this plant!

Our second and last obligate parasite is the "snow flower." (The buds often pop up early in the year, poking up through the snow.) Like *Rafflesia*, this type of plant has no leaves, no stems and no roots. It consists of nothing but haustoria threads living inside a fungus that lives on other plants. Since these plants live on a fungus, some people like to call them "fungus flowers." The snow flower takes its nourishment from a fungus that is taking its nourishment from a plant. Indirectly, the snow flowers are feeding on a plant, but through the fungus. Very strange, indeed.

These snow flower buds were found in Yosemite National Park in California.

ACTIVITY 1: "O" THAT RAGWORT IS A PROBLEM!

Ragwort is a wildflower in the aster family (same family as daisies). It has pretty yellow flowers and looks nice growing by the roadside. It is native to Northern Europe, but can now be found in places all over the world, including Australia, New Zealand, Argentina, India, northern Africa and some states in America. There are certain moths and flies that love to feast on the leaves and nectar. In fact, they won't eat anything else. These insects don't reflect the opinions of the animal kingdom in general, however. Ragwort is very bitter and most animals won't willingly eat it.

Farmers all over the world are on a mission to try to make this plant extinct (much to the dismay of insect enthusiasts). The bitter taste of ragwort is due to toxins (poisonous chemicals) it produces. These toxins help the plant by keeping it safe from hungry animals. However, as the plant dries out, the toxic chemical taste less bitter. If dried ragwort gets mixed in with horse or cow's hay supply, the animal won't be able to detect the ragwort in its food. They will accidentally eat the ragwort and the toxins will get into their bloodstream and poison their livers, making them very sick. In some places (such as the UK and some US states) if you find ragwort growing on your property you are required by law to destroy it.

One way you can identify ragwort is by counting the petals of its flowers. Ragwort flowers have 13 petals. There aren't too many things in the natural world that come in 13's. One of the few places where the number 13 shows up in flower petals. Other common petal numbers are 4, 5, 8, 10, and 21. Mathematicians think it is interesting that petal numbers roughly correspond to "Fibonacci" numbers: 1, 2, 3, 5, 8, 13, 21, 34... (add the two previous numbers to get the next one).

This ragwort's 13 petals correspond to 13 botanical "root words" from Latin or Greek. The easy part is that all of these root words end in the letter "O" which already appears in the center of the flower. Fill in the rest of the letters starting at the outside of the petal and going towards the "O." You may have to turn your paper sideways and upside down! (If you need a hint, a page number is given where you can find the answer.)

1) light *(pg 1)*
2) very small *(think of a scientific instrument that lets you see very small things)*
3) green *(pg 8)*
4) middle *(pg 38)*
5) one *(pg 31)*
6) turn *(pg 36)*
7) tree *(pg 40)*
8) life *(think of the branch of science that studies life)*
9) flower *(pg 44)*
10) naked *(pg 50)*
11) vessel or container *(pg 52)*
12) yellow *(pg 39)*
13) air or breath *(pg 8)*

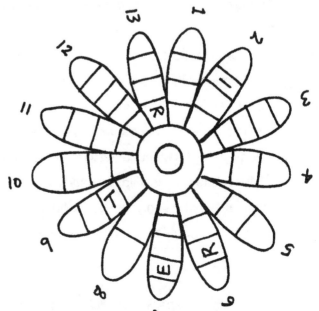

ACTIVITY 2:   MORE VIDEOS! (unless you watched them already)

Get comfy, go to www.YouTube.com/TheBasementWorkshop, and watch some fascinating videos on carnivorous plants.

ACTIVITY 3:   TRUE OR FALSE?

Can we trick you? See if you can determine whether each statement is true or false.

1) ___ Flytraps can survive wildfires.

2) ___ Bogs have mineral-rich soil.

3) ___ Various species of flytraps live all over the world.

4) ___ Flytrap leaves have no petioles.

5) ___ Flytraps have muscle cells.

6) ___ Nepenthes have parasitic ants that destroy their pitchers.

7) ___ Nepenthes were not discovered until the 20th century.

8) ___ All carnivorous plants have digestive glands.

9) ___ Pitcher plants can be found growing on several continents.

10) ___ Nepenthes plants have a symbiotic relationship with a particular species of tropical spider.

11) ___ Sundew trichomes can move.

12) ___ Carnivorous plants produce poisonous chemicals to paralyze their prey.

13) ___ The bladderwort's trap is probably the fastest-acting mechanism in nature.

14) ___ Bladderworts have no roots.

15) ___ Bladderwort traps can be used only once.

16) ___ Socrates died by drinking a potion made from the hemlock tree.

17) ___ A *Conium* plant makes cones.

18) ___ Some animals can eat deadly nightshade and survive.

19) ___ Sometimes animals are not bothered by plant toxins that are fatal to humans.

20) ___ Never eat wild raspberries.

21) ___ The mistletoe plant does not have roots.

22) ___ A hemi-parasitic plant can still do photosynthesis.

23) ___ Mistletoe plants ruin wild habitats.

24) ___ The *Rafflesia* has only two parts: haustoria and flowers.

25) ___ "Snow plants" are really a type of fungi.

This is a species of pitcher plant called the cobra lily.

LESSON 8: PLANT DISEASES

LEVEL ONE

Just like people and animals, plants can get sick. They can catch viruses and come down with bacterial and fungal infections. About two thirds of all plant disease is caused by fungi, so let's take a look at this category first.

Fungi are a bit like the Rafflesia plant. (If you read level 2 of lesson 7, you've already met this plant.) This parasitic plant has no roots, no stems and no leaves. The main "body" of the plant is an invisible network of fibers running through the host plant (the plant to which it is attached). You'd never know the Rafflesia even existed if it didn't produce flowers once in a while. Seemingly out of nowhere (but actually from that network of fibers) a flower appears. Rafflesia flowers grow to be the largest flowers in the world. But there sit the flowers, with no plant in sight!

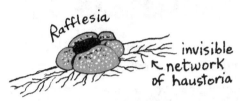
Rafflesia
invisible network of haustoria

Fungi work in much the same way. The "body" of a fungus is a network of fibers called a *mycelium*. (The word "mycelium" is Greek for "fungal body". Not much translating needed there.) The individual strands that make up the mycelium are called *hyphae* (meaning "filaments"). If you are talking about just one strand, you call it a *hypha*. That's the basic structure of a fungus. Pretty simple. The hyphae can be separated into individual cells with walls in between, or they can be like one very long cell, with nuclei and organs dotted here and there along the way. Fungal cells are similar to plant and animal cells in that they have a nucleus and the usual assortment of organelles—mitochondria, endoplasmic reticulum, ribosomes, Golgi bodies, and storage vesicles.

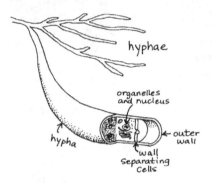
hyphae
organelles and nucleus
hypha
outer wall
wall separating cells

Mycelia are creeping around all the time and you are not even aware of it. It's only when the fungus decides to reproduce that you notice it. Certain fungal cells are able to produce what are generally called "fruiting bodies." The fungal fruiting bodies you are most familiar with are mushrooms. You might think of a mushroom as a little plant, but it's not. A mushroom is only a reproductive structure. The main body of the organism we call a mushroom is actually the hidden mycelium under the dirt. You can't see the main body of the organism. The mushrooms come and go, but the mycelia are there all the time. During periods of very dry weather, mushrooms disappear.

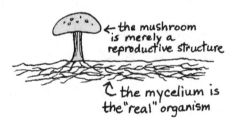
the mushroom is merely a reproductive structure
the mycelium is the "real" organism

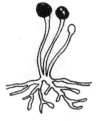

Another type of fruiting body you are familiar with is the blue, green, or black fuzz that grows on breads and fruits when they've been sitting too long. If you could look at the fuzz under a magnifier, you'd see that the fuzz is made of thousands of tall filaments with balls on their ends. The balls are similar to those sporangia we saw on moss plants. The sporangia break open and release millions of spores into the air. The spores can float in the air for a long time. Eventually they may land on a fruit or a slice of bread where they can grow into mycelia.

So, there's fungal mycelia in my sandwich?
Unless it's hot out of oven, yeah- probably a few. But they won't hurt you.

Fungi get their nutrition by using enzymes to dissolve the plant or animal tissue they are growing on. The hyphae release digestive enzymes into the immediate environment around them. The enzymes break down the tissues into tiny molecules that the fungal cells can then absorb. It's like external digestion. Fungi are very important to the environment because their digestion helps to recycle dead plant and animal material. Fungi, along with bacteria, are **decomposers**. We'd be buried miles deep in dead plants and animals if it were not for our tiny decomposing friends! However, there are certain members of the fungi kingdom who are not so helpful.

Fungi can attack plants. You've seen mushrooms and shelf fungi growing on trees. Other types of fungi cause black or brown spots on leaves.

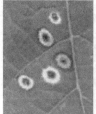

Any time you see large, round, dark spots on leaves, it's probably a fungal infection. The spots are round because the fungus starts out as a single dot then grows at the same rate in every direction.

Powdery mildew is another common fungal infection. It is often seen on lilac bushes and on garden plants such as squash and cucumbers.

"Rust" is the common name for a fungus that causese leaves to turn reddish-brown, as though they were rusting.

Cankers are infections that cause "open wounds" on trunks.

Another well-known fungal infection is called **Dutch Elm Disease**. This fungus has devastated the population of beautiful old elm trees in public parks and college campuses across Europe, the UK and North America since the 1930s. (An estimated 25 million trees died in the UK alone!) The fungus is carried from tree to tree by a beetle that eats elm tree bark. When the fungus gets into the xylem tubes, the tree reacts and tries to protect itself by sealing off that area. The xylem tubes begin making a gummy substance that intentionally clogs them up. This effectively stops the fungus from travelling up through the xylem tubes, but it also cuts off the water supply for the connected branches. Those affected branches will die not as a result of direct contact with the fungus but because they are not getting enough water. As the beetle bites into more parts of the trunk, more xylem becomes clogged. As more and more branches are affected, the entire tree will start to die.

One way to fight the disease is to try to get rid of the beetles. **Insecticides** (insect-killing sprays) were used during the 1950s and 1960s until these chemicals were proven to be harmful to other forms of life, not just beetles. **Fungicides** (fungus-killing chemicals) have also been used, but the results have been disappointing. The fungicides have not been able to get rid of the disease.

The most successful approach has been to find plants that are naturally resistant to it. Remember back in those lessons about plant reproduction we learned that one reason plants need to trade DNA (by using egg and sperm) is to produce offspring that are slightly different from the parents. All baby elm trees look and act like elm trees, but the baby plants have minor differences. One of these differences is their ability to survive attacks by various diseases. **Arborists** (professional tree growers) have found some elm trees that are more resistant to the Dutch Elm Disease fungus, and they've started to breed these hardy trees. Sick trees are destroyed and are replaced by these more resistant ones.

Did you know you can give a tree an injection? Dutch Elm fungicides are often injected into the roots.

If a plant in your yard or garden comes down with a fungus, the first thing you need to do is cut off all the parts that are sick. Trim off every leaf, stem and branch that looks even slightly affected. Dispose of the diseased parts in a way that won't spread the fungus around any more. (Throwing them out is probably best. You can compost them only if your pile is hotter than 130° F.)

Sometimes you can use a spray to slow down the fungus. (Sprays don't work for Dutch Elm Disease, but they are effective for other types of fungi.) Two very safe sprays you can make are baking soda spray (made from baking soda, vegetable oil, and a little dish soap) and compost tea spray. To make compost tea, you soak compost in water and pump air bubbles into it. The result is a solution full of good bacteria that will kill fungi without harming your plants. There are also sprays you can buy that contain sulfur and copper, but you have to be careful with these since they could be toxic to animals.

Perhaps the best thing you can do for plants that are fighting fungal infections is to try to keep them dry, if possible. You can't control the weather, but if you water your plants, don't spray the whole plant. Pour the water on just the roots. The extra water on the leaves only serves to help the fungi grow.

Day 2

The next most common infection seen in plants is viral infection. Human viruses you may be familiar with include rabies, polio, chicken pox, influenza and the common cold. The most well-known plant virus is called mosaic virus. It was first discovered on tobacco plants, so it is often called **tobacco mosaic virus**.

Mosaic virus gets its name from the mottled pattern it makes on leaves. It mainly attacks members of the nightshade family (which includes tobacco, potatoes, tomatoes, eggplants and peppers), but it can also attack cucumbers and some types of garden flowers. The virus rarely kills the plant, but causes enough damage that the plant becomes useless to farmers who are looking to make money from their harvests.

The virus was discovered in the late 1800s, though at that time there were no electron microscopes, so the scientists who discovered it never knew what it looked like. They knew it was extremely small—much smaller than a bacteria. They put juice from infected plants through strainers that could filter out even the smallest bacteria. After the juice had been through the strainer, they could be sure that it had no bacteria in it. When this bacteria-free strained juice was applied to healthy plants, they got sick. Obviously, some infectious agent was slipping through.

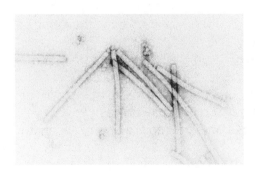

In 1939, the first electron microscope picture of the mosaic virus was taken. Then, in the 1950s, Rosalind Franklin (the scientist who produced the images of DNA for Watson and Crick) was able to gather enough information from her x-ray images of the virus to be able to make a model of it for the 1958 World's Fair. She figured out that the virus was long and hollow, like a drinking straw, and contained a single strand of RNA. The piece of RNA contains instructions that can tell a plant cell how to make mosaic viruses.

Viruses are like pirates—they land on a cell and take it over. They inject their RNA instructions into the cell. The cell's organelles then stop what they are doing and begin to follow these new instructions instead. The plant organelles begin to manufacture and assemble new mosaic viruses. Soon the cell is so full of viruses that it bursts open, releasing all the new viruses. Each one of those new viruses goes to another plant cell and takes it over. When the viruses get into the xylem and phloem tubes, they are quickly transported to other areas of the plant. As you might guess, it doesn't take too long before the plant is overwhelmed with viruses.

Plants don't have immune systems like animals do, but they aren't totally helpless, either. We've already seen how a Dutch Elm clogs its infected xylem cells to keep the fungus from spreading. Plants can also make chemicals that will interfere with the ability of a **pathogen** (a disease-causing fungus, virus or bacteria) to live and reproduce. Plants that are more successful at producing large volumes of protective chemicals, or better quality chemicals, will be the ones that survive the infection. Weaker plants die off and the stronger ones go on to reproduce and pass along these strong genetics to their offspring. Plant scientists have been able to speed up this natural process and breed plants that are more resistant to disease.

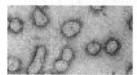 There are many other types of plant viruses besides mosaic virus. Most are long and thin like mosaic viruses, but some look more round. No matter what they look like, they all work the same way, taking over the cell's "machinery" and forcing the organelles to make viruses.

Once a plant is infected there isn't much you can do. Usually infected plants need to be destroyed so they won't infect other plants. Anything that has touched the plants (tools, gloves, etc.) will need to be washed with soap and water, or possibly even with bleach. Metal tools that might rust can be heated with a blowtorch.

Insects and worms can transfer viruses from plant to plant. (The viruses don't harm the bugs at all.) It's not possible to kill all the bugs that have touched the infected plant. The best you can do is to try to cut down the insect population as much as possible and hope for the best.

When we think about bacteria we should not think of them as "bad guys." Judging by all the advertisements for anti-bacterial soap, you'd think that a world without bacteria would be ideal. Not so! Most bacteria are friendly and are essential to the health of every type of organism on the planet.

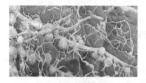 We met some nice bacteria back in lesson 6—the nitrogen-fixing bacteria who live in nodules on the roots of legume plants and take the nitrogen out of the air and put it into a form that plants can use. Without these bacteria the soil would run out of nitrogen. Other types of bacteria can protect plants against insect and fungal invaders. The bacteria found in compost piles break down dead plants (or animals) and turn them into fresh soil that is rich in nutrients.

Relatively few species of bacteria are considered to be pathogens (causing disease). It is estimated that about 70 percent of all bacteria are not harmful. However, the remaining 30 percent can be a problem. Perhaps you have come down with strep throat or pneumonia or some other illness that had to be treated with antibiotics. (Strangely enough, do you know where most antibiotics come from? They are made by fungi!) Plants can have unfriendly bacteria attack them and damage their leaves, fruits and stems. Sometimes the bacteria live in the soil and get into the plant through the roots. Other bacteria are carried by insects. When the insect bites the plant, the bacteria get in.

Unfortunately for plants, there are no antibiotic medicines you can give them. Once again, get rid of all diseased plants and plant parts. Don't put them in your compost pile unless you know your pile stays over 130°F (55°C). Burn them if you can, or dispose of them into the trash. Clean any tools that have touched the diseased plants.

Bacteria are very simple—they don't have all the fancy organelles that plant cells do. They don't even have a true nucleus. They've got a clump of DNA (the nucleoid), and thousands of ribosomes floating around in cytoplasm. Most bacteria have a cell wall outside of their membrane and many bacteria have some kind of protective capsule. Some have flagella that allow them to move around, but many do not. Some have plasmids.

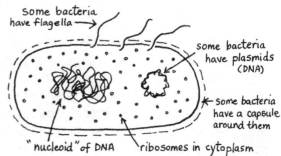

Crown galls on a willow tree

The most well-known example of a bacteria that attacks plants is the species of bacteria that causes **crown gall**. A gall is a bit like a callus on your skin. If something irritates your skin for long enough, your skin will make a thick lump in that spot. A gall is what a plant does when it gets irritated. In the case of crown gall, a big ugly, wrinkly lump forms. The crown gall doesn't outright kill the plant, though, as you can see from this picture. If the tree died, the bacteria would be homeless and hungry. The main problem with crown gall is that it likes to attack fruit and nut trees and grape vines. This causes problems for farmers who rely on these crops for their income.

The crown gall bacteria is an unusual species. It has a flagella (tail) and can swim over to the roots of a plant and burrow in. Then it injects a piece of DNA into the cell. The bacterial DNA is taken into the nucleus of the plant cell and attaches to the plant cell's DNA. The added bacterial DNA causes the cell to do two things: 1) make too much auxin, and 2) make special food for the bacteria. The extra auxin causes the infected plant cells to grow too much and the result is a large lump, almost like a tumor. (The species name for crown gall is *tumefaciens*.)

Recently, scientists have discovered ways to use the crown gall bacteria to do some genetic engineering. They took out that piece of transferrable DNA (contained in the plasmid) and put in some DNA from a firefly instead. What did they get? A plant that glowed in the dark! Seriously, it worked! The plant cell's ribosomes (little protein factories) had the information for how to make glow-in-the-dark chemicals, so they started making some. After that, the scientists tried putting in DNA that had instructions for how to make chemicals that kill bugs. The engineered plants started producing their own insecticides. Pretty

Crown gall bacteria attacking plant cell

cool, eh? But...wait a minute. What if people ate these plants? What would happen? No one is absolutely sure. There is a lot of controversy about this right now.

When you see a label on a food package that says "No GMOs" (Genetically Modified Organisms) this means that the plants and/or animals used to make the food did not ever have this type of genetic engineering done to them. Genetic engineering of plants is so common today that most foods you eat already contain genetically modified plants. (Corn and wheat are some of the most modified plants you eat.) Is this okay? Some scientists say it is perfectly harmless. Others aren't so sure. Would you want to know if your food had been genetically modified? Some governments are considering passing laws requiring food companies to put labels on all their products, stating whether or not they contain GMOs.

An "oak marble" gall

Galls can be caused by other things, too, not just bacteria. A gall is a plant's version of a skin callus, so anything that irritates a plant's epidermis can cause a gall. Fungi, viruses and insects can also cause galls.

The most well-known gall forming insect is the gall wasp. It's a tiny harmless wasp, not the big kind that can give a painful sting. (It looks more like a fly than a wasp.) In the spring or early summer, the female wasp deposits eggs into a leaf or stem. For reasons not entirely understood, the plant cells around the egg start to change their growth pattern, making a gall. This gall-forming process is similar to the crown gall in that the cells' DNA is changed. The cells follow molecular instructions for how to build a perfect home for a gall wasp larva. By the time the larva hatches, it is surrounded by a very cozy room filled with food. The larva munches away on the cells that line the inside of the gall. When it is mature enough, the larva will escape from the gall and fly off to enjoy its adult life out in the fresh air and sunshine. Some gall wasps spend the entire fall and winter in their galls and don't come out until spring. They live as adult wasps for only a few months—just long enough to find a mate and lay eggs (if they are female). Then the cycle starts again.

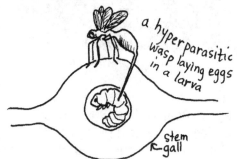
a hyperparasitic wasp laying eggs in a larva

stem gall

Some species of gall wasps lay their eggs inside already-formed galls. The females of these species have very long and sturdy ovipositors (with metal [zinc] tips) that can drill into even large, solid galls. The female's target is the larva in the center. She deposits one or more eggs in or near the larva. When these new wasp eggs hatch, they will eat the larva as their food source. These wasps are called "hyperparasites" because they are parasites of parasites. (And, believe it or not, there are other types of gall wasps that deposit their eggs onto these parasitic larva. That's hyper-hyperparasitism!)

Galls are very common and in some places they have even become part of human folklore. In medieval England, the custom was to open a gall as part of the St. Michaelmas festival (September 29) and use the contents of the gall to predict the coming seasons. If a "worm" (insect larva) or a fly was found, then the upcoming year would be pleasant. If a spider was found, the coming year would bring hardships with ruined crops. If the gall was empty it spelled disaster for the community, possibly even plagues. Obviously, there is no science behind these customs and if the year turned out as the gall predicted, it was just a coincidence. (Hopefully, some observant person discovered how to check for small holes in the sides of the galls. A small hole would indicate that the occupant of the gall had already escaped.)

Galls can occur on any part of a plant. Most are brown or green, but a few kinds are bright red.

Cola-nut gall on oak leaf

Nail galls on lime leaf

Spangle gall on oak

"Pineapple" gall on pine branch

Leafy goldenrod gall

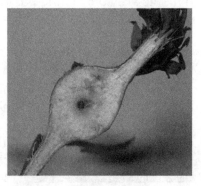
Goldenrod stem gall cut in half

ACTIVITY 1:   WATCH GALL WASPS IN ACTION

There is a fantastic video about gall wasps posted on the Botany playlist. Also, see some of the strangest galls in the world—they jump!

ACTIVITY 2:   WEBSITES ABOUT GALLS

Want to see a "poop gall"? This and many other strange galls are featured at this web address: http://waynesword.palomar.edu/pljuly99.htm

If you'd like to look at pictures of galls (without more info) here is a gallery of just photos: http://www.british-galls.org.uk/gallery.htm

ACTIVITY 3:   A THREE-ANSWER QUIZ

This quiz only has three possible answers: fungus, virus, bacterium. However, you will have to use these answers more than once.   (You can abbreviate with F, V or B.)   Sometimes only one of these will be the right answer, but other times two of them or all three of them will be correct. We are going to make the blank lines all the same size so you won't have any clues as to how many correct answers there are. (Note: We are using the word "pathogen" here in our clues, but remember that some types of fungi and bacteria are beneficial. We're just focusing on the pathogenic species.)

1) This type of pathogen attacks plants. _____

2) This type of pathogen contains DNA. _____

3) This type of pathogen sometimes has a tail-like thing called a flagella. _____

4) This type of pathogen doesn't qualify as being truly "living." _____

5) This pathogen is so small you need an electron microscope to see it. _____

6) This pathogen sometimes contains a plasmid (extra ring of DNA). _____

7) This type of pathogen can act as a decomposer, recycling dead plants. _____

8) This pathogen is often compared to a pirate because it takes over cells. _____

9) Some plants are naturally more resistant to this type of pathogen. _____

10) This type of pathogen can be used to do genetic engineering of plants. _____

11) This type of pathogen has organelles. _____

12) This type of pathogen makes reproductive structures. _____

13) Garden tools should be sterilized after contact with this type of pathogen. _____

14)   This type of pathogen can cause a plant to form a gall. _____

15) Plants and plant parts affected by this type of pathogen need to be destroyed. _____

16) This type of pathogen can be discouraged by using "compost tea." _____

ACTIVITY 4:   A SYLLABLE PUZZLE

     The answers to all these questions have been chopped up into individual syllables, then arranged alphabetically. All you have to do is put the words back together again!   The number at the end of the line is a helpful hint, telling you how many syllables to use. You might want to circle or cross out the syllables once you use them, so you don't get confused.

A, AN, AR, BAC, BI, BOR, CAN, CEL, CIDE, CO, COM, COM, DE, DEN, DER, DEW, ER, GEN, GOL, HY, I, I, I, I, IC, IC, IC, IL, IN, IST, IZE, KER, LEG, MID, MIL, MO, MY, O, OT, OV, PAR, PATH, PHA, PLAS, POS, POS, POST, POW, RE, ROD, SA, SECT, SIS, SITE, STER, TANT, TI, TO, TOR, UM, UME, US, VIR, Y

1) This microorganism can't reproduce on its own.   ___ ___ ___ ___ ___ (2)
It must "borrow" the organelles of a cell.

2) This is a pile of rotting plants, rich in friendly bacteria. ___ ___ ___ ___ ___ ___ ___ (2)

3) This describes the pattern on leaves infected with this virus. ___ ___ ___ ___ ___ ___ (3)

4) This chemical kills bugs. ___ ___ ___ ___ ___ ___ ___ ___ ___ ___ (4)

5) Both fungi and bacteria help to break down dead plants and animals. An organism that does this job is called a ___ ___ ___ ___ ___ ___ ___ ___ ___ ___ (4)

6) This is the main "body" of a fungus. ___ ___ ___ ___ ___ ___ ___ ___ (4)

7) This is one single strand of the answer to number 6, above. ___ ___ ___ ___ ___ (2)

8) This fungus likes to attack lilac bushes. ___ ___ ___ ___ ___ ___ ___ ___ ___ ___ ___ ___ ___ (5)

9) This infection looks like an open wound on a tree trunk. ___ ___ ___ ___ ___ ___ (2)

10) This is a person who specializes in taking care of trees. ___ ___ ___ ___ ___ ___ ___ ___ (3)

11) Some plants are natually more ___ ___ ___ ___ ___ ___ ___ ___ ___ to diseases than others. (3)

12) This is the body part of a female gall wasp that she uses to deposit eggs into a plant or a larva.
___ ___ ___ ___ ___ ___ ___ ___ ___ (5)

13) This type of plant lives in symbiosis with nitrogen-fixing bacteria. ___ ___ ___ ___ ___ ___ (2)

14) This is an extra ring of DNA found inside some bacteria. ___ ___ ___ ___ ___ ___ ___ (2)

15) The first virus ever discovered was found in this type of plant. ___ ___ ___ ___ ___ ___ ___ (3)

16) This type of chemical is used to fight bacteria. ___ ___ ___ ___ ___ ___ ___ ___ ___ ___ (5)

17) Any microorganism that causes disease can be called a ___ ___ ___ ___ ___ ___ ___ ___ (3)

18) A common weed that often gets stem galls (both leafy and ball-shaped) is the
___ ___ ___ ___ ___ ___ ___ ___ ___ (3)

19) This is what you should do to tools that have been used to cut out diseased plants.
___ ___ ___ ___ ___ ___ ___ ___ (3)

20) This kind of organism must live in or on a host organism. ___ ___ ___ ___ ___ ___ ___ ___ (3)

LEVEL TWO

Although plants sometimes get sick, their biggest problem isn't pathogens, it's their environment. A plant with healthy growing conditions—the right amount of light, water and minerals, and the absence of toxins—will be much less susceptible to infections than a plant that is struggling with drought or malnutrition. It's the same with people; nutrition is very important to maintaining good health.

What are ideal growing conditions for a plant? It depends on the plant. We've already seen that some plants thrive in desert conditions while others are adapted to watery environments. Also, not every plant needs a lot of sunshine—some do better in shady areas. All plants need minerals from the soil, but some plants need more of one thing and less of another. So the best we can do in this lesson is to offer some very general information that will apply to as many plants as possible.

Did you know that plants can get sunburned? In general, leaves are really good at soaking up sunlight with no harm done to them, but they can only do this if they have an adequate water supply. Even the hardiest leaf will start to burn if it runs out of water. Plants that are designed for shady environments don't even have to get dry to experience sunburn. The author of this book found this out the hard way, with an indoor palm and an outdoor fern.

One day I looked over at my palm and noticed that there were several leaves right in the middle of a frond that had gone brown. Some of the tips were also brown. I didn't immediately figure out what had happened because the plant had been moved away from the lamp. But as part of my investigation, I moved the plant back over near the lamp. It became obvious what had happened. These leaves had gotten more than their recommended daily allowance of light. No amount of watering could restore these leaves.

Fruits can also get sunburned. If you stop to think about the location of fruits on trees and vines, you'll notice that they are sheltered by leaves. (Think about fruit trees, berry bushes, or even bean plants. You have to reach in or under leaves to pick the fruit, don't you?) Sunburned areas on fruits are discolored and acquire a hard texture. Though not toxic, they won't sell very well at a store, so fruit and vegetable growers have to keep a watchful eye on their plants as the fruits ripen.

Getting the right amount of light is critically important for a plant. Two other very important environmental factors are water and nutrients. We are very aware of a plant's need for water; it wilts and we can see that it is thirsty. What we are less knowledgeable about is plant nutrition. Plants don't need to consume the raw materials that animals and people do. They do not need protein, fats or carbohydrates. They only need minerals.

A plant's diet consists of about 17 basic minerals, all of which are elements that can be found on the Periodic Table. The elements they need a lot of are called **macro**nutrients. They are nitrogen, phosphorus, potassium, sulfur, calcium, magnesium, and silicon. The ones they need less of are called **micronutrients**, and include iron, copper, boron, sodium, zinc, nickel, chlorine, cobalt, manganese and molybdenum. (Some species of plants like to have tiny amounts of other elements, too, such as aluminum.)

That's the complete menu for plants—less than 20 minerals, plus water. If the soil doesn't contain enough (or contains too much) of one or more of these minerals, the plant will not be as healthy as it should be. Poor growing conditions make the plant susceptible to all kinds of problems.

So how do you know if your plant is experiencing problems with its growing conditions? A good place to start is to look at the leaves. If they are dry and brown at the tips (A), your plant probably needs more water. If the leaves at the tips are okay but the leaves at the base of the branch are brown (B), your plant might be experiencing "salt burn." This can be a result of too much plant fertilizer (this applies even to indoor plants) or because the plant is receiving run-off water from roads or sidewalks (obviously an outdoor problem). Run-off water often has a lot of salty chemicals in it.

If the leaves are too yellow, look carefully at the veins. If the veins are still fairly green and the yellow is mainly between the veins (C), your plant is probably suffering from a lack of nitrgoen or magnesium. Adding some plant fertilizer to the soil can fix this problem. If yellow leaves appear only at the tips of the branches (D), the plant might be getting too much light. If the yellow leaves are near the bases of the branches (E), the plant could be getting too much water.

For indoor plants, keep the soil moist but not soggy. To estimate how much water is in the middle or bottom of the pot, tap the the pot. If you hear a solid "thud" sound, this indicates that there is still water in the pot. If you hear a hollow sound, your pot is dry and you need to add water.

If your plant's leaves are wilted, are they still green or are they shades of brown, black, or gray? If they are green, you might just need to water your plant. If watering the plant doesn't revive it, it may have a bacterial disease called, appropriately enough, "wilt." Cucumbers and squashes are susceptible to bacterial "**wilts.**" This type of bacteria is usually transmitted by beetles. You'll need to get rid of infected leaves and stems first, then deal with the beetles.

If the wilted leaves are not green, they could be infected with a fungus (if the leaves are fuzzy or powdery), a bacteria (if the leaves are brown and either crispy or gummy), or by insects (if the stems have telltale holes or chew marks). If you suspect a pathogen is the problem, trim off the infected leaves immediately. If the plant in question is an outdoor plant and you want to know exactly what is wrong, you might want to consult a diagnostic website like this one: www.extension.umn.edu/gardeninfo/diagnostics/

If an outdoor plant appears to be struggling to survive for no apparent reason, you might want to look at the roots. A tiny round worm called a ***root-knot nematode*** can take up residence in roots, causing root galls. Unlike the nitrogen-fixing nodules, these nematode galls hinder the plant's growth. The roots can't do their job effectively and the plant parts above the soil have trouble getting enough water and minerals. You need to remove the plant from that area and either burn it or throw it out. Don't compost the plant, as the nematodes will be able to survive for a long time in the compost and will infect any soil you put the compost

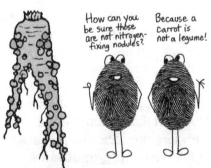

on. You can reduce the nematode population in the soil by covering the area with black plastic for a few weeks (cooking the worms to death), or by planting some marigolds in that area. Before the marigolds start making seeds, chop them up and plow them into the dirt. The rotting marigold stems and leaves will release chemicals into the soil that will kill the nematodes.

If your plant looks way too tall and skinny, it is probably not getting enough light. Remember, lack of light makes plant cells produce more auxin which causes more growth, enabling the plant to grow towards a light source. You might have to move the plant to a sunnier location, but do a little research first to find out how many hours of sun per day are best for this type of plant. You'll also have to observe your yard or garden on a sunny day and figure out which areas get full sun, partial sun, or full shade.

If your leaves have holes of any kind, they are probably being eaten by some kind of small animal. Insects are the most common leaf eaters, but slugs and mites will also damage leaves. There are hundreds of thousands of different kinds of tiny critters that eat plants. We can't study them all, so we've chosen just eight of the most well-known plant pests of all time.

WANTED

THE LOCUST
For severe crop damage throughout history in every part of the world

THE LOCUST

This member of the grasshopper family is famous for its tendency to form swarms. The largest swarm ever recorded was estimated to have over 12 trillion locusts in it! Swarms this large can sweep across farmland and consume every single green leaf in their path, leaving nothing but sticks and stubble behind. (Exactly the scene described by Moses in Egypt, and by Laura Ingalls in the American midwest.)

Oddly enough, locusts don't form swarms all that often. Usually, they exist as individuals minding their own business. When conditions get crowded and they start bumping into each other a lot (several times per minute) that's when they switch over to "swarm mode."

In ancient times there was little anyone could do to stop a swarm of locusts. Nowadays, farmers can use an insecticide made from a fungus. This particular type of fungus loves to attack grasshoppers, eating right through their hard outer shell. The fungus won't harm the crops.

WANTED

BOLL WEEVILS
For causing millions of dollars of damage to cotton crops

THE BOLL WEEVIL

This beetle migrated up from South America into North America in the late 1800s and early 1900s. By the 1920s it was devasting cotton crops in the southern American states. Up through the 1970s it was costing cotton farmers crop losses totalling over 300 million dollars every year.

In the 1950s and 1960s, DDT insecticide was sprayed on cotton fields, but this chemical was eventually banned in 1972. Now, a milder chemical is used: malathion. They also use environmentally-friendly traps baited with pheromones (the chemicals insects use to communicate with each other.) These traps are especially effective in the spring when the weevils are first emerging. For every 2 weevils you trap in the spring, you've prevented their potential 134 million off-spring! (They have a very short life cycle of only three weeks so they do a lot of reproducing over the summer.)

WANTED

THE GYPSY MOTH
For destroying 80 million acres of deciduous forests in the eastern US

WANTED

"CABBAGE WHITE"
For eating our cabbage and broccoli plants.

WANTED

APHIDS
For sucking the sap out of our favorite yard and garden plants

THE GYPSY MOTH

This pest is native to Europe and the UK. It was brought to America in the 1860s by a Frenchman named Professor Trouvelot. He thought this moth might be good for silk production so he started a little moth farm in his backyard in Boston. By the time he figured out that they were worthless for silk production, the moths had already escaped from his yard and had infested all the trees in his neighborhood.

The moths spread out quickly and within a few decades the forests of neighboring states were covered with them. A century later, the moths were destroying forests as far west as Wisconsin and as far south as Virginia.

At first, toxic insecticides were sprayed on the forests, but now they use sprays containing viruses and bacteria that attack only gypsy moth caterpillars. Sounds a little strange to intentionally spread viruses and bacteria, but apparently it's safer than using the chemical sprays.

THE WHITE CABBAGE BUTTERFLY

Sometimes mistaken for a moth, this little white butterfly lays eggs on the undersides of cabbage and broccoli leaves. Why it prefers the members of the cabbage family is unknown, but it does show a marked preference for plants related to cabbages (the mustard family, "Brassicaceae," also known by the name "cruciferous").

When the eggs hatch, the baby caterpillars start munching on the leaves. As the caterpillars grow, so do the sizes of the holes in the leaves. The caterpillars rarely kill the plant, however. The problem with these caterpillars is that they make their way into the part of the plant that we eat. (Worms in your broccoli—yuck!) However, these insects are very easy to defeat without causing any harm to the environment. You can spray the plants with a friendly bacteria that kills only these caterpillars, not other forms of life.

APHIDS

We met some aphids briefly when we were studying the vascular system. They have a specialized mouth part that drills into a stem until it hits a phloem vein. The aphid then stays put, letting the sap from the phloem fill up its stomach. Usually aphids don't take enough sap to kill their host plant. The biggest problem is that aphids transmit viruses and bacteria from one plant to another. The pathogens get sucked up along with the sap so that when the aphids move along to another plant, the pathogens go along, too.

Fortunately, there is a natural way to control aphids. Get yourself a big supply of ladybugs. (Yes, you really can buy ladybugs from online suppliers.) Parasitic wasps and lacewing insects will also eat aphids. Some gardeners just hose down their plants once a week to control aphids. You can also use natural plant oils, or insecticides made from fungi.

JAPANESE BEETLES

For skeletonizing the leaves of garden plants

THE SLUG

For chewing holes in leaves, and leaving yucky slime trails

SPIDER MITES

For sucking sap out of leaves and camping out in web tents

JAPANESE BEETLES

You have to admit, this villain is kind of pretty. If it were not for its appetite for our garden plants, we might like this insect as much as we like ladybugs and fireflies.

As their name suggests, Japanese beetles are from Japan. They came to the US in 1939 in a packet of iris bulbs. Once they were loose, they spread all over North America.

The Japanese beetle is not a picky eater and will munch on a wide variety of plants. Unfortunately, their favorites happen to be the same ones that we humans like to eat.

These beetles are called "skeletonizers," because they eat the soft parts of a leaf, leaving the veins. The leaf ends up as nothing but a network of veins—a leaf skeleton.

Many gardeners buy "bag traps," to hang in their gardens, but studies have shown that this can backfire and actually attract more beetles than they kill. The best bet is to use a natural (fungal) insecticide called "milky spore."

SLUGS

This creature is very different from most other garden pests. It's not even remotely related to an insect. Its closest relatives are snails and squids. Slugs must stay moist, so they stay out of the sun and come out at night. You'll never see them on your plants unless you go out with a flashlight after dark.

Slugs have big appetites. In one night a few slugs can do some pretty serious damage to a small plant. Other types of critters can eat holes in leaves, too, but only slugs leave slime trails. Yeah, it's yucky, but if you look carefully at a leaf and see a trail, you can bet there are slugs nearby. Just pick up the nearest big rock and you'll likely find the leaf-eating criminals hiding underneath it.

Chemicals that harm slugs can also harm humans, pets and wildlife. A non-toxic remedy is to go out at night and just start putting the slugs into a plastic bag. It's safe and cheap.

MITES

Mites are tiny relatives of spiders. Mites that live on plants are often called spider mites. They are super small—even smaller than the head of a pin. You can't see their body parts without using a magnifier. They look like tiny moving dots.

Like aphids, mites like to sip sap. They are so small, though, that a tiny vein in a leaf is big enough for them. Colonies of mites live on the underside of leaves, sipping sap and hiding inside web tents they've constructed.

Fortunately, mites aren't the worst pests you could have. Unfortunately, they are very resistant to insecticides. You can spray your plant with neem oil (a natural oil from the neem tree) or find an online supplier who can sell you bigger mites. Truly! You can buy predator mites that will eat spider mites. (We're betting you'll go with the neem oil.)

ACTIVITY 1: THE LAST VIDEOS

If you have not watched them already, watch the last few videos on the playlist. They are about how to solve some disease and pest problems in non-toxic, environmentally friendly ways.

* *

If you are interested in more specific information about plant diseases (a lot more detail than we went into in this chapter) try some online resources such as these:
1) Free downloadable fact sheets with color photos: http://ohioline.osu.edu/hyg-fact/3000/index.html
2) An online resource (not downloadable): http://www.extension.umn.edu/gardeninfo/diagnostics/

These sites feature plants that live in temperate climates (US, UK, Europe). If you live in a place where the climate is subtropical, tropical, or desert, don't worry—the Internet is a big place and the information you need is certainly out there somewhere. Search for "plant diseases" and also add key words about your climate (such as "tropical" or "desert"). There are plant experts all over the world, and they love to put information online to help people with sick plants.

ACTIVITY 2: "DEAR DR. GREEN"

In a quaint little town called Garden City, the newspaper runs a weekly advice column called "Dear Dr. Green," in which a local expert answers readers' questions about plants. Here are some recent questions that readers sent in. Can you impersonate Dr. Green and give these folks the answers they need? Write your answers in the blank spaces below the questions.

Dear Dr. Green,
I am 9 years old and just planted my first garden this summer. I am trying to take care of it and water it a lot. I have a problem, though. My watermelon vine looks really wilted no matter how much I water it. Can a plant be so thirsty that it can't get enough water? Will I have to water it day and night? Is there something wrong with the vine?

Sincerely,
Ollie Ocksenfree

Dear Ollie,

Dear Dr. Green,
I am a college student at Garden City College. Recently I saw men cutting down some of the big beautiful elm trees that line the main entrance to the campus. I was really mad. Those trees are historic. I think the maintenance crews need to be taught to respect history. However, my roommate

said that there might be a practical reason for them doing this. He said to write to you before I start my petition to the college against this tree cutting. Could there be any good reason for destroying beautiful historic trees?

Sincerely,
A political science student

Dear student,

Dear Dr. Green,
The bushes next to my driveway are starting to turn brownish-yellow. The first leaves to lose their green color were the ones down at the base of the stems. The leaves out at the end of the branches look the best. Our rainfall has been very good for this time of year so I think the bushes are getting enough water. The bushes even get extra water as it runs off our driveway. I am mystified as to why only some of the leaves are affected. What could be going on here?

Sincerely,
Ima Knotshure

Dear Ima,

Dear Dr. Green,
My lilac bush looks like someone dusted it with powdered sugar. Is a neighborhood kid playing a prank on me, or is this some kind of natural phenomenon? (And is there anything I should do?)
Mr. I. V. Grohsonmywahls

Dear Mr. Grohsonmywahls,

(Hint if you need it: Read page 84-85 again)

Dear Dr. Green,

I've been watching my next door neighbor's gardening habits for several years now. I've noticed that his garden looks different every year. He never plants the same thing in the same place two years in a row. Is he an organization freak, or does he know something about plants that I don't know? Why would someone do this?

An anonymous resident of Maple St.

Dear anonymous resident,

Dear Dr. Green,

I am having trouble with aphids on my roses. I can't spray insecticides on my plants because some of my kids have problems with chemical sensitivities. Help! What can I do? Am I doomed to be plagued by aphids?

Sincerely,
Gertrude Plotz

Dear Gertrude,

Dear Dr. Green,

My cousin, Egbert, says that if you touch a diseased plant, you'll catch the disease. Is he right?

Sincerely,
Billy

Dear Billy,

BIBLIOGRAPHY

The bibliography at the back of a book lets you see how much reading and research the author had to do in order to write the book. Just think—these are books and websites you did NOT have to read! You only had to read the condensed version. Not so bad, eh? (But if you are interested in reading them yourself, the ISBN number is given so that you can find them easily. (If you type that number into Amazon, for example, it will show you a copy of that book.)

Books intended for adults:

Biology of the Cell (Fourth Edition) by Sylvia S. Mader. Published by Wm. C. Brown Publishers, © 1993. ISBN 0-697-20857-5.

Biology (Tenth Edition) by Sylvia S. Mader. Published by McGraw Hill Higher Education, © 2010. ISBN 978-0-07-352543-3

What's Wrong With My Plant (And How Do I Fix It?) by David Deardorff and Kathryn Wadsworth. Published by Timber Press in Portland and London, © 2009. ISBN 978-0-88192-961-4

Botany for All Ages by Jorie Hunken. Published by Globe Pequot Press, © 1993. ISBN 978-1564402813

Books for young people:

100 Flowers and How They Got Their Names, by Diana Wells. Published by Algonquin Books of Chapel Hill, © 1997. ISBN 1-56512-138-4

Ferns: Plants Without Flowers, by Bernice Kohn. Published by Hawthorn Books, Inc., New York. © 1968.

How Did We Find Out About Photosynthesis? by Isaac Asimov. Published by Walker and Company, New York, © 1989. ISBN 0-8027-6886-5.

Science Explorer: From Bacteria to Plants, (a science text for grade 7), published by Prentice Hall, © 2005 by Pearson Education, Boston. ISBN 978-0-558-65259-3

Seeds and Fruits, by Holding B. van Dobbenburgh. Published by Smithmark Publishers, New York, © 1995. ISBN 0-8317-6122-9

Looking at Plants by David Suzuki. Published by John Wiley & Sons, © 1991. ISBN 0-471-54049-8

Here are websites the author used, in addition to the books:

General info:
Wikipedia.com (many, many articles)
http://universe-review.ca/R10-34-anatomy2.htm#ferns

Mosses:
http://umanitoba.ca/Biology/BIOL1030/Lab7/biolab7_2.html

Mosses, ferns, cross sections:
http://people.bethel.edu/~johgre/bio114d/lowervasculars.html

Ferns:
http://www.deanza.edu/faculty/mccauley/6a-labs-plants-02.htm
http://www.bbg.org/gardening/article/growing_ferns_from_spores

Stem cross section, including fern:
http://sols.unlv.edu/Schulte/Anatomy/Stems/Stems.html

List of monocots:
http://www.plantbiology.siu.edu/Greenhouse/MonocotList.html

Gymnosperms:
http://hcs.osu.edu/hcs300/gymno.htm
http://web.gccaz.edu/~lsola/NonFlwr/conif105.htm

Gymnosperms and angiosperms:
http://faculty.clintoncc.suny.edu/faculty/michael.gregory/files/bio%20102/bio%20102%20lectures/
seed%20plants/seed%20plants.htm

Flower structure:
http://www.differencebetween.com/difference-between-carpel-and-vs-pistil/
http://www.culturaapicola.com.ar/apuntes/libros/Polinizacion/flower.html
http://www.botany.uwc.ac.za/ecotree/flowers/flowerparts2.htm
http://www.finegardening.com/how-to/qa/hollies-fruit.aspx
http://www.whatcom.wsu.edu/ag/homehort/plat/viburnum2.html

Fruits:
http://scidiv.bellevuecollege.edu/rkr/biology213/assignments/pdfs/FruitLabKey.pdf
http://chemistry.about.com/od/chemistryexperiments/ss/ethyleneexp.htm
http://www.catalyticgenerators.com/whatisethylene.html

Pollination:
http://plantphys.info/plants_human/pollenemb.shtml

Flower dissection:
http://www.fs.fed.us/wildflowers/teacher/documents/k5_DesertGardeners_flowerDissection.pdf
http://www.fairchildgarden.org/uploads/docs/Education/Downloadable_teaching_modules/flower%20
power/Flower%20Dissection%20LabII.pdf
http://www.cbsd.org/sites/teachers/hs/jucollins/Lists/Advanced%20Science%20Calendar/Attach-
ments/240/flower_dissection.pdf

Seed dispersal:
http://www.theseedsite.co.uk

Plant adaptations:
http://www.mbgnet.net/bioplants/adapt.html
http://www.countrysideinfo.co.uk/wetland_survey/adaptns.htm
http://www.dep.state.fl.us/coastal/habitats/seagrass/

http://www.seagrasswatch.org/seagrass.html
http://reefkeeping.com/issues/2006-10/rhf/index.php

World record plants:
http://waynesword.palomar.edu/ww0601.htm
http://www.adventureandscience.org/high-plants.html

Poisonous plants:
http://aggie-horticulture.tamu.edu/earthkind/landscape/poisonous-plants-resources/common-poison-ous-plants-and-plant-parts/
http://www.poisoncontrol.org/plants.html
http://cal.vet.upenn.edu/projects/poison/common.htm
http://webecoist.momtastic.com/2008/09/16/16-most-unassuming-yet-lethal-killer-plants/
http://www.terrapermadesign.com/wp-content/userfiles/Trees-with-Edible-Leaves.html
http://artofmanliness.com/2010/10/06/surviving-in-the-wild-19-common-edible-plants/
http://www.rawfoodsupport.com/read.php?4,24008
http://www.rosefloral.com/blog/poisonous-plants
http://alloveralbany.com/archive/2008/05/09/tulips-really-are-edible-sort-of
http://www.chop.edu/service/poison-control-center/resources-for-families/berries-and-seeds.html

Plant diseases:
http://www.hickorytech.net/~flapper/thistlecontrol.html
http://www.buzzle.com/articles/plant-diseases-caused-by-fungi.html
http://dspace.jorum.ac.uk/xmlui/bitstream/handle/123456789/937/Items/S250_1_section3.html?sequence=4
http://www.fs.fed.us/ne/morgantown/4557/gmoth/
http://utahpests.usu.edu/htm/utah-pests-news/up-summer12-newsletter/root-knot-nematodes/

Photosynthesis videos I watched:
http://www.youtube.com/watch?v=ixpNw6mx3lk&feature=related
http://www.youtube.com/watch?v=m8v7prlscM0&feature=related (Brightstorm.com)
http://www.youtube.com/watch?v=2IygaV0_-B0&feature=relmfu (Brightstorm.com)
http://www.youtube.com/watch?v=hj_WKgnL6MI (N. Dakota State Univ., Virtual Cell series)
http://www.youtube.com/watch?v=3UfV060N27g&feature=channel&list=UL (N. Dakota State Univ.)
http://www.youtube.com/watch?v=-rsYk4eCKnA&feature=relmfu (Khan Academy)
http://www.youtube.com/watch?v=o1I33Dgcc_M&feature=related
http://www.youtube.com/watch?v=uwOCkEf37Lc&NR=1&feature=endscreen (Univ. of Kent)

Wow. I guess I shouldn't have complained so much.

Yeah, guess so...

ANSWER
KEY

LESSON 1
Level 1
Activity 5: (Crossword puzzle)
ACROSS: 1) chloroplasts 2) membrane 3) daughters 4) photosynthesis 5) elongation
6) energy 7) water 8) nucleus 9) chlorophyll 10) carbon dioxide
DOWN: 1) light 2) mitosis 3) eat 4) sugar 5) oxygen 6) DNA 7) vacuole 8) respiration 9) wall
Activity 6: Compare your drawing to the one in the chapter (Questions below: 1 magnesium, 4 nitrogens)
Activity 7: 1)D 2)A 3)B 4)F 5)H 6)C 7)E 8)G

Level 2
Activity 2: 1)J 2)I 3)B 4)F 5)G 6)D 7)A 8)H 9)C 10)E
Activity 3: 1)B 2)F 3)C 4)G 5)A 6)D 7)H 8)E
Activity 4: 1) Answers will vary. 2) ATP, NADPH high energy electrons 3) ATP synthase 4) respiration
5) light (photons) 6) Calvin Cycle (Light Independent Phase) 7) carbon dioxide, carbon
8) ADP 9) stroma of chloroplasts 10) 5 11) Melvin Calvin 12) 6 13) c 14) a
15) protons

LESSON 2
Level 1
Activity 1: 1) Muehlenberg 2) Engelmann 3) Michaux 4) Kellogg
Activity 3: 1)C 2)G 3)B 4)H 5)I 6)F 7)J 8)E 9)A 10)D
Activity 4: Answers will vary.

Level 2
Activity 1: 1) H   2) A   3) I   4) D   5) C   6) F   7) J   8) B   9) G   10) E
Activity 3: 1) China, 2) Italy, 3) Virginia, 4) India, 5) Tasmania, 6) Brazil
Activity 4: The prunus fruits all have one large seed that we sometimes call a "pit."
1) acorn squash (same species), 2) tomato (yam is monocot), 3) chestnut (both are Fagales)

LESSON 3
Level 2
Activity 2: 1) zygote   2) osmosis   3) sporophyte   4) bryophyte   5) thallus   6) gametophyte
7) gemma   8) wort   9) vascular   10) alternation of generations

Stupid plant joke missing words: moss, liverwort, argument, a, bryo-phyte (sounds like "fight")

LESSON 4
Level 1
Activity 3: The monocots are: corn, yucca, grass, orchid, tulip. The dicots are: oak, geranium, nasturtium, mint.

Activity 4: Vascular plants have a system of [pipes/tubes] that deliver water to their cells. They are made of two types of cells: [xylem] and [phloem]. The [xylem] tubes take water up from the roots and into the [leaves]. This process is called [transpiration]. (The reason this process works is because of the electrical attraction between [water] molecules.) The [phloem] tubes carry water that has sugars in it. This sugary water can go either up or [down] depending on where it is needed.   In northern climates, sap in maple trees rises from [the roots] up into the leaves. If you put a tube into the tree you can catch some of this sap and make [maple syrup] from it.

Most vascular plants make [seeds] but a few do not, such as the fern. Most vascular plants are either monocots or [dicots].   The monocots have one [seed leaf] when they first sprout, whereas the [dicots] have two. The monocots have [parallel] veins in their leaves.   The [dicots] have veins that resemble a palm shape.

The central part of a stem is called the [pith]. The outer cells are the epidermis. Just inside the epidermis is a layer of cells called the [cortex], In trees, the old, dead phloem cells become the bark.

Another way you can tell monocots from [**dicots**] is to look at their roots. Monocots have [**fibrous**] roots and dicots have a long [**tap roots**]. Roots are part of the vascular system. A [**cap**] on the end of the root tip protects it while it grows. You can remember that in trees the [**xylem**] is the part we called "wood" because you know that a musical instrument called [**the xylophone**] is made of wood.

Level 2

Activity 3: 1)T 2)F 3)F 4)T 5)T 6)F 7)T 8)T 9)T 10)T 11)F 12)T 13)T 14)F 15)T 16)F 17)F 18)T 19)T 20)F

LESSON 5
Level 1

Activity 2: We counted 45 rings (including the central "dot" which would have been the first year). The tree was 34 years old when a very wet summer occurred.

Level 2

Activity 1: (Crossword puzzle)

ACROSS: 2) carotene 6) stomata 7) lobed 11) abscission 12) whorl 14) pinnate 17) xanthophyll 21) apex 22) phloem 24) guard 25) petiole 26) xylem

DOWN: 1) deciduous 3) anthocyanin 4) cuticle 5) cambium 6) serrated 8) dendrochronology 9) margin 10) cordate 13) deltoid 14) palmate 15) woody 16) palisade 18) herbaceous 19) mesophyll 23) lamina

LESSON 6
Level 1

Activity 2: FRUIT: tomato, peas, beans, pumpkin, corn, zucchini, cucumber, pepper, eggplant, olive, avocado
VEGETABLE: spinach, lettuce, carrots, kale, cabbage, broccoli, beets, asparagus, celery, parsley, rhubarb

Activity 5: 1) zygote 2) stamen 3) anther 4) pistil 5) angio 6) style 7) fruit 8) embryo 9) harden 10) fern 11) filament 12) share 13) rhizome 14) receptacle 15) the wind 16) prothallus 17) double   Stupid joke: "Why did the botany student fail the test? He forgot the anthers!"

Activity 6: 1) photosynthesis 2) respiration 3) CO_2, H_2O, 1, O_2, H_2O 4) mitosis 5) nucleus 6) vascular 7) angiosperms, gymnosperms 8) monocot 9) moss/liverwort/bryophyte 10) osmosis 11) spores 12) male, female 13) xylem, phloem 14) pith 15) woody, herbaceous 16) fibrous 17) parallel 18) xylem cells 19) phloem cells 20) phloem 21) cambium 22) rhizome 23) petiole 24) apex 25) stomata 26) palisade 27) c 28) b 29) guard cells 30) dendrochronology

Level 2

Activity 1: 1) stigma (is female part, others are male parts)   2) almond (is dry fruit, others are succulents)
3) tomato (is a fruit, others are vegetables)   4) peanut (is a legume, others are nuts)
5) filament (is male part, others are female parts)   6) cabbage (is a leaf, others are stems)
7) apple (has multiple seeds, others have just one)   8) pineapple (is a multiple fruit, others simple)
9) dandelion (is not a legume like the others)   10) potato (is a tuber, not a true root like the others)
11) strawberry (not a true berry like the others)   12) sago (is a gymnosperm, others are angiosperms)
13) bark (is dead, the other tissues are living)   14) geranium (is a dicot, others are monocots)
15) serrated (describes edge of leaf, others describe placement of leaves on stem)
16) gemma (part of a moss, not a fern)   17) lamina (name for leaf, other words describe shapes)
18) moss (not vascular, others are vascular)   19) chlorophyll (is a molecule, others are organelles)
20) sodium (is not an element found in chlorophyll molecule)

LESSON 7

<u>Level 1</u>

Activity 1: 1) stomata, cuticle   2) areoles   3) C4, CAM   4) duckweed, plant   5) protein, starch
6) zygote   7) manatee   8) trichomes, epidermis   9) bottom, pad, red, spines
10) transpiration   11) burn   12) succulent, bulky, survive   13) gymno
PLANTS from left to right, top to bottom:
First row: agave, brain, cocoon, stone   Second row: ice, pencil, aleo, zebra
Third row: prickly pear, yucca, hen and chicks   Fourth row: saguaro, barrel, organ pipe, curiosity

<u>Level 2</u>

Activity 1: 1) photo   2) micro   3) chloro   4) meso   5) mono   6) tropo   7) dendro   8) bio
9) antho   10) gymno   11) angio   12) xantho   13) spiro

Activity 2: 1)T   2)F   3)F   4)F   5)F   6)F (pitcher is not destroyed)   7)F   8)T   9)T   10)F
11)T   12)F   13)T   14)T   15)F   16)F (not the hemlock tree, but rather the conium hemlock)
17) F   18)T   19)F   20)F   21)T (haustoria instead of roots) 22)T   23)F   24)T   25)F

LESSON 8

<u>Level 1</u>

Activity 3: 1) FVB   2) FVB   3) B   4) V   5) V   6) B   7) FB   8) V   9) FVB   10) B   11) F
12) F   13) FVB   14) FVB   15) FVB   16) F

Activity 4: 1) virus   2) compost   3) mosaic   4) insecticide   5) decomposer   6) mycelium   7) hypha
8) powdery mildew   9) canker   10) arborist   11) resistant   12) ovipositor   13) legume
14) plasmid   15) tobacco   16) antibiotic   17) pathogen   18) goldenrod   19) sterilize   20) parasite

<u>Level 2</u>

Activity 2: Student answers will vary, but here are the responses that Dr. Green probably would have given:

Dear Ollie,

It sounds like your vine might have a "wilt" disease. Wilt diseases are caused by bacteria. You should trim off all the branches of the vine that look wilted so the bacteria doesn't have a chance to spread to the rest of that plant or to other nearby plants. Put the diseased leaves in a trash bag and throw them out. (Or you can burn them if you live in a place that allows burning.) If the whole plant looks bad, you'll have to get rid of it. Sorry about your vine, but getting rid of sick plants is just part of learning to take care of a garden. Don't give up gardening!

Dear student,

Sounds like some of your elms have caught Dutch Elm Disease. Diseased branches must be trimmed off, and if the whole tree is sick it has to be cut down. This is very sad, but a sick tree can make all the others around it get sick, too. Hopefully the arborists will be able to plant replacement trees that are resistant to Dutch Elm Disease.

Dear Ima,

Since you mentioned that your bushes are next to the driveway, I think maybe they might be responding to an overabundance of salt in the soil. I'm betting you live in an area of the world where salt is applied to roads in the winter. The salty water probably runs off into your yard and goes into the soil around your bushes. Perhaps you could dig a landscaping trench that would take the salty run-off water away from your bushes?

Dear Mr. Grohsonmywahls,

Your lilac bush has a fungal infection called powdery mildew. This is very common. It's not likely to kill your bush. You could try spraying the bush with a baking soda spray or compost tea. Some people use neem oil on fungal infections, also. If you decide to try baking soda, buy potassium bicarbonate instead of sodium bicarbonate. (Potassium is better for plants than sodium is.) You might want to trim off any leaves that are seriously affected, but don't trim off so many that the bush will starve. Remember, the leaves are where the plant makes its food.

Dear anonymous,

Your neighbor is doing something called "crop rotation." This practice has been going on for thousands of years. There are two good reasons for rotating your crops. The first is for nitrogen fixation in the soil (by legume plants). The second is for disease control. Often, pathogens are specific to a certain type of plant. If your plants last season had a disease, the pathogen is probably still lurking in the soil and will attack any similar plants that are planted there. If you plant something different, the pathogen may be less likely to attack it. Hopefully, the population of that pathogen will decrease before you plant that same crop there again.

Dear Gertrude,

Aphids can become resistant to insecticides. They have a very short life cycle, which allows for the population to rapidly breed for resistance to things in the environment, such as chemicals. A nice way to control aphids is to purchase some ladybugs and release them near the aphids. Ladybugs love to eat aphids. If you don't want more insects around, trying hosing down your plants (with plain water) once a week.

Dear Billy,

You don't have to worry about catching plant diseases. Pathogens are very specific and can only attack a very narrow range of plants or animals. Animals can't get plant diseases, and plants can't catch animal diseases.

ACTIVITY
GUIDE

NOTE: If you would like to print out the pattern pages instead of photocopying them out of the book, you can download the PDF files for the images by going to www.ellenjmchenry.com. Click on FREE DOWNLOADS, then on PLANTS, then on "Printable pages for *Botany in 8 Lessons*." After downloading this file, you can print the pages using your computer printer or you can ask a print shop to print them for you.

SUPPLEMENTAL ACTIVITIES

LESSON 1

1) PLANT CELL "PENNY PITCH" GAME

This game can be played indoors or out. You can adapt the size and scale of all the game parts to suit your playing area. For small areas, make the model a few feet in diameter, and pitch pennies. For large areas, make the model very large and pitch bean bags or shoes. (You could even use an empty parking lot and draw the model with chalk.)

You will need:
- A large floor area (can be an area in a room, or as large as a parking lot outdoors)
- A long rope (to represent the cell wall)
- Small objects to represent ribosomes (dried beans, dimes, raisins—whatever you have on hand)
- Yarn (three colors: one for the cell membrane, one for the endoplasmic reticulum, one for the vacuole)
- Green fabric, felt or paper than can be cut into chloroplasts
- Fabric or paper scraps of various colors and/or textures, for other cell parts
- Objects to pitch, such as pennies or bean bags, depending upon the size of your playing area. Beanbags are obviously better for very large areas, pennies for smaller areas.
- Scissors

Set-up:

Use the ingredients listed above to make a flat model of a plant cell on the ground, using the diagram as a guide. The organelles can be in any position. You may give the students freedom to arrange the cell however they want to. (The cytoskeleton is not used, as it would make things too complicated. Also, some of the parts are discussed only in Level 2. You can adapt this game to Level 1 by using only the cell parts mentioned in Level 1.)

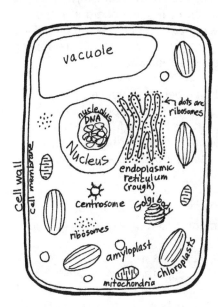

CELL WALL: Outer layer--provides protection and support for cell
CELL MEMBRANE: Thin membrane that controls flow of water and chemicals in and out of the cell
NUCLEUS: Contains DNA (the instructions a cell needs for everything it does and everything it has to manufacture)
NUCLEOLUS: Contains the DNA that tells how to make ribosomes
VACUOLE: Empty "bubble" helps to maintain shape of cell.
CHLOROPLAST: Where photosynthesis occurs (Makes sugar from light, carbon dioxide and water.)
MITOCHONDRIA: The energy producers of the cell
CENTROSOME: Assists cell in mitosis (reproducing by splitting in half)
AMYLOPLAST (a type of LEUCOPLAST): Stores sugar and starch molecules made by the cell
ENDOPLASMIC RETICULUM: A series of tubes connected to the nucleus (Rough ER has ribosomes surrounding it.)
RIBOSOMES: The "factories" that produce proteins the cell needs
GOLGI BODIES: Process and package proteins and fats made by the cell (they look sort of like a stack of pancakes)

How to play:

If you have a lot of players, divide them up into teams. Make sure all players are standing the same distance away from the cell. Call out the name of a team and then the name of an organelle. The members of that team all pitch their objects, trying to land on the organelle you just called out. The team receives a point for every "hit." Have the players reclaim their objects. Then call out another team and another organelle. Make sure all teams get a chance to aim for each organelle at some point in the game.

2) PHOTOSYNTHESIS GAME

You will need:
- A copy of the game board for each player
- Small "tokens" of at least three different kinds or colors, which will be used to represent carbon, oxygen, and hydrogen atoms. (Suggestions: small candies, different types of breakfast cereal, raisins, cranberries, nuts)
- One spinner (assemble and color the spinner according to directions) You will need scissors, glue, a paper fastener, and markers or crayons for this (and cereal box cardboard if you want to make the spinner sturdy enough to last for a while).

Directions:
This game can be played with any number of players. Divide the players up so that you have four teams. If you have only two or three players, the game will still work. Even one person can play it, although there won't be any competition, of course. (However, the satisfaction in having completed the task of photosynthesis might be enough.) The number of players per team does not have to be equal. Being on the same team simply means that all members of that team will receive the same spinner results on each round, and therefore will be doing the same thing at the same time. This can actually be very beneficial for those students who have trouble catching on to game formats. They can simply follow along with what their teammates are doing.

Each player/team is assigned a colored "arm" of the spinner. Each time the spinner is spun, the team (or individual player) will read the results from that color. For example, if you are on the red team, whatever the red arm lands on is your spin result. The blue arm is for all players on the blue team. Players on teams can take turns spinning the spinner, but the spin will be for everyone. There is no "down time" waiting for turns. All players do something each time the spinner is spun. (The exception being if you already have your slots filled for that item. If you already have a light token and light is spun again, you can't do anything on that turn.)

Each person decides what they will use to represent the atoms on their board: carbon, oxygen, and hydrogen. They will also need just one token to represent light. Make sure they choose their "code" ahead of time. For example: raisins for carbon atoms, Cheerios for oxygen atoms, small red candies for hydrogens, and a dried banana for light. Whatever the spinner arm lands on is what you build on your game board. If you or your team spins WATER, then you "build" one of the water molecules on the top portion of the board by putting two hydrogen tokens and one oxygen token right on top of one of the water molecules. You only need one light token, so if you land on LIGHT again, you just do nothing for that turn, since you already have light.

Once you have all the molecules filled up on the top half of the board, it then becomes a race (or a cooperation) to see how fast you can rearrange all the atoms to form the molecules on the bottom half of the board. Plants do this, too. They disassemble all the ingredient molecules and use them to form new molecules.

The advantage of using edible tokens is that whenever you have the bottom half of your board complete, you can reward yourself by eating the glucose molecule (and the other molecules, too, if you are still hungry!).

During the course of the game you will certainly hear the following comments. Here are some responses you could give.

"I keep spinning light. I don't need any more light!" *This is true for plants, as well. Plants living outdoors almost always have enough light. In fact, most of the sun's energy goes to waste. What limits photosynthesis is usually the amount of water available.*

"I don't have enough water. I keep spinning carbon dioxide." *This happens sometimes in real life, too. The weather can produce droughts. There is still plenty of carbon dioxide and light, but not enough water. If you keep spinning you are guaranteed to land on water eventually.*

"I have way too much water and not enough carbon dioxide." *Plants could possibly have this problem, though it is less likely than a water problem. Some people claim that breathing on your house plants helps them to grow faster since your breath contains carbon dioxide. There could also be atmospheric conditions in some places that would make carbon dioxide less abundant. Plants submerged in water are not able to take in air.*

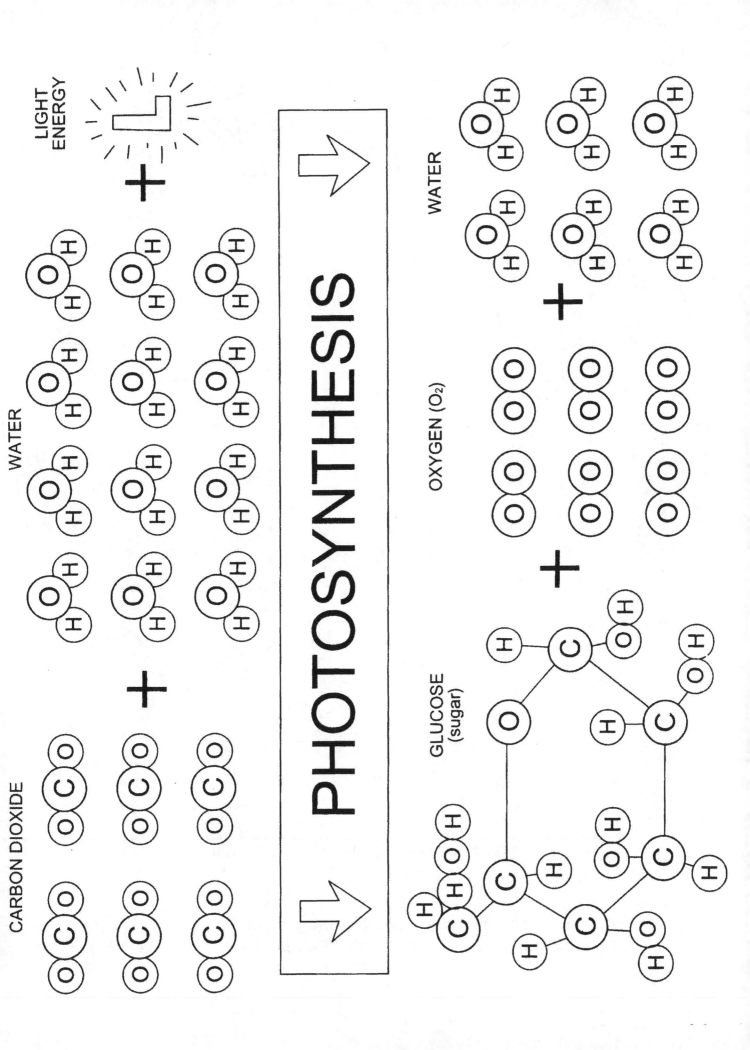

CARBON DIOXIDE

WATER

LIGHT ENERGY

PHOTOSYNTHESIS

WATER

OXYGEN (O_2)

GLUCOSE (sugar)

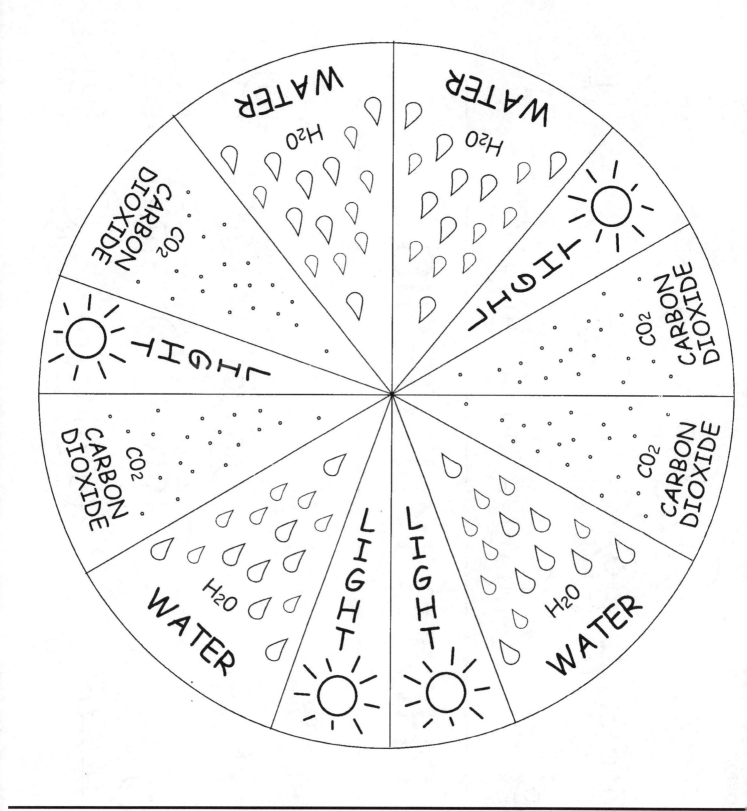

Do not cut out circle. Simply cut across this line.

GLUE THIS SPINNER SQUARE TO CARDBOARD IF YOU WANT IT TO BE
STURDY ENOUGH TO LAST A WHILE. (CEREAL BOX CARDBOARD IS FINE.)

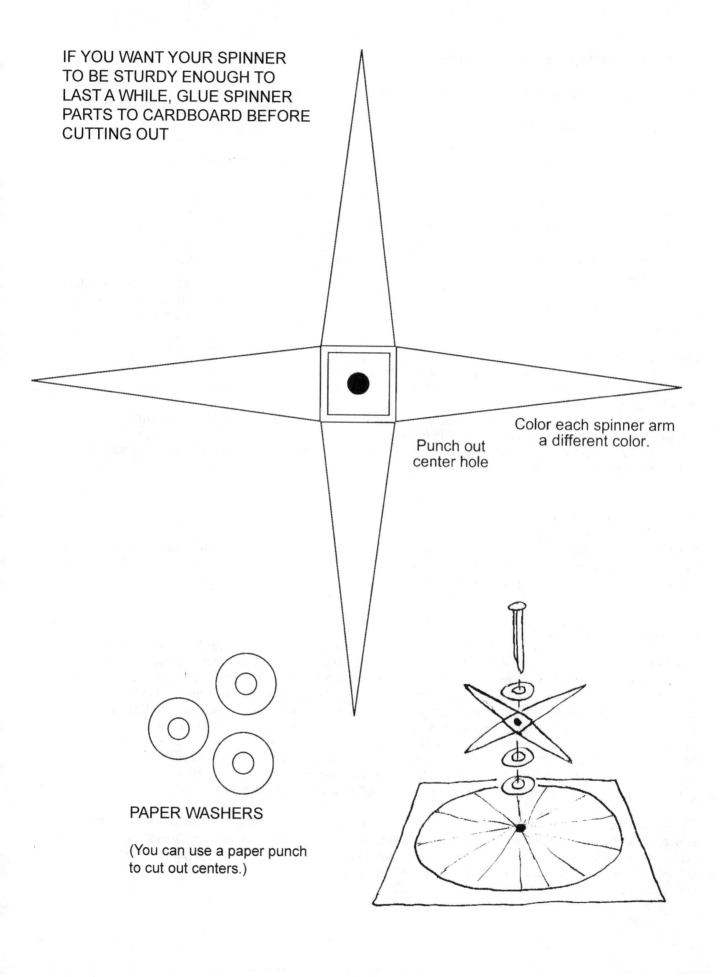

IF YOU WANT YOUR SPINNER
TO BE STURDY ENOUGH TO
LAST A WHILE, GLUE SPINNER
PARTS TO CARDBOARD BEFORE
CUTTING OUT

Color each spinner arm
a different color.

Punch out
center hole

PAPER WASHERS

(You can use a paper punch
to cut out centers.)

3) PHOTOSYNTHESIS RELAY RACE

The goal of this game is to reinforce the photosynthesis formula

WATER + CARBON DIOXIDE + LIGHT → OXYGEN + SUGAR + WATER

while at the same time allowing restless students to engage in active play.

The reverse side of the leaf will have an envelope that says "OUT."

You will need:
- Two pieces of green construction paper
- Four small (standard 3.5"x 6.5") envelopes
- Glue stick or white glue
- Marker
- Copy of the card pattern page with pieces cut out
- A flashlight for each team

Directions for assembly:
Cut two large green leaves. Cut the flaps off the envelopes, then glue an envelope on each side of each leaf, with the open side of the envelope facing out. Label the envelopes on opposite sides of the leaves "IN" and "OUT."

Photocopy the card pattern page onto card stock, if possible, to make the cards more durable. However, plain paper can be used as well. Cut out all the cards.

Optional: Decorate or color the cards to make them more readable at a quick glance. For instance, put a raindrop on the water cards.

How to set up the game:
You will need to prepare the leaves ahead of time by putting cards for WATER, OXYGEN and GLUCOSE in the OUT pocket of the leaves. Put WATER and CARBON DIOXIDE cards in neat piles at the start line. Put the leaves at a distance from the start line. (If your students need to stretch their legs, put the leaves really far away!) Put the flashlights next to the leaves.

How to play the game:
On the word GO, the first member of the team takes either a CARBON DIOXIDE or a WATER card, runs to the leaf, and puts it into the IN pocket of their leaf. He runs back and tags the next player. The second player takes the other card (whatever the first player didn't take, either water or carbon dioxide) and runs to the leaf. He puts this into the IN pocket, then runs back. The third player runs to the leaf, turns on the flashlight, shines it on the leaf briefly, turns it off (leaves the flashlight there), and then runs back. Now the leaf has had all the necessary ingredients for photosynthesis! The fourth player runs to the leaf and takes out just one of the cards in the OUT pocket and runs (taking the token with him) back to the team. The fifth player runs to the leaf, takes another card out of the OUT pocket and runs with it back to the team. The sixth player runs to the leaf and takes out the last card in the OUT pocket. When the last player gets back to his team with the last product of photosynthesis, the team is done. First team to accomplish all this wins the game.

Variations: This game is a lot of fun to play again and again if you change the method of locomotion to and from the leaf. Have them hop, skip, walk backwards, crawl, carry a ball between their knees, etc. This way they get the repetition of the photosynthesis formula without making them bored with the game. Even middle school and high school ages like the game when it is played with creative variations. It brings a lot of laughs, as well as a lot of learning.

WATER	WATER
WATER	WATER
CARBON DIOXIDE	CARBON DIOXIDE
OXYGEN	OXYGEN
GLUCOSE (SUGAR)	GLUCOSE (SUGAR)

4) STREAMING CHLOROPLASTS "FLIP BOOK"

You will need:
- Scissors
- White glue (can substitute glue stick if it is high quality, not "school" quality)
- Copies of the pattern pages printed onto white card stock
- Optional: colored pencils or crayons, fine sandpaper

Directions:

Do any coloring you want to do before you cut apart the pages or assemble the booklet. (However, coloring is still possible after the pages are cut and after the booklet is assembled, as long as the glue is dry enough so that the pages will not come apart.) The most important coloring is to make the chloroplasts green so that they will show up nicely when the pages are flipped. If you want to color other parts of the cell, you may do so, as long as you are consistent and do the same thing on every cell.

Cut out all the pages. Glue will be applied right where the numbers are. Use glue sparingly. Half a drop is enough if it is spread out! No oozing glue! Stack the pages, putting 1 on the bottom and working upward until the cover (which would be number 24) is on the top.

IMPORTANT: Match the edges on the right side of the book (the side away from the numbers). Don't worry if the number sides match up evenly. You want the side you will flip to be smooth. You can even use a piece of fine sandpaper to smooth the flipping edge once the booklet is dry. Hold that edge tightly, put the sandpaper on the table, and rub the booklet across the sand paper. The table will give you a firm surface on which to rub the edge of the booklet.

Let the book dry completely before sanding or flipping the pages.

PAGE 1 GOES ON THE BOTTOM.
WORK YOUR WAY UP TO 23 ON THE TOP, THEN THE COVER.

5) LOOK AT REAL PLANT CELLS UNDER A MICROSCOPE

If you have a microscope available (100x or greater) you can easily observe plant cells by using the thin membrane layer of an onion. Peel the tough, yellowish-tan layers off the outside of the onion. Before you get into the white layers, you will find an incredibly thin membrane—so thin you can easily see through it. This layer is perfect for viewing under a microscope. Put a small piece of this membrane onto a microscope slide and put it under 100x. You should be able to see rows and rows of cells.

6) EXTRA READING MATERIAL ABOUT PHOTOSYNTHESIS

If reading forms a large part of your educational program, you may want to consider purchasing a copy of the book How Did We Find Out About Photosynthesis? by Isaac Asimov. This book is written for ages 9-13 and tells the story of how scientists across the centuries (starting back in the 1700s) have gradually learned more and more about how plants work.

7) SIMPLE COMPUTER ANIMATION OF CALVIN CYCLE

This is a very short overview of the Calvin Cycle with a simple quiz at the end where you drag and drop the correct terms into the boxes. Good review after reading level 2 of the text.

http://sjbscience.weebly.com/uploads/2/7/5/3/2753626/calvin_benson_v2.swf

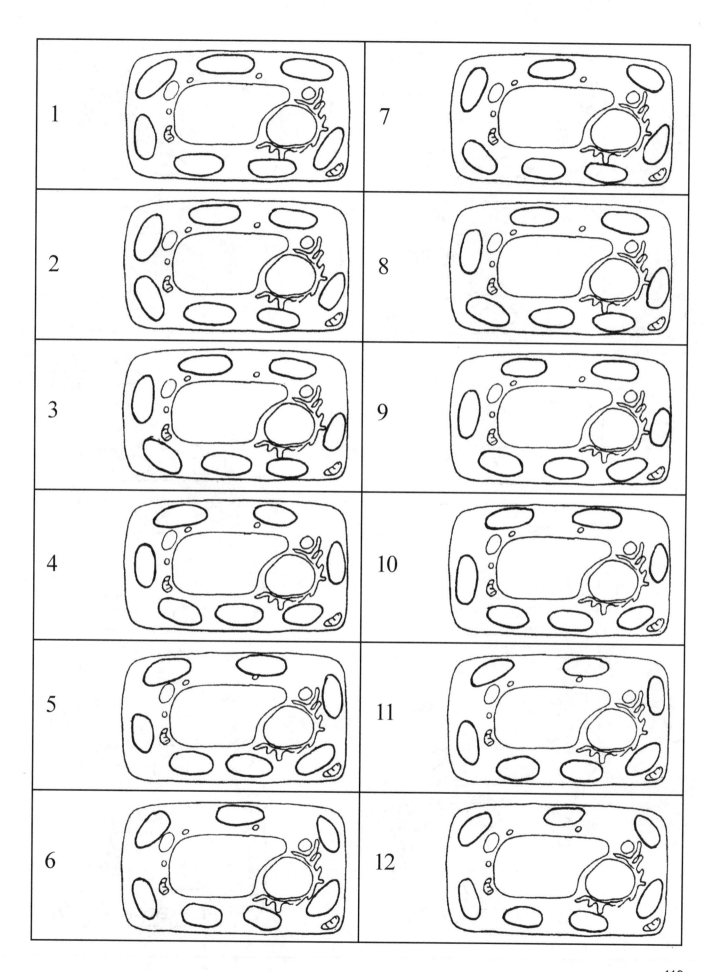

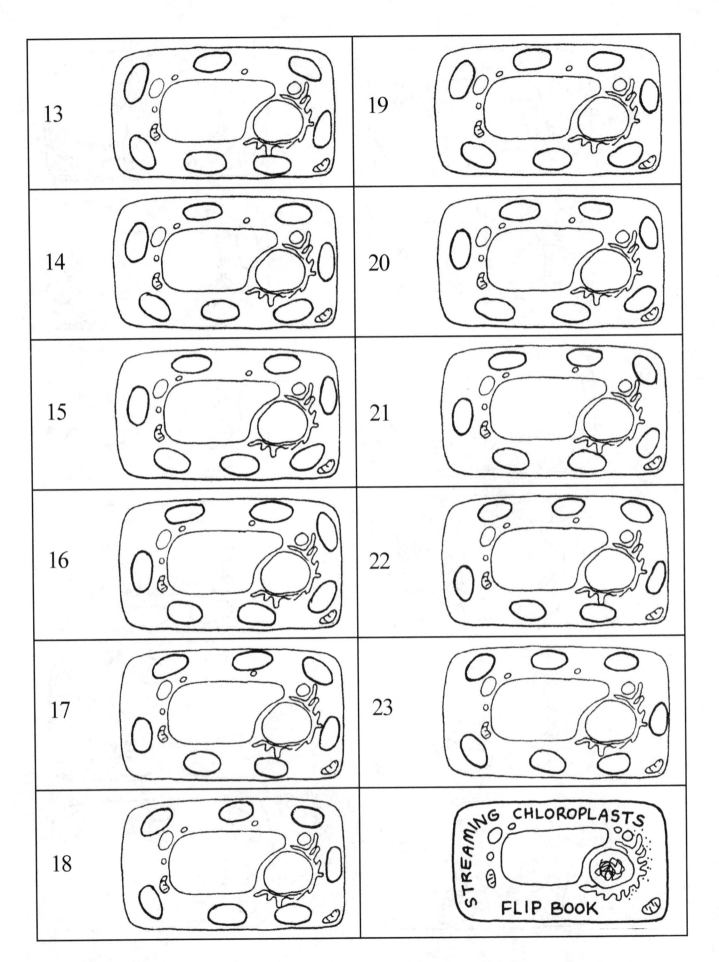

13

19

14

20

15

21

16

22

17

23

18

STREAMING CHLOROPLASTS FLIP BOOK

COPY ONTO WHITE CARD STOCK

7) ATP "POP GUN"

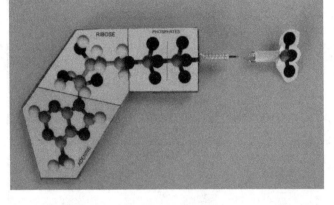

Here is a fun way to help your students remember what ATP is and what it does. This toy has a lot of science packed into it! The gun is labeled showing the chemical structure: adenine (the same adenine found in the rungs of DNA), ribose (very similar to the ribose sugar found in the "backbone" of DNA), and three phosphate groups. The third phosphate acts as the "bullet" and pops off, just like in real ATP. So the gun itself, without the bullet, is ADP.

The springs that launch the phosphate bullet represent the repelling forces between the oxygen molecules on the phosphates. The oxygens have a negative charge. According to the basic rules of chemistry, "like" charges repel and opposites attract. So the oxygens don't want to be next to each other. This repelling force is overcome, however, by the strength of the chemical bond, represented by the metal clip that holds the phosphate bullet in place until released. There is a fine balance between holding and repelling.

You will need:

- A copy of the following pattern page (there are two guns per page, so you'll only have to make one copy per two students)
- A piece of corrugated cardboard for each gun (the piece must be large enough so that you can orient the corrugate line to go parallel to the barrel of the gun)
- Optional: a sharp craft knife (a kitchen knife with serrated edge) for cutting the cardboard
- Two ball point pens per gun (the kind of pen that has a <u>clicking button</u> at the top, not the kind that has a removable cap)
- Three paper clips per gun
- White glue (a glue stick if you are using regular paper—glue stick will wrinkle the paper less)
- Needle nose pliers (pliers with a very pointed end)
- Scissors
- Tape: Masking tape is best, duct tape is a little thick but would work, clear tape is third choice because it will be hard to glue patterns on top of it. (If all you have available is clear tape, don't let this stop you from doing the project.)
- Possibly helpful: A tube of all-purpose craft glue (the smelly stuff that comes in a tube and promises to stick to plastic, wood, paper and metal) This is just in case you have trouble getting the springs to stay in.

Construction:

1) Copy the pattern page into heavy card stock if possible. (If you can't get card stock, you can make do with regular paper.) If you want your students to label the atoms, there is a labeling guide on page 222.

2) Cut out the gun patterns. Cut off the third phosphate on the end; it will be turned into the bullet. You can simply cut a rectangle around this phosphate, or you can trim around the shape more closely. Trimming can be done as the last step. For right now, set these pieces aside.

3) Take one of the gun patterns you have cut out and place it on top of the corrugated cardboard. You must be very careful to place the pattern so that the corrugate lines are going parallel to the barrel. Cut out the cardboard shape. Do not glue the gun pattern on top yet. This will happen in a later step.

4) Take apart the pens. Salvage both springs and one of the ink tubes. Take one spring and put it on the end of the ink tube and secure in place with a tiny strip of tape.

5) Slide the ink tube into one of the slots in the barrel section of the corrugated cardboard gun. Make sure it is secure. If it wants to slip back out, put a dab of all purpose glue on the tube before sliding it back in. (If you have no glue available, you can secure it at the end with a thin strip of tape. Tear the tape lengthwise so that it is only a third of its original width.)

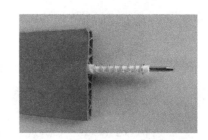

6) Take two of the paper clips and bend them just slightly on one end. Tape the paper clips right at the end of the barrel so that the end of the clip sticks out just a bit. You should be able to squeeze the clips together a few millimeters and have them bounce back to their original position. This will be the release mechanisms that fires the phosphate bullet.

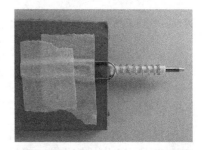

7) Now you can glue the pattern pieces to the sides of the cardboard. You have now finished the ADP section of the project. Remember, ATP without that third phosphate is ADP. See the picture on the previous page for an image of the completed ADP gun.

8) Cut a piece of regular paper 3 centimeters square (1 1/4 inches). You might be able to use a scrap of your card stock, but since this square will be rolled up, the card stock might be too thick. Set the spring on the edge of the paper, with one edge of the spring flush with the end of the paper, and roll the paper around the spring. The tricky part of this step is to make the roll snug but not so tight that the spring can't move inside the tube. The spring will need to be able to contract and spring back inside the tube. Once you get it wound just right, secure the roll with tape.

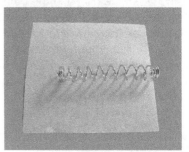

9) Pinch the end of the tube that has a bit of extra space. Secure with tape.

10) Take the remaining paper clip and snip off the small inner portion so that you are left with a long U shape. Make tiny bends in the ends that form angles of about 45 degrees. It is important to make these bends as small as possible. If they are too long you will have trouble releasing the bullet. You may have to make small adjustments to these hooks later on if your gun will not fire properly. (Some troubleshooting is to be expected!)

11) Tape this U-shape onto the paper tube so that the ends stick out over the open end of the tube. Secure with tape.

12) Glue the phosphate pieces back to back at the end of the bullet tube. Don't use too much glue. If there is glue seeping out, you've used too much. Press and hold the phosphates for at least about twenty seconds. White glue usually sticks well enough after twenty seconds that you can let go.

13) Now you are ready to try out the gun. You will probably have to make small adjustments to get it to fire perfectly every time. (But it can be done, and they often will shoot the bullet a distance of several meters (over 10 feet).

How to fire the gun:

Slide the bullet onto the end of the ink tube. The two springs will compress (representing the repelling forces of the negatively charged atoms that do not want to be next to each other). Pinch the two clips at the end of the barrel so that they get closer together. This should give you enough space to be able to slide the hooks over the clips. Slowly release tension on the end clips. The tension of the end clips pushing outward should keep the bullet hooks in place. When you let go, the bullet should stay in place.

To fire the gun, simply press the barrel's end clips together. The bullet should shoot quite a distance.

An extra feature you can add:

In a real ATP molecule, the release of the third phosphate is caused by a water molecule. It pops apart into an H and an OH. (These split-up pieces are called ions.) The H has a positive charge and is written like this: (H^+). The OH has a negative charge and is written like this: (OH^-). These two pieces can "plug" the electrically awkward "gaps" left behind by the third phosphate when it goes flying off. (After all, electrical bonds are broken when an atom leaves a molecule. Often there are some unhappy atoms or electrons left behind!)

You can make a hands-on way to remember how a real ATP fires its phosphate. Cut two paper circles and label one (H^+) and the other (OH^-). Tape one circle to your thumbnail and one to the nail of your index finger. (Or you can take a permanent marker and draw these letters on the fingernails. Permanent marker scrubs off fingernails fairly easily.)

With your thumb and index finger labeled correctly, you can scientifically fire your ATP gun using a water molecule. When water splits something apart it's called *hydrolysis*. "Hydro" means "water," and "lysis" means "split." (Actually, to be perfectly accurate, your thumbnail (with the OH on it) would have to go flying off with the phosphate bullet!) If the students simply remember that water is involved in splitting off the third phosphate, that will amaze all their future teachers until they get to AP biology or college biochem.

TROUBLESHOOTING TIPS:

1) If your bullet will not stay clipped, you need to check two things. First, make sure that the hooks on the end of the bullet are bent in far enough. They don't need to be completely at a right angle, but they need to be at enough of an angle that they catch onto the ends of the paper clips adequately. Second, you may need to adjust how much the end paper clips are bent. They need to be far enough apart that they can apply adequate outward pressure on the bullet clips.

2) If your bullet won't release and fly, check to see if the clips on the end are spread too far apart. You might have too much tension on the bullet hooks. Also, your bullet hooks might be too long. You may need to clip them a bit.

3) If your bullet doesn't go very far, check to see if both springs are operating as they should. If only one spring is providing impetus, the bullet will only go half as far as it should. Check to see if the spring inside the bullet is stuck. This spring should be able to contract and release even though it is inside the paper tube.

NOTE: Tips 1 and 2 are demonstrated on a video posted at www.YouTube.com/TheBasementWorkshop, Botany playlist or Project Demo playlist.

ONE FINAL SCIENCE NOTE:

To state the obvious, your ATP gun is not very powerful. It launches a tiny, lightweight paper bullet. It might be able to knock down a small paper target but it certainly isn't going to cause any damage to anything. Real ATPs are a bit like this, too. They release only a miniscule amount of energy. Your body must make and use trillions of ATPs every day. If you could collect all the ATPs your body makes and uses in one day, you'd find that your bucket full of ATPs would weigh almost as much as you do. That's millions of ATPs per second.

The fact that ATPs release only a small amount of energy is not a bad thing. If they released a lot of energy they would damage cells. ATPs are the perfect size for cellular tasks.

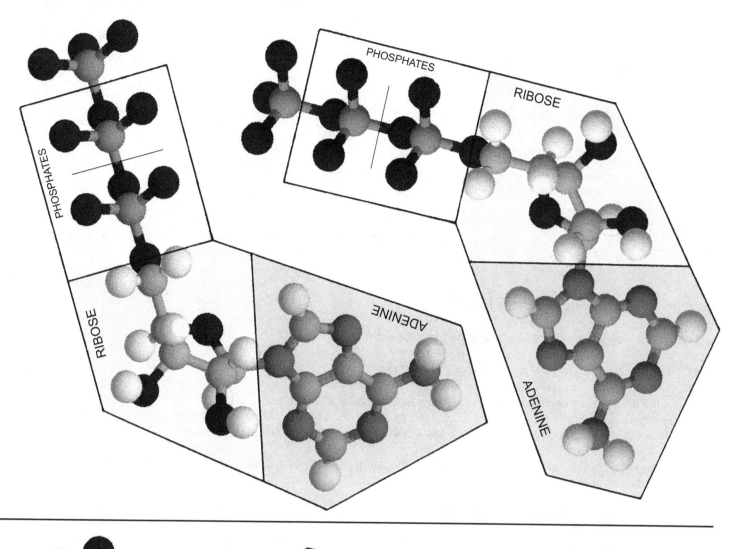

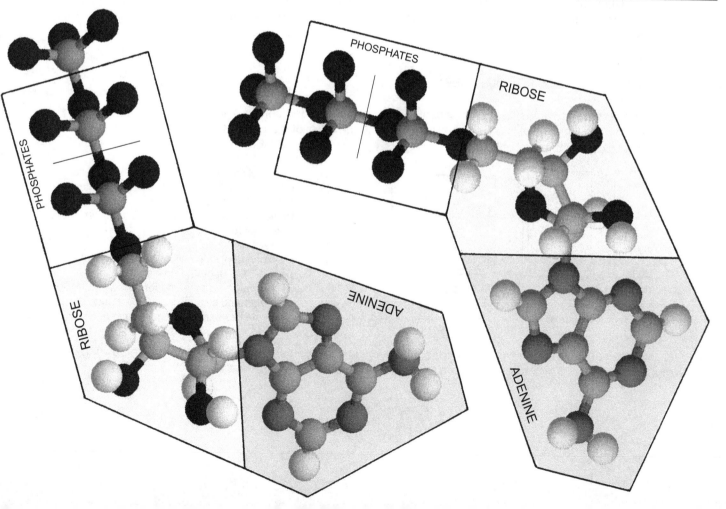

8) ANOTHER GAME ABOUT PHOTOSYNTHESIS: "C3"

This game correlates with the photosynthesis information in level 2, so if you are only doing level 1 you'll have to skip this activity. (You can always come back to it at some point in the future!)

You will need:
- Copies of the following pattern pages (see options below)
- Glue stick and/or clear tape (wide packaging tape if possible)
- Scissors
- A number cube (dice)
- A large plastic bag (such as a gallon-size ziplock) for storing all the pieces (and maybe some small bags, too, so you can keep all the colored pieces sorted)

Options for making the game board:

There are several ways you can make the game board.

1) The first option is to use the black and white pattern pages (following) and have your students add color. Copy the pages onto heavy card stock if you want the board to be durable. The circles in photosystems 1 and 2 should be mostly green (chlorophyll) but should also include a few yellow or orange (or even red) circles to represent other pigment molecules. (NOTE: Biology books usually use red to represent phospholipid heads. There is no particular reason for this. You may make your phospholipid circles a different color if you wish.)

2) The second option is to use the color pages provided at the back of this booklet. You can cut them out of the book and assemble them.

3) The third option is to acquire a digital copy of the game by going to www.ellenjmchenry.com and clicking on FREE DOWNLOADS, then on PLANTS, then on "Printable pages for *Botany in 8 Lessons*." This will give you a digital copy of the pattern pages. You can print these pages using your own computer printer, or you can get a print shop to print them for you.

PUTTING THE GAME BOARD TOGETHER:

For best assembly results, trim off each page as recommended below. Then overlap the pages as suggested. You'll end up with a white border all around the edge of the game (though the border is not necessary and can be trimmed off).

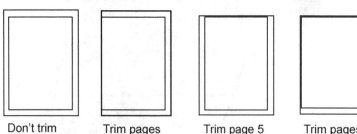

Don't trim page 1 at all.

Trim pages 2, 3 and 4 like this.

Trim page 5 like this.

Trim pages 6, 7, and 8 like this.

Apply some glue stick onto the right hand edge of page 1. Set page 2 onto the glued strip so that the patterns line up. Apply glue to the right hand strip of page 2, then set page 3 onto it, lining it up. Do page 4 the same way.
Then apply glue stick to the bottom of page 1. Set page 5 onto it so it lines up. Then apply glue to the bottom of page 2 and the right hand side of page 5. Set page 6 on. Continue like this with pages 7 and 8.

Once you have everything tacked together with glue stick, you should run some clear tape down the seams on the back of the board. Packaging tape is ideal because it is extra wide.

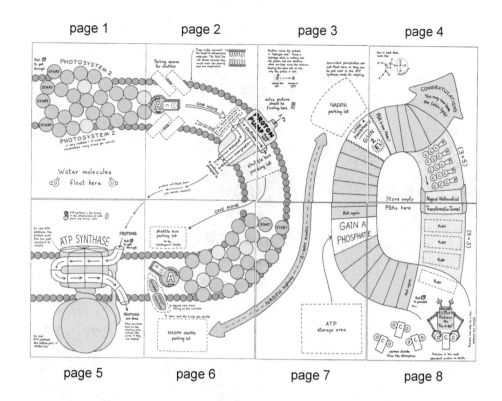

page 1   page 2   page 3   page 4

page 5   page 6   page 7   page 8

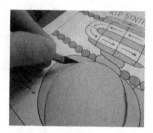

Cut slits along the sides of the ATP synthase. The ATP molecules will slide into the slit just far enough to hide the third phosphate.

Assembly of tokens:

Make a copy of the token page for each player. If possible, print each player's page onto a different color. If you want the tokens to be durable (re-usable) print them onto card stock. (Most computer printers will accept card stock.) If you have only white paper, just tell each player to add color (or a design) to all their tokens so they can identify them.

Make one copy of the WATER MOLECULES page per game (not per player). You can print on white card stock, or you can choose a color (a pastel color, perhaps) that does not match any of the players' colors.

Assembly of shuttles, truck, PGA(L) and RuBP:

This is the basic folding method for all tokens.

You can apply some glue stick to the inside of the bottom.

All tokens are sized so that a piece of clear tape will fit around the ends.

When finished, the tokens should be like this.

Assembly of photon:

Apply glue stick to inside of token. Press and hold so that it looks like the picture on the the right.

Assembly of ATP:

Apply glue stick to inside, between the A circles.

Fold a piece of tape all the way around the end of the last P (as shown), to form a "pocket" that will hold the individual P.

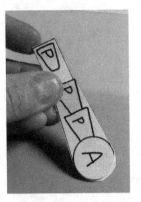

Slip the individual P into the "pocket."

Assembly of water molecules:

Fold the paper molecule in half and put a strip of tape across the center. Fold tape over on both sides. Put pairs of electrons and protons into the oxygen circle. (Remember, a hydrogen atom is nothing more than one electron and one proton.)

How to set up the board:

1) The photon tokens are placed on the start circles of photosystem 2.
2) Place an electron on the chlorophyll A in photosystem 2.
3) The assembled water molecules are placed inside the thylakoid, under photosystem 2.
4) Protons are placed around the outside of the proton pump. (2 for each player)
5) The plastoquinone Qb shuttles are placed in their "parking spaces" outside of photosystem 2.
6) The plastocyanin shuttles are placed in the parking area beneath the proton pump.
7) The assembled ATPs are inserted into the slots in the bottom of the ATP synthase machine so that the third phosphate is hidden. (This makes them look like ADPs that are waiting to be turned into ATPs.)
8) The NADPH trucks are placed in the parking area underneath photosystem 1.
9) The RuBPs (with the 3-carbon and 2-carbon molecules in them) are placed on the indicated rectangles in the Calvin Cycle.

10) The PGA(L)s start out empty and are placed inside the Calvin Cycle circle.
11) Individual carbons are placed on the C rectangles in the carbon dioxide molecules near Rubisco. It does not matter whose carbons go on which rectangles. Just choose any rectangle.

NOTE: There is a video posted on the Botany playlist showing how to set up and play this game. If you have trouble following these written directions, the video might be a big help.

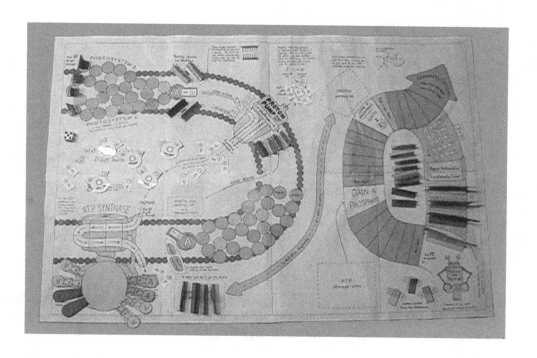

How to play:

Stage 1: Going through photosystem 2

Put your photon token on one of the start circles. Roll the number cube (dice) to get through the photosystem. Only one photon per circle. You can only move to a circle that is touching the circle you are on. In other words, you have to follow a path of touching circles. (Nothing special happens when you land on an orange or yellow circle. Treat them the same as green ones.)

You can't land on a circle that already has a photon sitting on it; you'll have to go around it if you can. There might be times when you are temporarily blocked and can't move. But don't worry, everyone will get through eventually! When you get to the end, you land on chlorophyll A.

The reaction center consists of two chlorophyll A molecules that are in close association with each other. All the gathered energy is focused down to these two molecules, which vibrate in such a way that an electron is released. When you land on chlorophyll A, you release the electron that is sitting there. You can pick up this electron card and move it to your shuttle. Then you will need to replace the electron you took. You take apart a water molecule and use one of its electrons. If there is already a water molecule torn apart from someone else's move, you can use that remaining electron.

After moving the electron to the shuttle, you will need to move your photon back to a start circle and repeat the whole process again, so that your shuttle contains two electrons.

Stage 2: Moving the shuttle to the proton pump

You don't need the number cube for this move. On this turn, the first thing you do is put two protons into the shuttle if you have not done so already. Then you simply move your shuttle across the arrow to the proton pump. The electrons will go through the pump and end up in the smaller shuttle on the other side. The protons from the shuttle, plus two protons from outside the pump, will go through the pump and into the lumen (inside) of the thylakoid. All of this happens as part of this turn. At the end of this turn, your large shuttle will be empty and will be back at its original starting place, 4 protons will have been pumped into the lumen, and your two electrons will be in the small shuttle.

Stage 3: Generating 2 ATPs and getting your shuttle over to photosystem 1

To generate ATPs, you roll the number cube to move protons along the track that goes through the ATP synthase machine. When a proton comes out the other side, an ATP can be removed from the bottom and moved over to the ATP parking lot near the Calvin Cycle.

One move is required to get your small shuttle down to the waiting area above the chlorophyll A of photosystem 1. Upon arrival, take the two "tired" electrons out of the shuttle and lay them somewhere inside the parking lot. They will wait there until they get a chance to go over to chlorophyll A and get recharged.

Stage 4: Loading your NADPH truck

To load your NADPH truck, you will need to move your photon through photosystem 1. Put your photon on one of the two start circles, and transfer one of the "tired" electrons from the shuttle onto chlorophyll A. (If both start circles are occupied by other players' photons, you'll have to wait a turn. However, chances are good that one of them will be open.) The rules from photosystem 2 apply to photosystem 1. One photon per circle, etc.

When your photon lands on chlorophyll A, move the electron card to the carriers (ferredoxin and NADP reductase). Then move your other "tired" electron to chlorophyll A. Remember, electrons are non-specific and don't actually belong to any player, so if another player lands on chlorophyll A before you do, they can take the electron you put there and replace it with one from their shuttle. (In real life, the action of photosystem 1 is so fast that it's more like a blur of electrons flying around.)

On your next move, you may take the electron off the carriers and put it into the truck.

Now you must put your photon through the photosystem again to get another electron. Once you have two electrons, pick up a proton and put it into the truck also.

On your next move, drive your truck (containing two electrons and one proton) up to the NADPH parking lot at the top of the Calvin Cycle.

Stage 5: Fixing carbon

Take the 3-carbon and 2-carbon molecules out of your RuBP and place each one in a PGA token. Pick up the single carbon atom (from the carbon dioxide molecule) and put it into the tray with the 2-carbon molecule so that the tray now has 3 carbons. You now have two 3-carbon PGAs.

Stage 6: Going through the Calvin Cycle

Choose one of your PGAs and roll the number cube to proceed around the oval. When you get to the GAIN A PHOSPHATE space, stop there and put a phosphate from an ATP into the PGA token. (Just stick it in — it won't match the other one sticking out to the side, but that's okay.)

When you get to the GAIN 2 E's space, put the two electrons and also the proton from the NADPH truck into the PGA token. Remove the phosphate (yes, you just put it in, but take it out now) and set it anywhere. The phosphate can float right there near the parking lot or it can be put down next to the synthase machine. It can go anywhere because in reality, phosphate molecules are floating around all over the place inside cells.

After losing the phosphate and gaining the electrons and proton, the PGA is now officially PGAL. Use the number cube to move it out of the cycle. It is now free to be used by the cell to make glucose or for other purposes.

NOTE: If you have limited time, you can choose to end the game here, with just one PGAL made. If you have enough time, require that 2 PGALs be made, so that a glucose molecule can be manufactured. (Glucose is a 6-carbon sugar, so two 3-carbon PGALs are needed.)

Stage 7: Making a second PGAL

Move the empty NADPH truck back down the road to the parking lot under photosystem 1. You will need two more electrons and another proton. Where do you get super-charged electrons? That's right — you'll have to go back to the beginning of the process and move photons of light through the photosystems.

However, on this second time around you can speed things up by DOUBLING THE VALUE OF THE NUMBER CUBE. In other words, if you roll a 3, you can turn it into a 6, and a 6 becomes a 12. Not bad!

You will probably already have a second ATP waiting. If not, you'll need to make another one.

The game is over as soon as one player gets his second PGAL made.

NOTES THAT CAN BE READ ALOUD TO THE PLAYERS BEFORE THEY BEGIN THE GAME:

This game is about the most common kind of photosynthesis, C3. Two other types of photosynthesis, C4 and CAM, are used by plants that need to survive dry weather conditions. (Some microscopic organisms such as bacteria and algae also do photosynthesis, and they have their own variations of it.) C3 photosynthesis is the most common type of photosynthesis and is therefore the one that students are expected to learn the most about.

You'll notice that the numbering of the photosystems seems backwards. You go through photosystem 2 before you go through photosystem 1. This is because photosystem 1 was discovered first. When another photosystem was discovered, they had to call it photosystem 2. We've been stuck with those names ever since.

The circles in the photosystems represent pigment molecules. They are drawn as circles, omitting the hydrocarbon "tails," just to make the board look less confusing. Most of the circles represent chlorophyll, but a few are other pigments such as carotene and xanthophyll. The job of the other pigments is to respond to wavelengths of light that chlorophylls miss.

The reaction center consists of two chlorophyll molecules working together. (We've drawn the "tails" on these since we had to have a place to put the electron card.) Notice that the chlorophyll A molecule in photosystem 2 is "P680" and in photosystem 1 it is "P700." The numbers 680 and 700 are wavelengths of light in nanometers. These are the wavelengths at which you find peak absorption by these molecules.

Photosystem 2 is not very stable and usually falls apart in a matter of seconds. The chloroplast must be constantly repairing the photosystem 2's and manufacturing new ones. Photosystem 1 is much more stable and can remain intact for a few days before needing to be repaired or replaced. (Solar energy researchers are learning how to harvest the electrical energy generated by photosystem 1. They've actually built organic solar panels out of living plant cells. It will be a long time until these biological panels are ready to be installed on our roofs, but the initial research looks very promising.)

The game board has two parts—the light-dependent processes in the thylakoid membrane, and the light-independent Calvin Cycle. It is important to remember that although the Calvin Cycle looks circular here on the game board, it would not be an identifiable circle in a cell. You don't see the Calvin Cycle when you look at a cell. You see thylakoids, but you don't see Calvin Cycles. The circle just helps us to understand some very complex chemistry that is going on everywhere in the stroma of the chloroplast.

During the game, you will have some loose electrons, protons and phosphates floating around. In the game there will be just a few of these, but in reality, the chloroplast is full of loose molecules and ions. The large quantity of available molecules and ions assures that at least some of them will end up where they need to be. A proton doesn't know that it needs to go down and go through the ATP synthase machine. The inside of the thylakoid gets so full of protons that they eventually end up getting pushed through the synthase machine. There are so many phosphates and ADPs floating around in the vicinity of the synthase machine that some of them happen to get trapped in the turning machinery and are snapped back together. The phosphates and ADPs don't "know" to go over to the machine to recharge. It's more like they accidentally bump into it. Also, the NADPH shuttle doesn't "know" to go back down and pick up more electrons. There are so many of them drifting around that there is a constant supply available for recharging. However, the game board would be way too cluttered if we attempted realism and had oodles of shuttles and molecules floating around everywhere. It's better to keep the game board neat and tidy and just move a few pieces around the board.

One final note—as complicated as this game board might seem, it is highly simplified. We've said this before, but it bears repeating: *photosynthesis is extremely complicated.* There are biochemists who spend most of their lives studying just one part of this process. Some details about photosynthesis still remain a mystery!

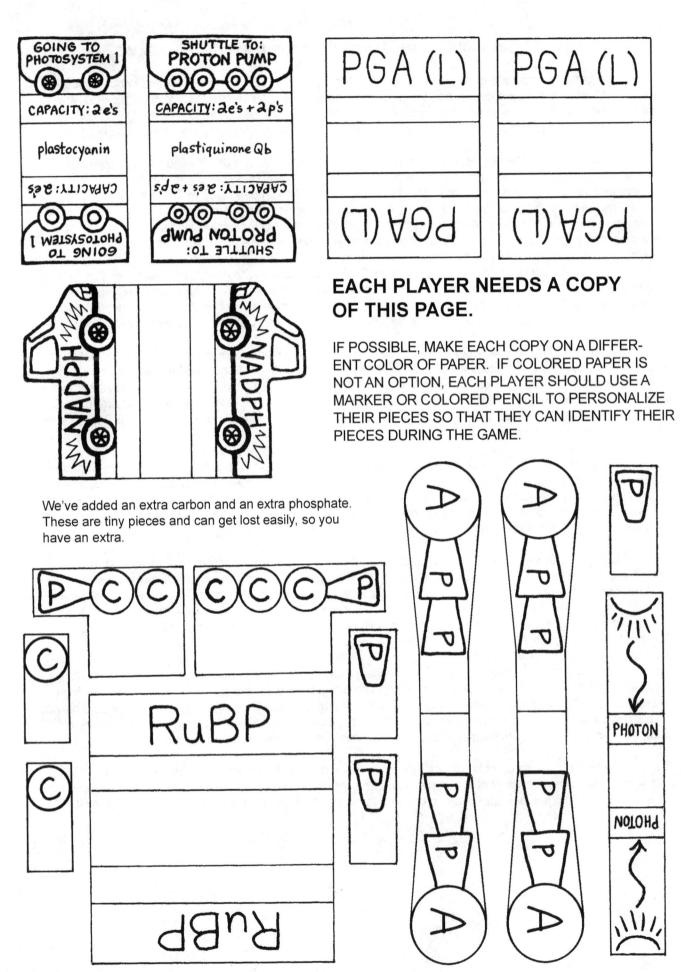

GOING TO
PHOTOSYSTEM 1

CAPACITY: 2 e's

plastocyanin

SHUTTLE TO:
PROTON PUMP

CAPACITY: 2 e's + 2 p's

plastiquinone Qb

PGA (L)

PGA (L)

NADPH

We've added an extra carbon and an extra phosphate.
These are tiny pieces and can get lost easily, so you
have an extra.

**EACH PLAYER NEEDS A COPY
OF THIS PAGE.**

IF POSSIBLE, MAKE EACH COPY ON A DIFFER-
ENT COLOR OF PAPER. IF COLORED PAPER IS
NOT AN OPTION, EACH PLAYER SHOULD USE A
MARKER OR COLORED PENCIL TO PERSONALIZE
THEIR PIECES SO THAT THEY CAN IDENTIFY THEIR
PIECES DURING THE GAME.

RuBP

PHOTON

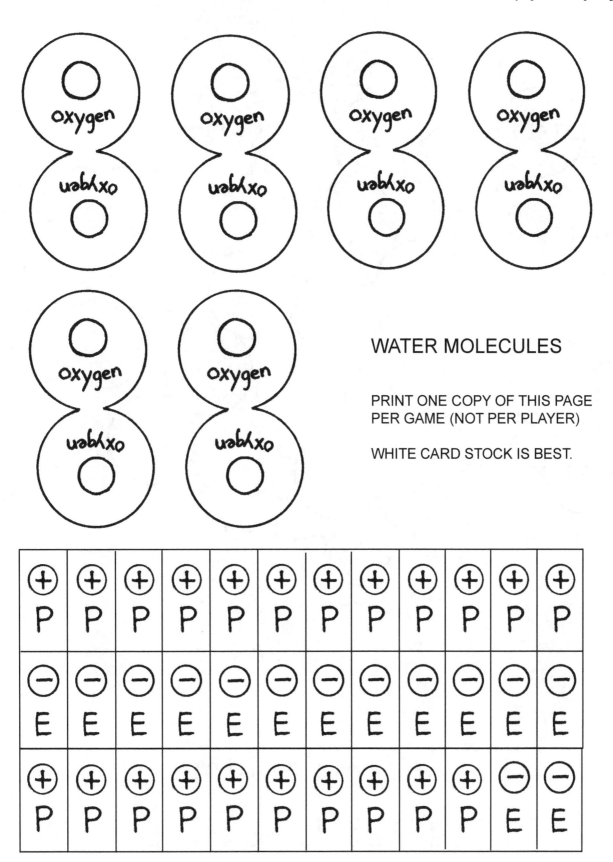

WATER MOLECULES

PRINT ONE COPY OF THIS PAGE
PER GAME (NOT PER PLAYER)

WHITE CARD STOCK IS BEST.

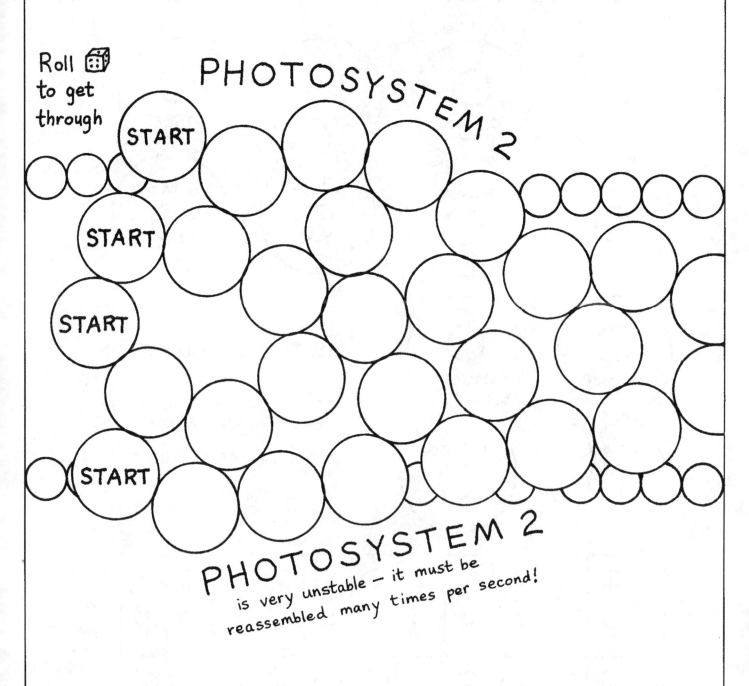

Roll 🎲 to get through

PHOTOSYSTEM 2

START

START

START

START

PHOTOSYSTEM 2
is very unstable — it must be
reassembled many times per second!

Water molecules
float here

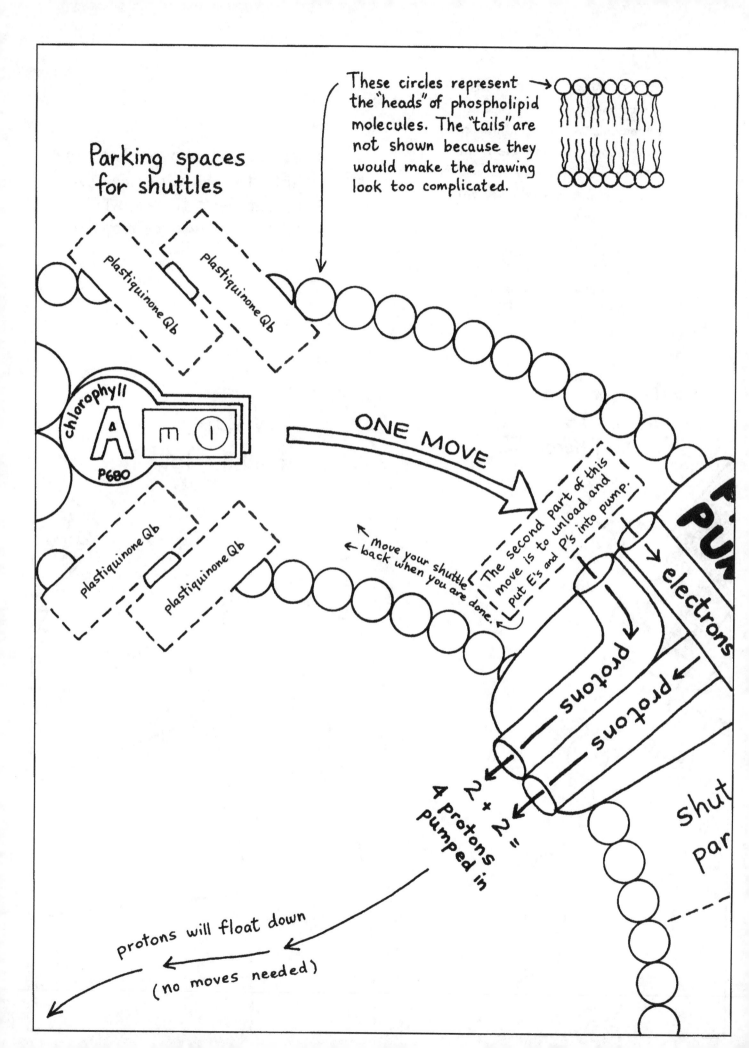

Another name for protons is "hydrogen ions." Since a hydrogen atom is nothing but one proton and one electron, when you take away the electron (making the atom into an ion), only the proton is left.

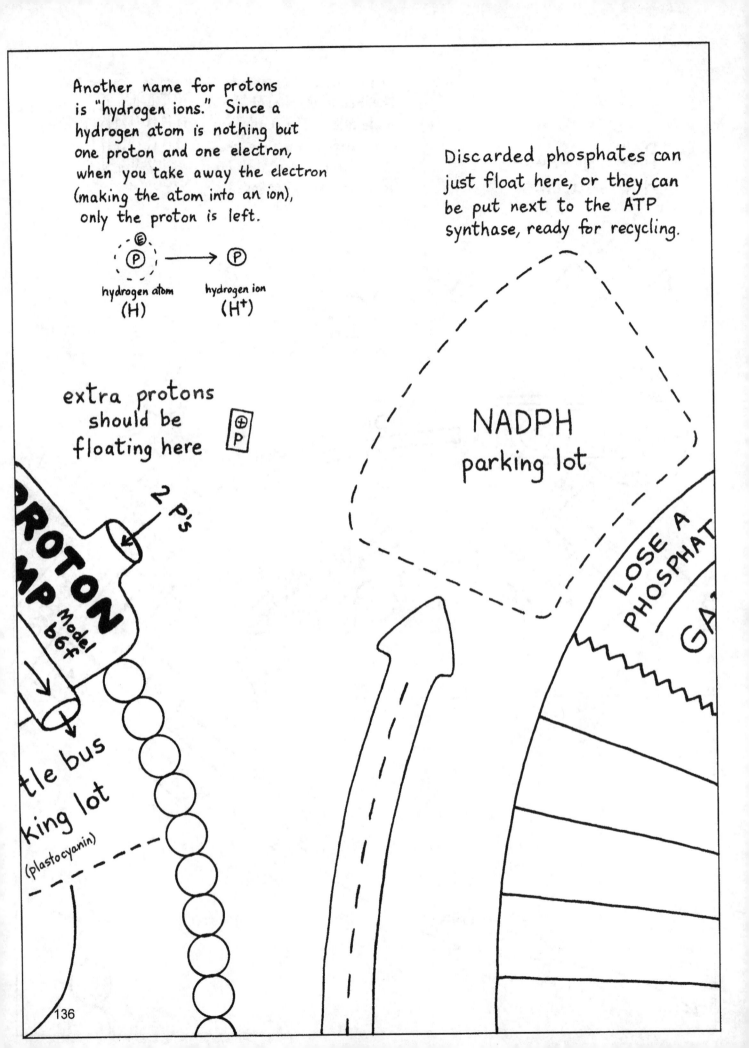

hydrogen atom
(H)

hydrogen ion
(H⁺)

Discarded phosphates can just float here, or they can be put next to the ATP synthase, ready for recycling.

extra protons should be floating here

NADPH parking lot

2 P's

PROTON PUMP Model b6f

LOSE A PHOSPHAT...

GA...

tle bus king lot

(plastocyanin)

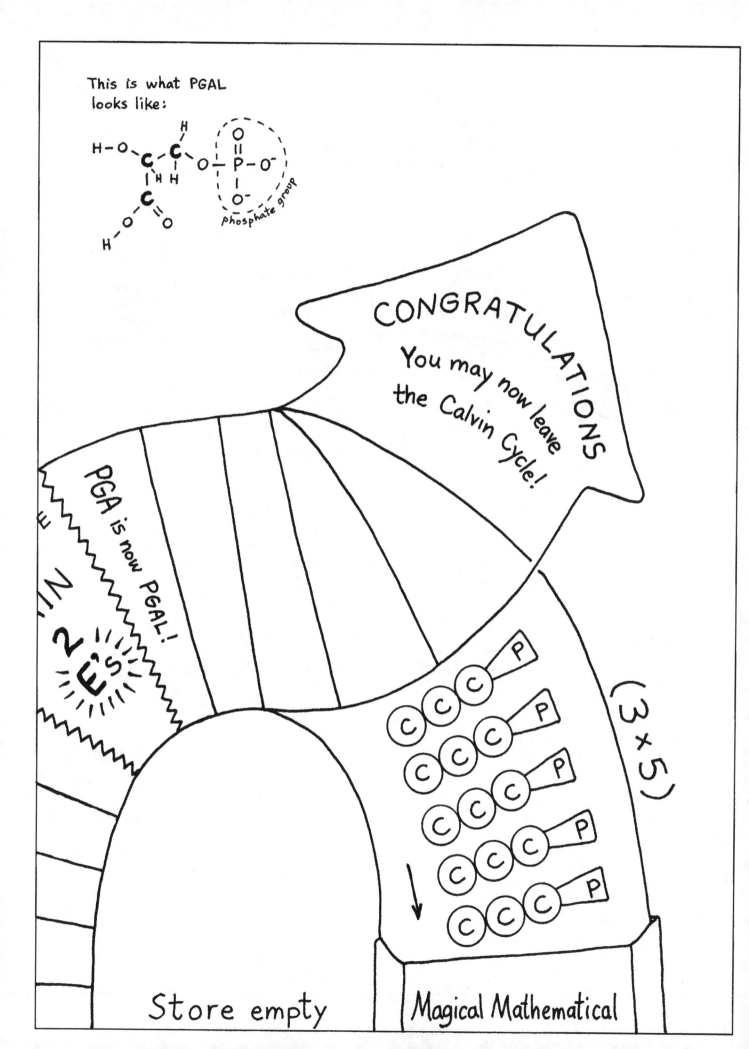

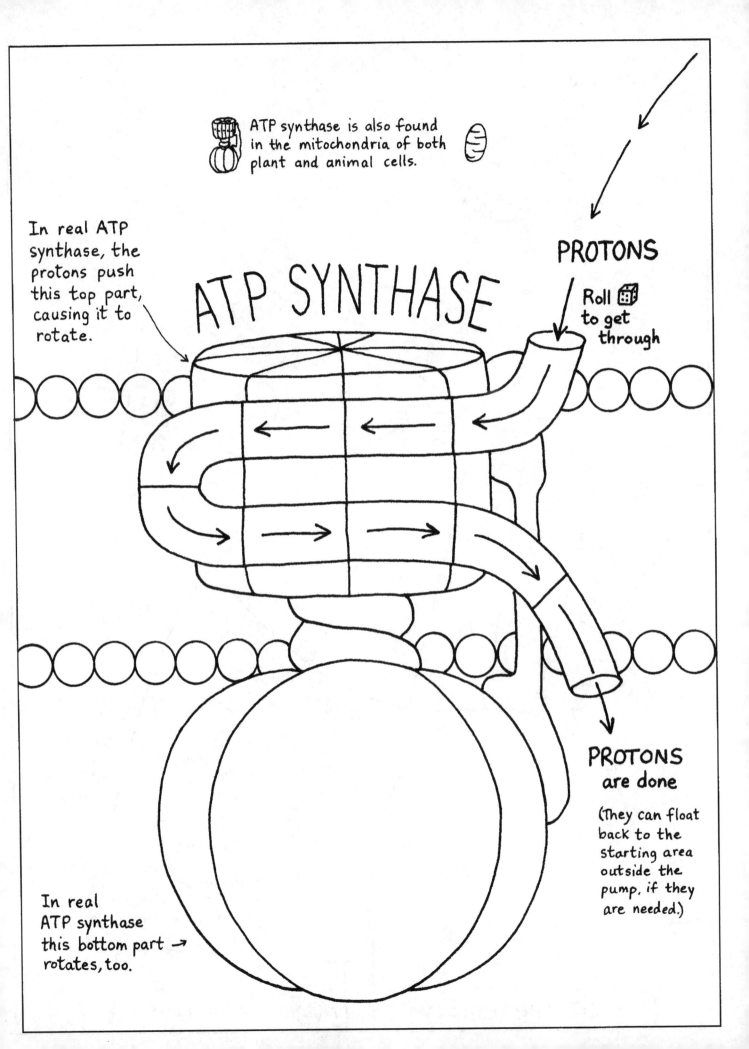

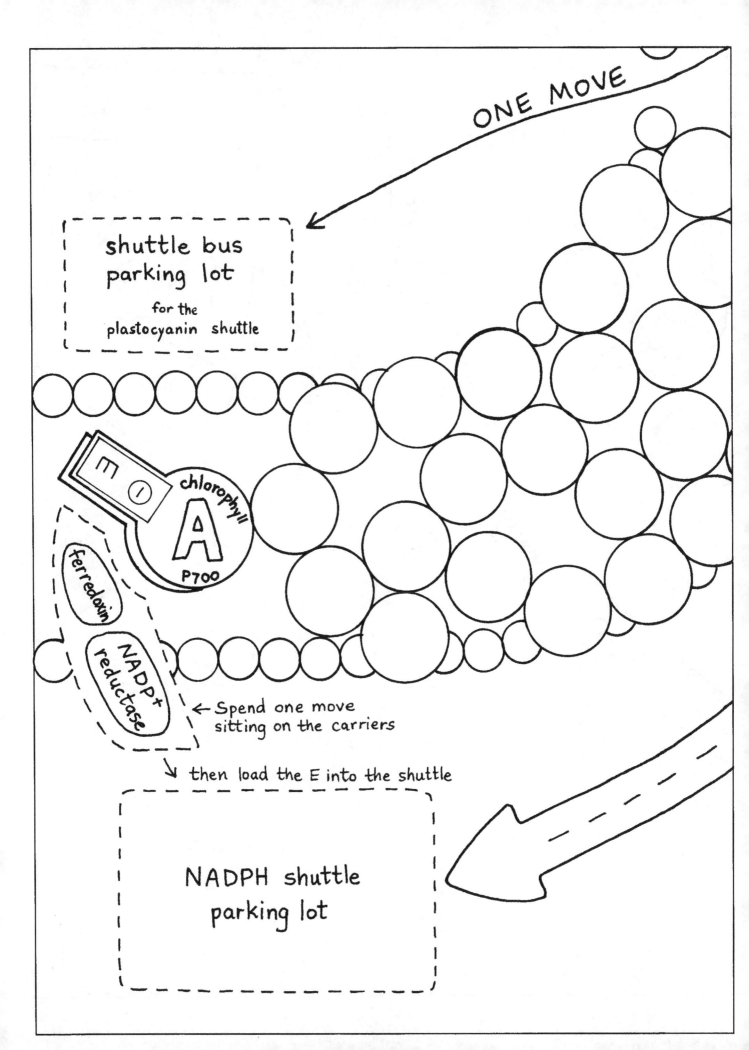

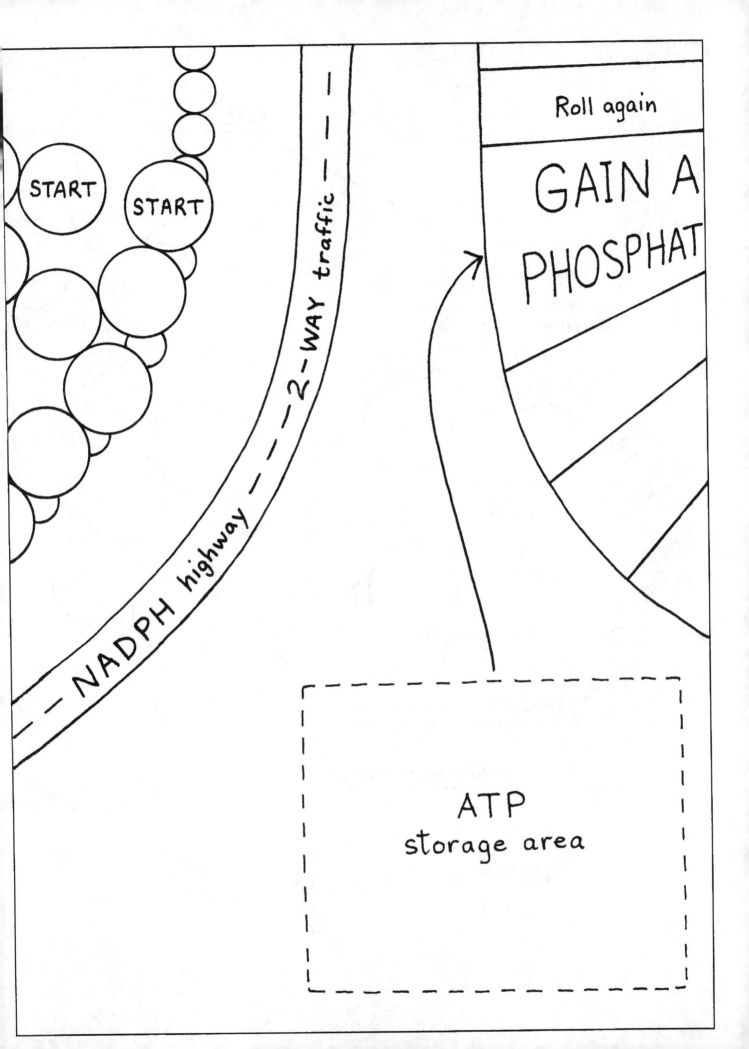

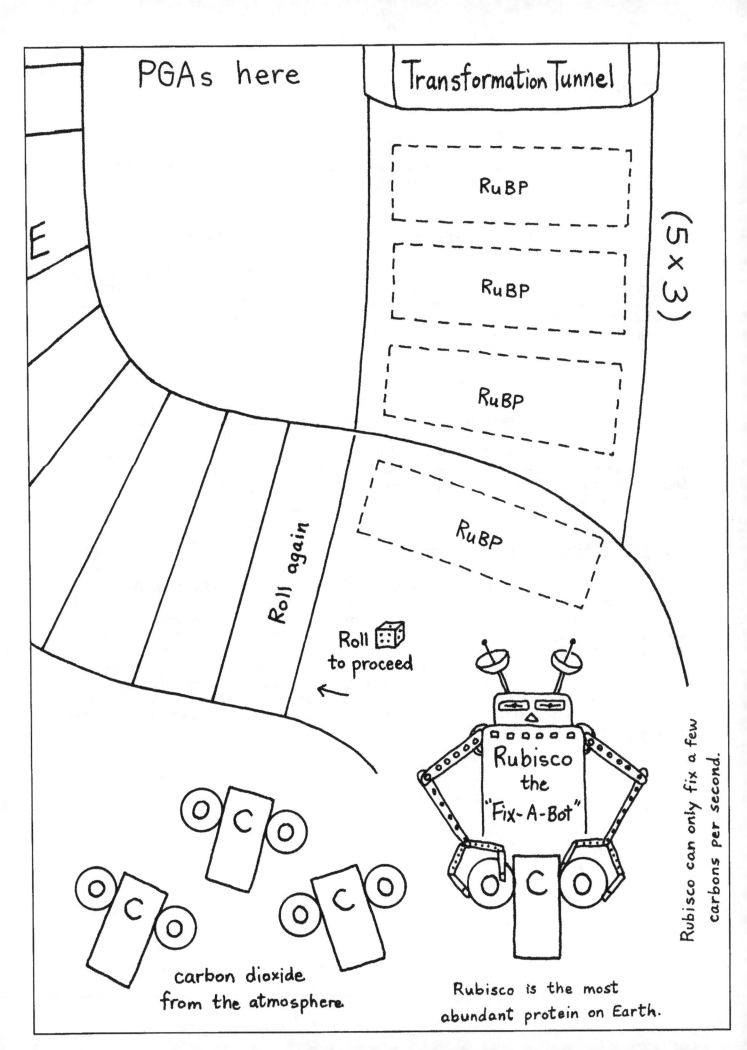

LESSON 2

1) LEARN HOW TO PRONOUNCE SCIENTIFIC LATIN

To learn more about how to pronounce Latin plant names, check out this site by the Florida Department of Agriculture: **http://botanicallatin.org/latinhandout.doc**

2) WANT TO HEAR MORE STORIES ABOUT HOW FLOWERS GOT THEIR NAMES?

To learn more about the names of flowers, you might want to read this book: 100 Flowers and How They Got Their Names by Diana Wells. (If your library doesn't have it, you can find inexpensive used copies on Amazon.com.) There's only about a page per flower—just enough info to keep you interested but not enough to bog you down. This book isn't intended for a juvenile audience, but literary-type kids might think it's interesting. Read just one or two flowers per day—maybe even as a short bedtime story!

3) A BOOK ABOUT PLANT FAMILIES

If you've got a future botanist in the family, you might want to consider purchasing this book: Plant Families by Carol Lerner. (The hardback version is ISBN 0-688-07882-6.) It is intended for a young audience, but has more than enough information to satifsy most adults, even those of us who enjoy science. The left side of each page has information about a popular plant family and the right side has beautiful botanical illustrations. The plant families include: buttercup, mustard, mint, pea, parsley, "pinks," arum, rose, composite, lily, grass and orchid.

3) A GAME ABOUT PLANT FAMILIES

If you like card games and are willing to spend $12.50 plus shipping, I recommend the following: **"Shanleya's Quest; A Botany Game"** by Thomas Elpel. The game is designed to go with a book by the same name, but can be used independently of the book. This book covers basically the same information as the book listed above in (3), though this one goes into a little more depth and is written around the theme of Native North American folklore.

The cards feature photographs of the flowers of members of various plant families. You learn to recognize members of the same plant family while playing games with the cards. The game is usable for students of any age, from elementary to high schoolers. (There is a video advertisement for this game on the Botany playlist. I posted the ad because there is so much information in it that it's worth watching it even if you don't buy the game.)

LESSON 3

1) WATCH OSMOSIS IN ACTION

You will need:
- A strip of paper towel
- A small bowl of water

Cut a strip of paper towel that is about 1/4 inch wide (half a centimeter) and 3 inches long (8 centimeters). Hold the strip of paper towel over the water so that the end you aren't holding is just touching the surface of the water. Hold it there and wait and watch. Do you see the water gradually moving up the paper towel? What is fighting gravity and causing the water to move up? (Osmosis!)

2) WATCH A "HAIR CAP" MOSS OPEN AND CLOSE

You will need:
- A hair cap moss (They prefer sandy soil and are often found by the sides of roads.)
- Water
- Hair dryer or fan

When conditions are dry, a hair cap moss folds up and looks like this:

When conditions are moist, a hair cap moss opens its "leaves" like this:

If the hair cap moss is closed when you find it, open it up by putting water on it. If it is open, gently dry it with a hair dryer or fan. If you use a hair dryer, be careful not to burn the moss. Once it is dry, open it again by putting water on it.

NOTE: There is a short video on the hair cap moss posted on the Botany playlist.

3) BUILD A "MOSS-A-RARIUM" (A TERRARIUM THAT FEATURES MOSS)

Back in the late 1800s, there was a gardening fad where people collected mosses and made special wooden outdoor terrariums for them. They were called "mosseries." You don't see mosseries much any more, but mosses are still considered an important part of outdoor landscaping, and mosses are almost essential for indoor terrariums.

You can easily put together a small terrarium using mosses and other natural objects you find on a walk through the woods. You will need some kind of glass or ceramic dish. You can use a glass bowl (such as a fish bowl or small aquarium) or you can use some other interesting dish you have around the house. Collect some small mounds of moss from places around your neighborhood. Take just a small amount of moss—only the amount you need. (Moss does grow back, but it takes a while.) Also collect some interesting rocks or pebbles, gnarled sticks, small plants or anything else you would like to add to your terrarium for artistic effect. Put some dirt on the bottom of the container, then arrange your moss, pressing it down firmly into the dirt. (Dirt that is the same or similar to what the moss was originally growing in might work best.) Arrange the other objects in and around the moss. You might want to use the Internet to find pictures of terrariums. You might get some great ideas from seeing what other people have done. Don't forget to keep your "mossararium" moist.

If you would like to establish an outdoor moss garden, the Botany playlist has a video showing how to do this. The film was made by a professional gardener who specializes in mosses.

LESSON 4

1) DISSECT XYLEM TUBES OUT OF A PIECE OF CELERY

You will need:
- Celery
- A tall glass of water
- Food coloring (red or blue would be best)
- Knife
- A pin
- Optional: X-acto knife with sharp point, or a dissecting scalpel
- Optional: magnifier

Put some drops of food coloring (at least 20 drops) in about two inches of water and let the celery soak in it for at least an hour. Take the celery out and make a clean cut at the bottom of the celery and observe. You should see little colored dots toward the outside edge of the celery. These dots are the xylem tubes. You will notice that they are spaced exactly the same distance apart and look very orderly. This is because celery is a dicot. Cut a small section of stem see if you can dissect out the xylem tubes using a pin or the point of a knife or scissor. (This should not be too difficult to do.)

Follow-up ideas:
   1) Take a fresh stalk of celery, cut a section, and dissect out the xylem tubes. Then put just these xylem tubes into the food coloring and see what happens. Can you trace the progress of the colored water as it goes up the xylem tubes? How fast does it go?
   2) Set up a celery transpiration race. Find two stalks of celery that are as identical as possible—same number and size of leaves, same width and length. (You might have to pull a few leaves off one of them to make them the same.) Put each in a glass of water that contains food coloring. Let one celery be the control and put it in a quite area, undisturbed. Set the other celery in front of a fan or a hair dryer set on low. Predict ahead of time what should happen and why.
   3) Use other types of stems. Does the dye highlight the xylem tissue? How are the bundles arranged?

2) MEASURE A GROWING ROOT

You will need:
- A corn or bean seed (corn is ideal)
- A moist paper towel
- A waterproof ink pen

Sprout a corn seed by placing it in a moist paper towel and leaving it there for a few days. When the root is about half an inch long, make some pen marks on the root at very regular intervals (every 1/16 inch [2 mm] or so). Put the sprout back into the moist towel and leave it there overnight. The next day, look at the pen marks. Where are the marks now? Which part of the root grew the fastest? Check the root again the next day, and the day after that. Do you see the same result? (As you can see from the sample photo, results should suggest that most of the growth occurs at the tip.)

3) PLAY A TRICK ON SOME ROOTS!

You will need:
- Some small dicot seeds (Radishes are ideal. Next best might be spinach, beet, carrot or lettuce, but you could use cucumber or squash seeds since they are fairly flat. Don't use grass seed.)
- Some moist paper towels
- A piece of fairly stiff clear plastic (or you can use an empty CD case)

- Rubber bands
- A piece of heavy cardboard (or thin plywood) the same size as the piece of plastic

You will make a "sandwich" of these materials, laying down the cardboard or wood backing board first, then some moist paper towels, then the radish seeds, then the clear plastic. Rubber-band this "sandwich" together tightly enough that the seeds don't fall out when you set it upright.

ALTERNATIVE:
Use a CD case

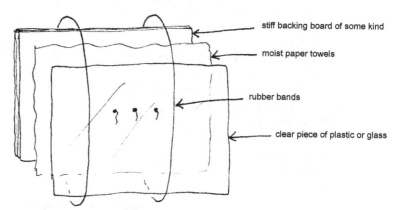

- stiff backing board of some kind
- moist paper towels
- rubber bands
- clear piece of plastic or glass

Put this finished panel in a window with the clear side facing the light. Make sure the paper towels stay moist. All you need to do is apply water to the edges. Osmosis should spread the moisture to the center of the towel. After the seeds have sprouted and grown about an inch (2 cm), turn the panel 90 degrees. When the roots have grown another inch (2 cm), turn it 90 degrees again. Keep repeating this every day, or every other day. You will end up with a root system with a pattern of 90 degree turns. The root always knows which direction is down!

What would happen if seeds were grown in a gravity-free environment? (This experiment was performed inside the space shuttle. The roots grew in random directions.)

4) MAKE VASCULAR STEM COOKIES

You will need:

- Cookie dough (standard sugar cookie recipe, or your own adaptation if you have students with special nutritional requirements)
- Food coloring (or use a natural substitute)

Divide the dough in half. Leave one half uncolored and then split the remaining half in half; make one half red and the other half blue. (If you don't have red and blue you could substitute other colors.)

Divide up the red and blue dough into smaller chunks and roll these chunks into long, thin cylinders about 1/4 inch thick (about 1/2 cm). These will represent the phloem (red) and the xylem (blue). Roll out the plain dough into a rectangle. Place a red and blue strip together, put them on the rectangle and then roll it just a bit. Do this again, placing a red and blue cylinder next to each other (as xylem and phloem tubes are found next to each other, in a vascular bundle), then roll it a bit more. Keep repeating this until the cookie is all rolled up. Then cut the roll into thin slices and bake at 350 degrees F for 8-10 minutes. They will cook quickly. (If they start to brown, the colors won't look as bright.)

If your bundles are scattered randomly, call them monocot cookies. If your bundles are very neatly spaced in a symmetric way (like a dicot cross section) call them dicot cookies. Either way, the students should have a better understanding of what they are looking at when they see a cross section picture. Some kids have trouble visualizing what a cross section is. This activity should help their understanding.

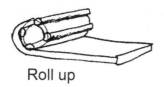

Roll up

then

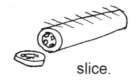

slice.

LESSON 5

1) GROUP PROJECT: MAKE A LEAF CROSS-SECTION MURAL

You will need:
- Pieces of paper cut into 3-inch (8 cm) strips
- Clear tape (or glue stick)
- Colored pencils
- Picture of leaf cross section from this chapter (as a reminder of what to draw)

Give each participant one strip of paper. The goal is to make this strip look like a piece of leaf cross section. (Use the picture in the text as a guide.) You might want to demonstrate this first, to make sure they understand the scale of how big the cells should be. They'll have to fit all the layers within those 3 inches. You might want to have them pencil in light guidelines so they don't run out of room for one of the layers. When the cross sections are finished, tape them together end to end to form one long cross section.

If you don't have a large group, adjust the size of the mural accordingly, or have the student(s) draw more than one section.

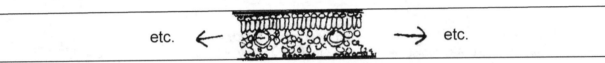

How long do you think this leaf mural would have to be to represent one actual inch of a real leaf? Plant cells are approximately 1/750 inch wide, so you will have to draw a section that is 750 cells wide. If you can draw 100 cells per foot of paper, the mural would have to be 7 feet long!

TIP: A group photo of everyone standing behind the leaf mural makes a nice keepsake for portfolios.

2) PRESERVING (PRESSING) LEAVES

You will need:
- A variety of leaves
- A leaf press (or a stack of heavy books)
- Sheets of newsprint paper or white construction paper (or other fairly absorbent paper)

Some leaves preserve better than others. Clover leaves, for example, seem to work better than dandelions. Leaves with high water content will be difficult to preserve in good condition.

A simple leaf/flower press can be made with two pieces of fairly thick plywood, four bolts, and four wing nuts. Stack the two pieces of wood together and drill holes in the corners, just large enough for the bolts to slip through. Stack all your leaves and papers, put them between the pieces of wood, then insert the bolts and tighten the wing nuts.

To preserve leaves without a press, place your leaves between sheets of paper. Paper that is a bit rough (such as newsprint or white construction paper) is better than regular paper because it will absorb more water. You can use ordinary paper if your leaves are fairly dry (like clover leaves). Stack the papers carefully (don't put too many leaves on a page) and put them under a stack of heavy books. Let them sit under the books for several weeks. Some leaves might be dried enough to use in just one or two weeks if they were fairly dry to start with. Take them out carefully, as they could be brittle. You can use them for craft projects or as part of a lap book about plants.

If you would like more specific directions and extra tips, there are numerous web sites that give information on this subject. Just do a search and choose a site that gives you the information you want.

3) TREE LEAF BINGO

You will need:
- A copy of the two tree leaf sheets for each player
- One copy of the KEY sheet (the one that has the "WIND" cards)
- Scissors
- Tokens of some kind for the players to place on their squares (pennies work well)

Set up:
1) Each player cuts out his leaf squares. There are a total of 24 leaves.
2) Each player receives a supply of pennies or other small tokens.
3) The "caller" cuts out the squares of the KEY page and puts them in a box or bag so they can be drawn out one at a time.
4) Decide whether you will play a 3x3 square or a 4x4 square. Each player takes either 9 or 16 cards and arranges them into a square. The rest of the cards remain as a personal draw pile. You will need them during the game.

How to play:
The caller randomly pulls out leaf cards and calls out the names. If a player has that card in his square, he puts a penny/token on it.

If the caller draws out a WIND card, the players must remove all the squares that show that kind of leaf unless those squares are weighted down with a penny/marker. The player then fills these empty spaces with cards from his draw pile. This happens every time a WIND card is drawn. Yes, the game board keeps changing! But whatever has a penny/token on it cannot be blown away by the wind.

SPECIAL NOTE: You will need to decide whether you want your players to study the leaves before you start to play. Ideally, this game would be a fun way to review after the students have done some other leaf identification activities. However, previous study is not necessary and the players can just learn as they go. You might want to have the caller show the KEY cards to the players during the first round, with the caller showing each leaf as it is called. Then, as rounds progress, see if the players can remember them without the cards being shown. Either way, the players will learn (or review) and have fun!

Here are the terms the players will need to know in order to play.

PINNATE: Leaves that have many small leaflets branching off the main stem. In this game the pinnates are the locust, the black walnut, the mesquite, and the "tree of heaven."
SIMPLE PALMATE: Leaves whose shape resembles the palm of your hand and whose major veins all radiate from the same point at the bottom. In this game the simple palmates are the maples, the sassafras, and the sweetgum. (You might want to compare the tulip tree and the sugar maple to see the difference between palmate and lobed. Note the way the large palmate veins all originate from the base of the leaf.)
COMPOUND PALMATE: Leaves that have a palm shape, but also are composed of more than one leaflet. The compound palmates in this game are the shagbark hickory and the Ohio buckeye.
LOBED LEAVES: Simple leaves that have definite lobes. In this game the lobed leaves are the oaks, the tulip tree, the gingko, and the sassafras.
DELTOID: Triangle-shaped leaves. In this game, the deltoids are poplar, cottonwood, and quaking aspen.
SERRATED EDGES: Edges that are spiky or jagged, like a serrated knife. In this game the serrated leaves are the poplar, beech, quaking aspen, cherry, cottonwood, willow, shagbark hickory, Ohio buckeye, sweetgum, red maple, and black walnut.

NOTE:
If you happen to live in a part of the world where these trees are uncommon, you could substitute your own homemade cards showing leaves from trees you have in your area. You could draw your own pictures or print some using Google image search. (You might even be able to use actual leaves, pressed and glued to cards.)

Quaking Aspen

Red Maple

Sassafras

Cherry

Black Walnut

Shagbark Hickory

Southern Magnolia

Sugar Maple

Cottonwood

Dogwood

Sweet Gum

Tree of Heaven

Tulip Tree

Holly

Locust

White Oak

Willow

Red Oak

Ohio Buckeye

Pin Oak

Beech

Gingko

Mesquite

Poplar

WIND

Takes away all
serrated edges
unless weighted

WIND

Takes away all
monocots
unless weighted

(ginko is only monocot)

WIND

Takes away all
pinnate leaves
unless weighted

WIND

Takes away all
compound leaves
unless weighted

WIND

Takes away all
palmate leaves
unless weighted

WIND

Takes away all
deltoid edges
unless weighted

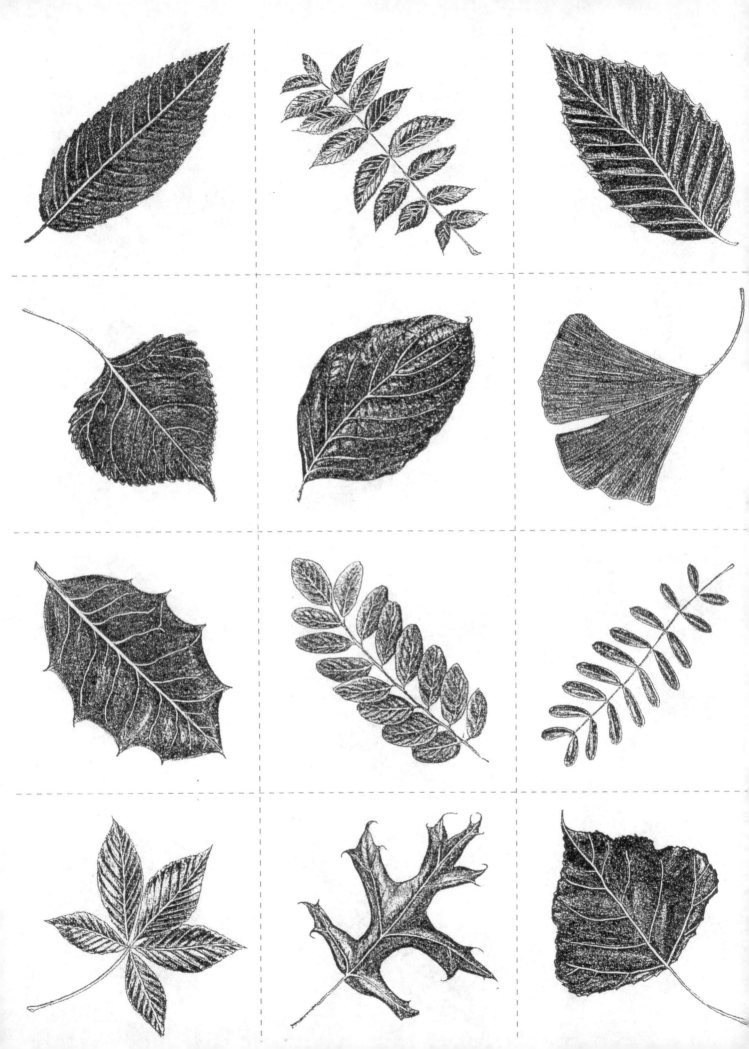

4) LAB EXPERIMENT: USE ANTHOCYANIN TO TEST SOIL pH

NOTE: This is more of a chemistry experiment than a botany project. Feel free to skip it if you want to.

You will need:
- Purple cabbage
- Pot of boiling water
- Some clear glass jars (can substitute with bowls if you don't have clear jars)
- A few spoons
- Some soil samples (just a few spoonfuls of each, gathered from very different environments)
- Optional: baking soda, vinegar, orange or lemon juice, soap, wood ash

Background information:

We read about how the hydrangea plant will develop different colored flowers depending upon the acidity of the soil. Scientists measure acidity using a scale called the pH scale. The "p" stands for the word "potential" and the "H" stands for "hydrogen." When an acid is put into water, it releases hydrogen ions. (An ion is an atom that has an electrical charge.) The pH scale goes from 1 to 14, with 1 being strongly acidic, 7 being neutral, and 14 being extremely alkaline (which is the opposite of acidic). And just to confuse you, alkaline substances can also be called "bases." You often see the words "acid" and "base" used as opposites.

Things that are acidic have a sour taste and a strong smell. Examples of acids include vinegar, lemons, unripe fruit, tea leaves, and carbonated beverages. Bases (alkaline substances) have a soapy texture and a bitter taste. Soap is a base—that's why it feels soapy and tastes so bad. Other bases include baking soda, oven cleaner, medicine used for indigestion, and laundry detergents.

Different types of soil have different pH levels. Some soils are acidic. The soil under a pine tree is likely to be more acidic than soil found in a grassy field. Some plants love acidic soil. Other will die in it. Farmers test the soil in their fields often to keep track of the acidity or alkalinity. If the soil gets out of balance, they can add substances like potash or peat to bring the pH back to the level that is best for the crops they are growing.

In this experiment you will use anthocyanin to test the pH of soil samples.

Preparation:

To obtain anthocyanin, boil some purple cabbage leaves (perhaps three or four leaves—the exact number is not important) in about a quart of water (don't bother measuring the water; it doesn't have to be exact). Let the water cool and dispose of the leaves. You should then have about a quart of bluish-purple water.

How to do the experiment:

To test the soil samples, put a spoonful of soil into a clear glass jar, then add enough anthocyanin water to cover the soil. The water will remain purple, or it will turn red if the soil is acidic. The water will turn blue if the soil is neutral, and it will turn green if the soil is alkaline. If your soil samples do not produce a wide variety of colors, try the anthocyanin on lemon juice, a carbonated beverage, baking soda and soap. A small sample will produce the same result as a large one. Plan your experiment so that you don't run out of anthocyanin water too soon. (Or you can just boil more cabbage leaves.)

5) EXTRA COLORING PAGE (OPTIONAL)

You will need:
- Copies of the following pattern page
- Colored pencils, crayons or watercolor paints

If you've got students who love to color, here's an extra page you might find helpful. You can use bright colors and make each color represent a type of cell, or you can make it more realistic and use various shades of green or yellow. If you want to use bright colors, here's a suggestion for a color scheme (or use your own). Make a "color key" in the blank space at the bottom left so the viewer knows what the colors represent.

White: air spaces
Yellow: epidermis (top and bottom)
Red: phloem (inside vascular bundle)
Brown: sheath (covering of vascular bundle)

Orange: cuticle
Green: palisade layer and spongy mesophyll
Blue: xylem (inside vascular bundle)
Purple: guard cells

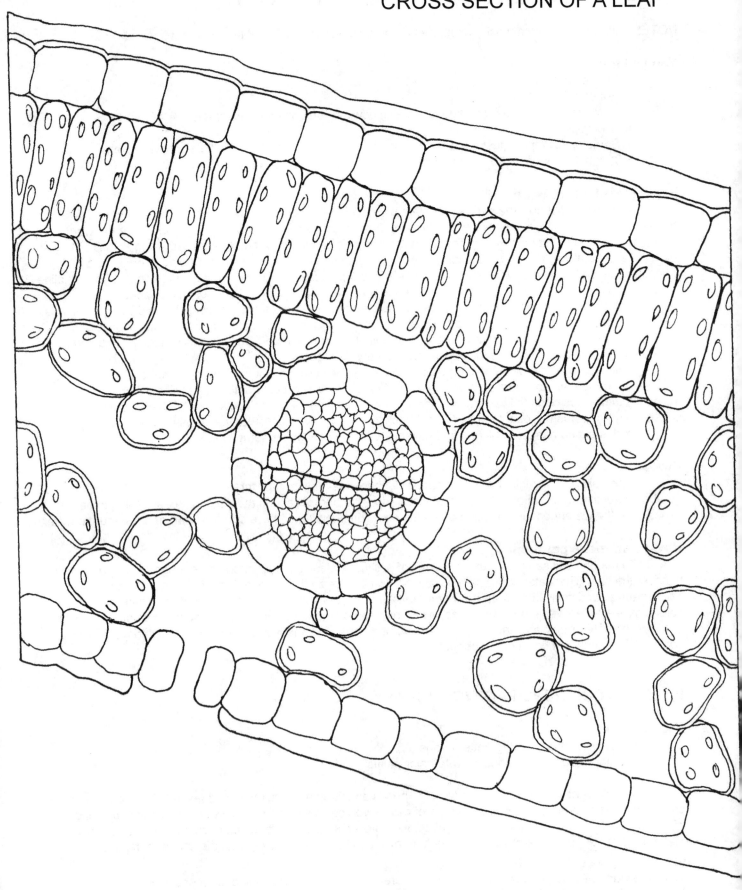

6) MAKE A SCIENTIFIC WORK OF ART

You will need:
- Any type of art media you wish to use.

Some students solidify their learning by using their knowledge to make or do something. This activity will particularly benefit kinetic learners, but it's also a good experience for any type of learner.

Micrographs (pictures taken with microscopes) can be amazingly beautiful, not just scientifically accurate. You may have noticed this as you browsed through some micrographs during this chapter and the last one. (For reasons unknown, some of the most colorful and spectacular images result from using the key words, "pine needle cross section.")

Have your students choose one type of cross section (a dicot or monocot stem, a root tip, a fern stem, a deciduous leaf, a pine needle, etc.), and make it into a painting, drawing, or craft. (In my travels through Google images recently I came across a picture of a crochet project based on a cross section of a plant stem. It was several feet wide!)   If you would like an opportunity to review plant cell anatomy, you could also add pictures of cells to the list of options.

Here is a list of media you might want to consider:

Pencil or colored pencil
Pen and ink (black ink)
Pen and ink with watercolor washes added
Watercolor or acrylic paint
Mosaic (paper, ceramic tiles, found objects...)
Fabric or felt (either sewn or glued)
Collage (variety of objects or patterned papers)
Quilling (tiny paper strips rolled up tight)
"Stained glass" paints (transparent when dry)

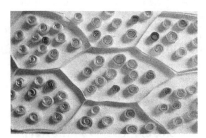

A paper quilling project

* * * * * * * * * * * * * * * *

Take a look at the work of a fabric artist who uses micrograph images as the inspirations for her designs:
http://www.squidoo.com/MeltedCells?utm_source=google&utm_medium=imgres&utm_campaign=framebuster

Try finding other examples by using Google image search and key words "art inspired by microscopic images."

* * * * * * * * * * * * * * * *

Here is a helpful set of guidelines you can give to the students:

RULES FOR YOUR PROJECT:

1) It must be a microscopic view and it must be scientific. If questioned about what the shapes represent, you must be able to give accurate answers.

2) You cannot use a computer except to print off some sample photos to work from. (No "Photoshopping" images to create your art.)

3) It must be artistic, not just scientific. Start out with designing your whole space. Don't just stick some objects on a blank page. There's no "blank space" in a piece of art.

4) You may use "artistic license" when choosing shapes and colors. For example, you are not required to make chloroplasts green.

LESSON 6

1) DISSECT FLOWERS

You will need:
- Flowers (simple, not compound, and larger ones are easier to work with)
- Pins
- Tweezers ("forceps" in scientific jargon)
- Magnifiers
- Razor blade or sharp craft knife
- One sheet of white paper per student (put the flowers on the white paper so small parts don't get lost)
- A copy of the FLOWER DISSECTION LAB worksheet for each student

Acquiring flowers:

A good source of large flowers is a florist shop. Several times a week, florists throw out large numbers of flowers. Any flower that is slightly damaged or a little wilted gets pitched. These "damaged" flowers are still fine for use in science class. Florists will usually be able to supply you with as many flowers as you want. Try to get as many different types as you can. You can also supplement with wild flowers or garden flowers if it happens to be the right time of year.

TIP #1: Some flowers will be much harder to work with, such as roses, daisies, asters, and irises. The easiest to work with are tulips, lilies and the gladiolus.

TIP #2: Have the florist identify the flowers for you. Write down the names if you think you'll have trouble remembering them. This will help the students fill in the answers for the first question on the lab worksheet.

Notes for each lab question:

1) If you don't know what kind of flower it is, use a flower identification book or an online flower identification program. Try one of these: **www.flowerpictures.net** or **www.shootgardening.co.uk/plant/select**.

2) The number of petals on a flower is a key to its identification. If the flower has too many petals to count, you can just write "many."

NOTE ABOUT COMPOSITE FLOWERS: Look carefully at flowers such as daisies and asters. All those petals are actually individual flowers that form a **composite** flower. Each "petal" is called a **floret** and has its own ovary. All the florets are attached to a broad, flat receptacle called a **head**. Often, the large petals around the outside of the head lack reproductive parts and are considered sterile. The inner petals, which may look very different from the outer ones, are the florets that will produce seeds.

3) Not all flowers contain stamens. There are a few kinds of flowers that are either male or female. In orchids, the male and female parts are fused into a column with a **pollina** on the end. The pollina has large packets of pollen that get picked up by insects.

If at all possible, look at some of the pollen grains under magnification.

4) Once again, most flowers have pistils, but a few do not. Male flowers do not have pistils. Odds are good that you will have obtained flowers with both male and female parts, however. Only 5 percent of plants have flowers that are either male or female. If you suspect your flower is either male or female and want to investigate further, try using the Internet to search "list of dioecious angiosperms."

5) If you cannot see separate petals and sepals, you might have a flower with **tepals**. Tepals are a fusing of petals with sepals. It is likely, however, that your flowers will have separate petals and sepals.

6) This activity will be impossible if you have a composite flower with ovaries almost too small to see. If this is the case, just assume each ovary has one ovule and will make one seed. For large pistils, cut the ovary lengthwise. You should be able to see one or more ovules. Then take one of the halves and cut it the other way to see a cross section view. This may help you to see more ovules in some cases, depending on your flower.

7) Make sure the section is pretty thin. You will probably need a magnifier or microscope to view the vascular bundle sections. If you don't have magnification high enough, but you do have some leaves from the flower, use the vein pattern on the leaves to determine if it is a monocot or dicot. If you have a long enough piece of stem, or extra flowers with stems still attached, you might want to soak the stems in colored water for a few minutes. The xylem cells will take up the water and make it easier to distinguish xylem from phloem.

8) The artwork does not have to be perfect. You might want to require labeling of the parts.

FLOWER DISSECTION LAB

1) **What are the names of your flowers?** (common names or scientific names, or both)
   Flower 1: _____
   Flower 2: _____

2) How many petals does the flower have? Are the petals all basically the same shape?
   Flower 1: _____   Y/N
   Flower 2: _____   Y/N

3) How many stamens does the flower have? How long are they? (estimate in centimeters) What color is the pollen? (If the grains are too small to see, just write "too small.")
   Flower 1: _____, _____, _____
   Flower 2: _____, _____, _____

4) Find the pistil and stigma. Does the flower have more than one stigma? What shape is/are the stigma(s)? How long is the style?
   Flower 1: Y/N, _____, _____
   Flower 2: Y/N, _____, _____

5) Find the receptacle, sepals and ovary. Is the ovary above, below, or in the middle of the sepals?
   Flower 1: _____
   Flower 2: _____

6) Cut the pistil down the middle lengthwise. Observe the inside of the ovary. Does it appear to have more than one chamber? How many ovules do you see? (If there are too many to count, write "many.") Each ovule will become a seed, so if you see things that look like seeds, those are the ovules.
   Flower 1: Y/N, _____
   Flower 2: Y/N, _____

7) Cut a thin section of stem. Observe it under magnification and find the vascular bundles. Is the flower a monocot or dicot? (If your flower has leaves attached, you can use those as clues, also.)
   Flower 1: _____
   Flower 2: _____

8) Draw a sketch of each feature:

| STAMENS | PISTILS |
| Flower 1 | Flower 2 | Flower 1 | Flower 2 |

2) TEST THE STRENGTH OF A GERMINATING SEED

You will need:
- Plastic cups (small to medium size)
- Plaster (and also water and a mixing container)
- Some large seeds (beans are ideal)

A baby plant might seem like a very weak little thing, but thanks to its ability to tap into the power of water pressure, it is amazingly strong. If your students have never seen this demonstration before, they will be impressed.

Put the seeds in water and let them soak for an hour or two. Then mix up a batch of plaster and pour it into the paper cups. Pour each cup about halfway full (2 to 3 inches, or 5 to 7 cm). Push a seed down into the plaster in each cup, as if you were planting it. The seed should be in the middle of the plaster.

Now all you need to do is wait and see what happens. You don't need to water the seed. The seed will have taken in water when you soaked it and will continue to take in water from the plaster as it hardens. In less than a week the seed should crack the plaster and sprout up out of it. If this does not happen, the seed might have been non-viable (destined not to grow no matter what). Some seeds might take a little longer than others, but every one I've ever seen has eventually popped its way out of the plaster (to the amazement of its owner!).

3) LOOK AT POLLEN UNDER A MICROSCOPE

If you happen to have access to a microscope, here is a fun lab to do. It's easy and usually gives good results. If you will be doing the flower dissection lab, you could use those flowers' pollen for this lab.

(NOTE: If you can't to get the pollen to germinate, just watch the videos of this on the Botany playlist.)

You will need:
- A microscope
- Glass slides (concavity slides are ideal—they have a little depression in the middle)
- Cover slips for the slides
- An eye dropper
- Pollen
- A pinch of sugar
- Water
- Optional: petroleum jelly if you will be using the "hang drop" slide method described below

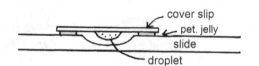

The recommended method for viewing pollen is to make a "hang drop" slide. If you don't have any concavity slides and need to use regular slides, you can make do. If you simply make a standard wet mount with a drop of water under a cover slip, you'll probably get adequate results.

For either method, you'll need some 10% sugar water. (Put a pinch of sugar into a spoonful of warm (not hot) water.) The sweet water is designed to simulate the natural sugars produced by the pistil, causing the pollen grains to start making their tubes.

For a "hang drop" slide, put a drop of sugar water on the center of a cover slip. Sprinkle some pollen into the drop and make sure it gets mixed in. Don't let the water spread out too much. Put a ring of petroleum jelly around the depression. Set the cover slip upside down onto the ring of petroleum jelly so that the drop of water is suspended, hanging from the underside of the cover slip.

If you are using a regular slide, just put a drop of sugar water onto it, sprinkle the pollen, then put a cover slip on top. Don't push down on the cover slip.

Try 100x power first, then a higher magnification if you have one. Even on 100x you should be able to see the different shapes. Pollen grains vary greatly in their geometry. Students are usually surprised at how interesting they are. You'll have to be patient to see the germination happen. Pollen tubes grow slowly.

If you don't have access to a microscope, you can use the Internet to find some spectacular pictures. The pictures that look 3D were taken with electron microscopes that use electrons instead of light. Pictures that look flat were taken using ordinary microscopes.

VARIOUS TYPES OF POLLEN GRAINS

This picture was taken with a scanning electron microscope. The image is in black and white because the SEM does not take color photographs. If you see a 3D image of pollen that is in color, the color has been added using a computer program. Regular light microscopes can record colors, but the images look fairly flat compared to this one.

4) DO AN EXPERIMENT WITH RIPENING FRUIT AND ETHYLENE GAS

There are many variations of this experiment ranging from extremely simple to very complex. The more difficult versions of the experiment use iodine to help quantify exactly how ripe a fruit is. (Iodine will stain starch but not sugar, so the darker the stain, the less ripe the fruit is.) After reading the information on ethylene and reading through the three experiments, you may be able to design your own ethylene experiment, also.

Background information:

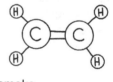

Ethylene gas is a very small molecule consisting of two carbon atoms and four hydrogen atoms. It is colorless, odorless and harmless (non-toxic). Although ethylene gas is a natural substance produced by plants, it can also be found in exhaust from combustion engines, in leaks in natural gas pipelines, and in cigarette smoke.

Plant cells produce ethylene gas in places that are growing fast, ripening, or dying. Ethylene can break down plant cell walls and cause the cells to collapse. Starches are converted to simple sugars, causing the phenomenon we call ripening. When a fruit becomes detached from its parent plant, chemical signals are set off that trigger the production of ethylene. Very ripe (or rotting) fruits produce a lot of ethylene. Flies, especially fruit flies, can smell ethylene and are attracted to it, which explains those clouds of insects around your ripe cantaloupe or bunch of bananas.

People who cultivate plants can find ethylene bothersome—it can make leaves turn yellow and drop off, and can cause stems to shorten and bend. These are not positive outcomes if you are growing ornamental plants. In other areas of agriculture, ethylene can be very helpful. Fruit farmers can use artificially produced ethylene to control the rate at which their fruit ripens. If you've ever heard of tomatoes being "gassed," you need not fear—the gas is just harmless ethylene. Getting fruits and vegetables from the field to your refrigerator is a tricky business. Ethylene gas is a key component in the process of transporting produce to stores. (Temperature and transit time are also important.)

Some plants produce more ethylene than others. Plants that produce a lot of ethylene in their fruits include apples, pears, bananas, avocados, tomatoes, melons and peaches. Cherries and berry plants produce much less.

A) A SIMPLE EXPERIMENT:
NOTE: You can skip this experiment and do B or C instead.

You will need:
- Four or more pieces of the same kind of fruit (apples or bananas work well)
- A plastic bag large enough to hold the fruit and be tied shut

Divide the fruit into two groups. One group will be the "control," meaning that you won't do anything to it. The other group will be the experimental group. Put the experimental fruit into a plastic bag and tie it shut. Now all you have to do is wait. What will happen?

Both groups of fruit will be producing ethylene gas. The control group is sitting on the table with no plastic around it. The ethylene it produces will drift off into the air. The ethylene gas produced by the fruit inside the bag will be trapped. The concentration of ethylene will rise inside the bag as more and more ethylene is produced. The more ethylene produced, the more the fruit is stimulated to produce more ethylene.

The fruit inside the bag should ripen much more quickly than the fruit sitting on the table.

B) A SLIGHTLY MORE COMPLICATED EXPERIMENT:
Have you ever heard the expression, "One bad apple spoils the whole barrel"? Well, it turns out to be true! That one bad apple begins producing lots of ethylene. The apples next to it sense the ethylene and begin to ripen and spoil faster than they would have otherwise. Then those apples affect the ones next to them. Next thing you know, you've got a whole barrel of spoiled apples.

In this experiment you will test the ability of a ripe fruit to influence the fruits around them.

You will need:
- A few ripe bananas
- Some unripe apples or pears (or yellow-green tomatoes)
- Some plastic bags large enough to hold the fruit and be tied shut

Select a few unripe pieces of fruit to be your control group. These fruits will sit on the table and do nothing. Select a few unripe fruits to be the experimental group. Place each experimental unripe fruit into a bag with a ripe banana and seal them or tie them shut. What do you think will happen over the next few days?

The probable outcome of this experiment will be that the fruit that is bagged with a ripe banana will ripen much more quickly because of the ethylene gas produced by the ripe fruit. If this does not happen, you can consider factors that might have caused your result. Were all the unripe fruits equally unripe? Perhaps the fruits in the control group were slightly more ripe. Were your bananas ripe enough? Perhaps your bananas did not release enough ethylene. Was the temperature chilly around the fruits? Cold temperatures slow down the ripening process, and reduce the effects of ethylene.

C) A MORE COMPLICATED EXPERIMENT:
This experiment requires iodine. In the US, you can't buy iodine is stores anymore. A good place to purchase iodine for science experiments is **www.hometrainingtools.com**. They sell a small bottle of iodine solution (sometimes called Lugol's solution) for less than $5. (For quick access to the ordering page for this item: **www.hometrainingtools.com/iodine-solution-lugols-30ml/p/CH-IODINE/**)

NOTE: You might want to try this variation of the experiment even if you can't get iodine. Just do the visual inspection of the fruit.

You will need:
- A bunch of green bananas
- A bunch of ripe bananas
- Some unripe apples or pears (or yellow-green tomatoes)
- 8 plastic bags large enough to hold the fruit and be tied shut
- Your refrigerator
- Iodine solution (mildly poisonous—do not get any in or near your mouth, and avoid contact with skin)
- An eyedropper
- Paper towels (iodine will stain your table or counter top)
- A knife (for cutting the fruit slices)

NOTE: If you can't get bananas, you can substitute other high-ethylene fruit such as apples, pears, avocados, peaches, and tomatoes. You'll need both ripe and unripe pieces of the fruits you choose.

ON A TABLE:
1) a green banana
2) a green banana in a bag
3) an unripe piece of fruit
4) an unripe piece of fruit in a bag
5) an unripe piece of fruit and a green banana in a bag
6) an unripe piece of fruit and a ripe banana in a bag

IN THE REFRIGERATOR:
1) a green banana
2) a green banana in a bag
3) an unripe piece of fruit
4) an unripe piece of fruit in a bag
5) an unripe piece of fruit and a green banana in a bag
6) an unripe piece of fruit and a ripe banana in a bag

Which of these is your control group? (the green banana and unripe fruit sitting on the table, unbagged)

Let your experiment run for 4-7 days. (Halt the experiment before your fruit gets overly rotten!) Examine all the groups and come to some conclusions. Did temperature play a role in the ripening time of the fruit? Which played a greater role—temperature or ethylene?

After visual examination, do the iodine test. Cut a slice of each fruit. (Cut the slices before you get out the iodine. You don't want to get iodine on the rest of the fruit, rendering it inedible. Those experimental fruits (with no iodine on them) should be eaten, not wasted!) Put a few drops of iodine on each slice. Wait one minute and then check the results. Iodine turns black in the presence of starch, but not sugar. The more sugary (more ripe) a fruit is, the less black it will turn. A very unripe piece of fruit will stain black. The iodine on a very ripe fruit will stay yellow. Do your iodine results match your visual assessment of what happened?

6) DETERMINE THE GERMINATION PERCENTAGE FOR A PACKAGE OF SEEDS

You will need:
- A packet of seeds (any type, but larger ones will be easier to work with)
- One or more egg cartons
- Potting soil

Not all seeds germinate. As we all know, life is not perfect and sometimes things go wrong. It's no different with plants and seeds. There are many things that could go wrong during the process of seed formation or during the time during which the seeds are dormant. Commercial seed packets often have a failure rate as high as 20-30%.

This experiment requires some precision and accurate counting. You have flexibility in determining how many cartons to use, what type of seeds to use, and how many seeds to sow in each compartment.

Put some potting soil in each egg compartment. Put one or more seeds in each compartment. Plant the same number in each compartment. (One per compartment would be ideal, but you can double up or even plant three per.) It is crucial that you plant exactly the same number in each compartment. It's also imperative that you count the total number of seeds you planted.

Keep the soil moist and warm. The back of the seed package should give you an estimate of how long it will take for the seeds to germinate. Don't begin your final count until the sprouts are well up out of the soil. (Give slow seeds a chance to germinate before you count.) When you are sure that no more seeds are going to come up, look at the compartments and count how many sprouts should have come up but did not.

To determine the mathematical percentage, divide the number of seeds that did not come up by the total number of seeds you planted, then multiply by 100. How did your packet compare with the average failure rate of about 20%?

EXTENSION IDEA: Have the student write a list of everything they can think of that could go wrong with a seed and cause it not to germinate. Look back over the processes described in this chapter and think of what might go wrong. (What if the cotyledons can't break out of the seed coat? What if an insect damages the seed? What if only one sperm got into the ovule? What if the polar nuclei only had one nucleus? What if...)

7) DO A STENCIL ART ACTIVITY ABOUT GERMINATION (for younger students)

If you are working with younger students (10 and under) you might want to take a look at an activity posted for free download on The Basement Workshop website. Go to **www.ellenjcmchenry.com**, click on FREE DOWNLOADS, then on PLANTS, then on "Germination Stencil Activity."

8) ENGINEER A FLYING SEED

Seeds sometimes need to travel away from the parent plant in order to survive. There are many mechanisms for dispersal of seeds. This activity focuses on seeds that are designed to travel through the air.

You will need:
- Sheets of paper
- Tissue paper
- Scissors
- Tape and/or glue
- Some medium-sized, lightweight seeds (flat seeds such as pumpkin or squash will be easier to work with)
- Optional: a fan if you want to simulate wind

Try to obtain some real examples of seeds designed to fly, such as maple "helicopters," dandelion "parachutes," or any similar mechanisms that you may have available. Let the students experiment with these and see how they float or glide or twirl. (TIP: Make sure the students have seen the video on the playlist about seeds that take to the wind. They might get some good ideas from watching the video.)

Allow the students to choose what kind of mechanisms they would like to build. If there is time, encourage them to make several different models. They need not use the patterns suggested here, but these are the ones that are commonly recommended for this type of activity. Encourage experimentation. Perhaps after a few flights they might think of a way to improve their design.

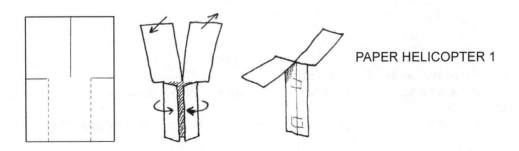

PAPER HELICOPTER 1

PAPER HELICOPTER 2   EXPERIMENT WITH TISSUE PAPER, ALSO

Remember, they are not limited to these designs. (What about a one-blade copter?)

Tape or glue the seed onto the paper mechanism. (Remember, the goal is to make the seed fly!) If the first pattern (helicopter 1) seems to require a bit of weight at the bottom, provide paper clips.

Establish a starting line. If you are using a fan, set the fan so that the wind will be blowing from behind the starting line toward the finish area. If you would like to quantify the distance of the flights, mark off increments of measurement on the floor. You might also want to provide a chair at the starting line so that the participants can launch their seeds from as near to the ceiling as possible. (Or you can have the launch done by an adult if that works better for you.) You might also want to time the flights, in addition to measuring distance on the floor. If you want to practice graphing skills, have the students make a simple graph plotting time aloft versus distance traveled.

Allow multiple trials. Encourage the students to think of ways they might adapt their mechanisms to make the flight longer.

Take as much time as possible to analyze the results during and after the event. Which models stayed airborne longest? Was there one strategy that yielded the best results?

8) TEST THE DURABILITY OF SOME SEEDS

Seeds are tough. They can survive harsh conditions in their environment—drought, flood, freezing temperatures, and extreme heat. Some seeds are more durable than others, of course. Plants that grow in the tropics can't be expected to produce seeds that can survive Arctic winters (though they might!).

In this experiment, you will test a seed's ability to survive various conditions.

You will need:
- Several packets of seeds, all of them identical
- Boiling water and a large spoon
- Refrigerator and freezer
- Moist paper towels for germinating the seeds (or some small cups and potting soil)
- Paper (or masking tape) and pen to make labels for the seeds

This experiment will require you to germinate seeds. You can use wet paper towels, or you can use little cups with dirt in them. Choose the option that works best for you.

Preparation:
Divide your seeds into 8 groups. You need several seeds in each group because there is a chance that some of the seeds are not viable. The more seeds in each group, the more accurate your results will be.

One group will be your control group. The other groups will receive an experimental treatment.

GROUP 1: Control
GROUP 2: Overnight in the freezer
GROUP 3: 1 hour in the freezer
GROUP 4: 10 minutes in the freezer

GROUP 5: 3 seconds in boiling water
GROUP 6: 10 seconds in boiling water
GROUP 7: 60 seconds in boiling water
GROUP 8: 10 minutes in boiling water

The day before you plan to do this experiment, put GROUP 8 into the freezer. (Longer than overnight is fine, and they can be put into a small plastic bag if you wish.) An hour before you plan to start the boiling water,

161

put GROUP 3 into the freezer.

When you are ready to start the experiment, put a pot of water on the stove. While the water is coming to a boil, put GROUP 4 in the freezer. Then think about how you will keep track of the groups of seeds. You might want to label some small cups, or put labels on index cards and set the seeds on the cards, or write in permanent ink on the paper towels. Whatever is convenient for you is fine. (It will be easier than you think to get the groups mixed up and forget which is which!)

When the boiling water is ready, put GROUP 5 on the large spoon and immerse in the water for 3 seconds. Put GROUP 6 in for 10 seconds, GROUP 7 for a minute, and GROUP 8 for 10 minutes.

Now you are ready to begin the next phase. You will have decided already how you intend to germinate the seeds. Put each group into a germination container, whatever it might be, and make sure the group is labeled. Keep the seeds appropriately moist. Make sure all the groups get the same amount of water and light. Wait and watch. (Check the seed packet to see how long germination should take.)

The control group should definitely germinate. Compare the other groups to the control group. How did each group fair? Did any fail to come up at all? Were any of them delayed? How did the freezer group compare to the boiled group? Did the length of exposure make a difference?

9) PLAY A CARD GAME ABOUT FLOWER ID: "FOLLOW THE GARDEN PATH"

This activity is about learning to identify common garden flowers. There are several ways to make the game cards. The first option is to use the picture cards (in color) available at ww.ellenjmchenry.com. Click on FREE DOWNLOADS, then on PLANTS then on "Follow the Garden Path." Download the patterns and print them onto heavy card stock paper. Cut apart the cards and write the name of the flower of the back of each card. Feel free to substitute your local names for the flowers if they differ from what is printed on the cards. (The names printed on the cards are the names generally used in North America.)

Another option is to make the cards from scratch. You can use pictures from a garden catalog, photographs from the Internet, or even your own photos. You can customize the game to your area of the world. Put each photo onto a card and write the names of the flowers on the backs of the card.

The rules for play are included in the download. (In a nutshell, the cards are divided up between all players, then they take turns laying down cards, but first they must recite the names of all previous cards.)

10) PLAY A CARD GAME ABOUT FLOWER CLASSIFICATION: "FLOWER FLIP"

This activity is also posted as a free download at www.ellenjmchenry.com.

This game is about how flowers are classified using both color and shape. As simple as it may seem on the surface, flower classification can get very complicated and involve numerous Latin terms. A few of the more common Latin terms are written on some of these cards.

NOTE: The distinction between *regular* and *irregular* is included in the game, but **not** the distinctions between *perfect* and *imperfect*, *simple* and *compound*. These latter characteristics are difficult (or even impossible) to determine by looking at a picture. For example, students would probably guess that a daisy is a simple flower because it looks simple. However, it is a compound flower with each petal being considered a separate flower. This can only be discovered by dissecting a daisy under high magnification.

If you would like to include these terms in your game, discuss each flower card ahead of time (this may involve a bit of research) and determine how each should be classified. (TIP: Make an official list that can be referred to during the game.)

PERFECT FLOWERS contain both male and female parts; imperfect flowers have just one or the other.
SIMPLE FLOWERS have only one reproductive system.
COMPOUND FLOWERS are made of tiny individual flowers, each having their own reproductive system.

LESSON 7

1) FUN GAME: "Don't Sink the Lily Pad!"

You will need:
- Aluminum foil
- A pan or large bowl of water (several inches deep is best)
- Scissors
- A large bowl of pennies (a couple of dozen for a small pad, several hundred for a pad that is the size of a dinner plate) You could also used dried lima beans or other small objects.

How to prepare:
Cut three foil circles: a small one (just a few inches across), a medium-sized one (more like 4 or 5 inches across) and a large one (7 to 10 inches across). Fold up the edges to make it look like a real Amazon lily pad. Refer to the picture in the chapter to see that these pads have a very steep "lip" all around the edge. (Tip: The higher the lip, the more pennies you will be able to place on the pad before it sinks.)

How to play:
Place the smallest pad in the pan of water. It should float very well. Let the players take turns placing pennies on the pad. The idea is to be able to place a penny without sinking the pad. (You could pretend that the pennies are frogs or birds that might be found sitting on a lily pad.) The person whose penny sinks the pad is the loser. (You can avoid having a loser by just making it fun to see how many pennies each lily pad will hold.) As the game progresses, the players will start seeing strategy—how to add pennies without upsetting the balance of the pad. Players who like physical science will like this game.

After trying the small pad, move up to the medium pad, then the large pad.

During the game, ask the players what they notice about how the pad holds weight. What happens when the pad finally gives way? Where is the weakest point on the pad? (Usually the lowest point on the lip.)

As an additional investigation, puncture a small hole in one of the pads and try it again. How much difference does a small hole make? Puncture a few more tiny holes. Any difference? What about a large hole?

2) MAKE A PAPER MODEL THAT SHOWS HOW A CACTUS STEM EXPANDS

You will need:
- Paper
- Scissors
- Tape

 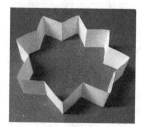

Cut two long strips of paper (from the long side of a piece of paper). Fold them back and forth ("accordion" style). Tape the ends together and adjust the shape so it looks like the one in the picture.

Experiment with the model. Demonstrate how a cactus is able to expand suddenly.

3) PLAY A GAME ABOUT POISONOUS PLANTS: "Where Sheep May Safely Graze"

The name of this game comes from a piece of music written by J. S. Bach (Canon No. 208). He probably wasn't thinking about poisonous plants when he wrote it, but the title was just too tempting to resist.

The board is designed for 1-4 players, so if you will have more than 4 players, make two (or more) copies of the game board. All players can still play as a group, but on separate boards.

You will need:
• Copies of the game board pieces and copies of the sheep tokens (one sheep per player)
• Tape (a glue stick might also be helpful for assembling the sheep tokens)
• Scissors
• Optional: colored pencils or markers so players can color their sheep in order to identify it

How to set up the game:
Tape together the two game board pages. Cut out, fold and assemble the sheep tokens. Each player should either write his name on the sheep, or color the fleece so that he will be able to keep track of his sheep.

How to play the game:
The object of the game is to get your sheep across the long meadow without eating any poisonous plants. This will be difficult because three out of four plants in each row are toxic to some degree. Only one is considered by botanists to be edible. Not all the toxic plants are equally toxic. Some will just cause stomach upset or headaches, others will kill you. As with all things, "The dose makes the poison," as Paracelsus stated back in Renaissance times. In most cases, the amount you eat has a lot to do with the outcome. Each plant has been given a numerical estimate of how toxic it is, using a scale of 0 to 3. (This is not an official number you'll find anywhere. These numbers were created for this game and should not be construed as scientifically valid toxicity estimates.) Edible plants have a toxicity score of 0, so the goal is to end up with a score as close to 0 as possible.

Disclaimer at this point: Even though the token is a sheep, I've erred on the side of choosing to define edibility by human standards, not grazing animal standards. In most cases, humans and animals will react in a similar manner, but if there was any discrepancy, the human factor was given more consideration since the players are humans who might find this information helpful at some point in the future.

This game requires a leader (most likely the teacher/adult in charge, but it could be a student, especially if you have an older student and some younger ones). The leader will give the correct answers after each move and will also be able to add some extra information at his/her discretion from the extra info sheet.

All players move at the same time. The leader calls out the number of the row the sheep will be grazing, moving from 1 to 12. The players then place their sheep on the plant in that row that they hope is edible. (There can be more than one sheep on a square.) After all sheep have been placed, the leader reads the answers and gives the toxicity rating for each plant. The players write down their score for that row. As they progress up the rows, they keep adding up their points so that after row 12 they will have a final score. The lowest score wins.

Where Sheep May Safely Graze

azalea	hibiscus	rhododendron	hydrangea
gooseberries	asparagus berries	pokeweed berries	yew berries
tulip bulbs	orchid bulbs	daffodil bulbs	hyacinth bulbs
maple tree leaves	dogwood tree leaves	cherry tree leaves	oak tree leaves
raw kidney beans	raw lima beans	raw green beans	raw Mung beans
cherry pits	grape seeds	apple seeds	pear seeds

6	potato leaves	potato stems	green potatoes	red potatoes
5	tiger lily	lily of the valley	Jack-in-the-pulpit	calla lily
4	violets	buttercups	foxglove	larkspur
3	ferns	ivy	holly	cattails
2	white snakeroot	jimson weed	ragwort	nettles
1	wild carrots	dandelion leaves	rhubarb leaves	tomato leaves

Three of the plants (or plant parts) in each row are toxic. One is edible.

Good luck, sheep!

Where Sheep May Safely Graze

This page is an extra in case you want to make your own game, or add additional rows to the other pages.

potato leaves (1)	potato stems (1)	green potatoes (1)	red potatoes (0)
Potatoes belong to the Solanaceae family, the nightshades. All nightshades produce solanine chemicals, at least to some degree. This chemical is most abundant in the green parts of the plant.	Since potato stems are green, they contain some solanine, a chemical that can affect both the digestive system and the nervous system. Cooking does not destroy this chemical.	Eating a few bites of green potato won't make you terribly sick, but eating a lot of them isn't good for you. The green color indicates the presence of solanine, a toxic chemical.	The tubers of potato plants do not contain much solanine as long as they are white or red in color.

tiger lily (0)	lily of the valley (2)	Jack-in-the-pulpit (1.5)	calla lily (3)
Tiger lilies are edible and are sometimes used to garnish salads and desserts. They belong to the family of daylilies, which are chemically different from other plants we call lilies.	Though it looks great in your flower garden, all parts of this plant can cause abdominal pain, vomiting, and reduced heart rate. Eating a large amount can be deadly.	This plant contains saponins, which cause severe irritation to the mouth, throat and stomach. In severe cases, swelling causes problems with breathing. When cooked properly, the root can be edible.	This type of lily contains oxalic acid (also found in rhubarb leaves) and causes digestive distress. The acid can affect other organs, also, and a dose of as little as 5 grams can be fatal to small children.

violets (0)	buttercups (1)	foxglove (2)	larkspur (2)
Violets are often used to add color to a green salad. They are high in vitamin C.	These lovely flowers can be a danger to grazing animals. They can cause cholic in hoofed animals and digestive distress in all animals. They can also irritate the skin.	This plant contains digitoxin, a chemical that will make you nauseated, then cause serious heart problems. However, in small doses this chemical is used as a heart medication.	The toxins in this plant cause problems to muscles and nerves, and can be fatal. This plant causes problems in grazing animals. In late summer, the plant becomes less toxic.

ferns (.5)	ivy (1)	holly (1.5)	cattails (0)
People in Asia eat fern fiddleheads with no apparent ill effects. However, all ferns have been shown to be carcinogenic and they are probably contributing to Japan's high rates of digestive cancers.	Ivy leaves and berries are mildly poisonous, causing digestive discomfort and labored breathing. Their bitter taste helps to keep humans from eating them.	Holly looks nice as a holiday decoration, but don't eat it. It will give you nausea, vomiting and diarrhea.	All parts of the cattail are edible. Some people grind the roots into a flour. The stems are tender and taste like cucumber. The brown spikes can be eaten like corn on the cob.

white snakeroot (2)	jimson weed (3)	ragwort (2)	nettles (0)
All parts of this plant are toxic due to a chemical called tremetol, which causes severe trembling and vomiting and can be fatal. The toxin can pass through a cow's udder and into its milk causing "milk sickness."	Like deadly nightshade, jimson weed contains a chemical called atropine, which interferes with the normal functioning of the nervous system. In very small amounts, this chemical can be used as a medicine.	This plant is most dangerous to grazing animals. It is bitter and therefore unlikely to be consumed by humans. It causes liver damage because of its many alkaloid chemicals.	Though they have a reputation for being nasty stingers (because of the hairs on their stems), cooking them removes the sting and makes them completely edible.

wild carrots (1)	dandelion leaves (0)	rhubarb leaves (1)	tomato leaves (1)
The carrots we grow in our gardens are far removed from their wild cousins. It is advisable not to eat things you find in the wild that look like carrots. They can be poisonous.	Dandelion leaves are a great source of vitamins, minerals, and fiber. All parts of the plant are edible, either cooked or raw. Many people use the leaves as salad greens.	Rhubarb leaves contain oxalic acid, which can cause kidney damage, convulsions and coma. However, you'd have to eat quite a few of them to achieve these extreme effects.	These contain solanin, which can cause stomach upset and nervous system distress. Tomatoes are in the nightshade family of plants, Solanaceae, along with Atropa belladonna, jimson weed, and potatoes.

azalea (2) The azalea is a small rhododendron. The nectar of the azalea flowers is also toxic, so if bees make honey from azaleas, the honey will be toxic.	**hibiscus (0)** Hibiscus plants are famous for their huge flowers. Since the flowers are edible, they can be used as disposable plates!	**rhododendron (2)** Rhododendrons are the larger group of plants to which azaleas belong. Rhododendrons are large bushes with huge ball-shaped flowers. As long as you look and don't taste, you're OK!	**hydrangea (1.5)** Hydrangea are distantly related to rhododendrons, but contain the same toxic chemicals found in the *Prunus* family (fruits with pits). These chemicals mainly affect the digestive system.
gooseberries (0) Gooseberries are one of the few simple, round berries that are edible. They are related to currants and are native to Europe and Africa. They are used in salads, desserts and jams.	**asparagus berries (1)** Asparagus berries are somewhat controversial, but the general consensus is to refrain from eating them, as they have been reported to cause toxic effects.	**pokeweed berries (1.5)** The pokeweed plant is a common weed. The ripe berries are dark purple and can be used as a natural dye. Eating more than a few berries can cause nausea and headache.	**yew berries (2)** These bright red berries are found on bushes that have soft, flat needles, like an evergreen. Eating more than a few berries can cause vomiting, diarrhea and dizziness. Eating a lot of them can be fatal.
tulip bulbs (1) Most of the tulip bulb is moderately toxic. During WW II people in Holland ate the outer parts of tulip bulbs when faced with starvation. The knew the central part of the bulb was toxic and did not eat it.	**orchid bulbs (0)** Orchids are not closely related to these other bulbs, so their chemistry is different. All parts of the orchid plant are edible and the flowers are often used in salads and desserts.	**daffodil bulbs (2)** Daffodils are related to tulips but their bulbs seem to be more toxic than tulip bulbs. Eating daffodil bulbs causes intense vomiting and diarrhea.	**hyacinth bulbs (2)** Related to tulips and daffodils, hyacinths are also to be avoided. The alkaloid chemicals cause intense digestive misery, and can also affect other systems of the body.
maple leaves (2) These are more of a danger to grazing animals than people, as horses find them tasty and people do not. The leaves get more toxic as they wilt and turn colors. Only a few pounds of them will poison a horse.	**dogwood leaves (0)** The leaves and berries of the dogwood tree are non-toxic.	**cherry leaves (2)** The leaves of the cherry tree contain the same toxic chemicals found in the seeds. Horse owners are very careful to keep cherry tree leaves out of their animals' pastures.	**oak leaves (1)** Oak leaves contain high levels of tannic acid, which causes digestive upset and possibly other symptoms at high doses. It can cause grazing animals to cholic. Pigs are not affected.
raw kidney beans (2) Raw kidney beans contain a substance called lectin, which is beneficial to the plant, but not to you. Even 4-6 raw beans can cause great distress to your digestive system. Boiling beans for 10 min. destroys the lectins.	**raw lima beans (1)** Raw lima beans contain a substance called linamarin, which is fairly toxic. When boiled for just 10 minutes, this chemical is broken down and becomes harmless.	**raw green beans (.5)** We've all eaten a few raw green beans once in a while. Don't panic! A few won't harm you. Just don't eat a bushel of raw beans or you'll get some distressing digestive disturbances.	**raw Mung beans (0)** Mung beans belong to the genus *Vigna* and come from India. The other beans in this row are genus *Phaseolus* and are native to the Americas. Mung beans can be eaten raw or cooked.
cherry pits (1) All members of the *Prunus* family have cyanogenic glycoside chemicals that attack the cells in your digestive system. A large does of these chemicals can affect other organs, as well.	**grape seeds (0)** Grape seeds are not only non-toxic but they are beneficial. Grape seed extract is a powerful anti-oxidant, protecting your cells from dangerous molecules called "free radicals."	**apple seeds (.5)** Apple seeds contain small amounts of a toxic cyanide chemical, but you'd have to eat hundreds of seeds to produce any noticeable symptoms.	**pear seeds (.5)** Pear seeds have the same issue as apple seeds, since they are somewhat related. Again, eating an occasional apple or pear seed is not a problem.

LESSON 8

1) DO SOME EXTRA RESEARCH ON GARDEN PESTS

You will need:
> • Blank WANTED poster (you can create your own, find one online with Google image search, or use the two small posters provided at the back of this book)
> • Books or websites about plant pests

You may want to ask your student(s) to do some extra research on one or more plant pests that are common in your area. A fun way to present the information they learn is by making their own WANTED poster.

Here are some ideas for more plant pests: thrips, earwigs, whiteflies, scale insects, ants, tomato or tobacco hornworms, leafhoppers, coddling moths

2) LEARN MORE ABOUT PLANT NUTRITION

If your student(s) want to learn more about why plants need the nutrients they do, you can find this information listed on the Wikipedia article about plant nutrition, or you might want to use this website for kids: www.ncagr.gov/cyber/kidswrld/plant/nutrient.htm. This site lists only 13 of the nutrients but the information is very good and is age-appropriate.

3) AN EXTRA RESOURCE ABOUT POISONOUS PLANTS

If your student(s) enjoyed the game about poisonous plants and would like to learn more about the darker side of botany, take a look at this book on Amazon: Wicked Plants by Amy Stewart. You can use the "Look Inside" feature to preview the book to see if it is right for your student(s). The text consists of over 70 very short "chapters" on each plant, so you can pick and choose which plants you want to read about. The writing style is very entertaining and the author includes lots of fascinating historical anecdotes and funny stories.

4) LOOK AT MOLD UNDER A MAGNIFIER

You will need:
> • A magnifier (10x minimum, 20x-30x is ideal)
> • Some bread or fruit mold

This is a very simple activity, but if you've never done it, you've got to try it! Mold is fascinating if you view it up close. You can clearly see the filaments with sporangia on top in various stages of development. It's like an alien forest, not like yucky scum.

5) TAKE A FIELD TRIP, OR ENJOY SOME VIRTUAL OUTINGS

A nice way to end a unit is with a field trip. If you have any greenhouses, organic farms, botanical gardens, or agricultural research centers you can visit, your students are now prepared to understand what is going on at these places, and be able to ask really good questions!

If you can't get out, enjoy some virtual field trips on the Botany playlist.

GENERAL REVIEW ACTIVITIES

1) CARD GAME: "Plant Pile Up"

You will need:
- Copies of the cards on the following pages (printed onto card stock is best)
- Scissors
- Copy of the answer key

Preparation:
Copy the pattern pages onto card stock, then cut apart the cards.

How to play:
Shuffle the deck, then distribute 5 cards to each player. The remaining cards stay in the deck and become a draw pile. Turn one card over to begin the first discard pile.

The object of the game is to get rid of all your cards. You may only discard one card per turn, unless you use a "Start New Pile" card. (When you lay down a "Start New Pile" card, you may then immediately discard one of your cards onto it.) If you cannot lay down a card, you must pick one up.

The discard piles will alternate between picture cards and word cards. If you have a question about which cards qualify for which descriptions, consult the answer key.

2) BOTANY SCAVENGER HUNT

Each student will need a copy of the scavenger hunt and a gallon-size resealable plastic bag for collecting specimens. Set a time limit for the collection period. You can make this time period whatever suits your needs. You could do it all in one afternoon as part of a field trip, or you could do it over the course of several weeks, allowing students to have enough time to look for things as the plant life around them grows and changes. They'll have a better chance at finding more of the items if a larger time frame is allowed. If you decide to allow several weeks, the bags will need to be refrigerated. If you are doing this in a group setting with regular weekly meetings, you might want to ask the students to bring in whatever they have found each week, checking them off the list, then disposing of them. Send the bags back home empty. This will prevent problems with bacterial overgrowth.

For an additional fun challenge, have a LARGEST LEAF contest. (A good way to measure the leaves is to measure the widest dimension and the longest dimension and then add the two numbers.) The winners of the contest can have additional points added on to their total score.

Prizes:
If you are doing this as a group, you may want to award prizes according to point values earned. One method that works very well is to have a prize table with point values assigned to all the prizes. Students may "spend" their points at the prize table. To make it fair, line them up in order of how many total points they earned, letting the students who earned the most points go first. However, each participant only gets to take one prize the first time through the line. This ensures that there will still be a nice selection of prizes available for even the last person in line. Then let them file past the table a second time, taking one more item. Then a third pass, etc., until everyone has spent all their points. This method of awarding prizes rewards those who worked hard without disheartening the other participants.

3) FINAL REVIEW / TEST

A final review/test form is at the end of this section. Please note that the first two pages cover information found in just the level 1 sections. The third page can be added for students who also did the level 2 sections.

HAS CHLOROPLASTS	HAS CHLOROPLASTS	HAS CHLOROPLASTS
HAS A VASCULAR SYSTEM OR IS PART OF A VASCULAR SYSTEM	HAS A VASCULAR SYSTEM OR IS PART OF A VASCULAR SYSTEM	IS AN ANGIOSPERM
IS PERENNIAL (ADULT PLANT SURVIVES FOR SEVERAL YEARS)	MAKES SPORES	MAKES FLOWERS
HAS AN ADAPTATION THAT ALLOWS IT TO SURVIVE IN ITS ENVIRONMENT (NAME THE ADAPTATION)	HAS AN ADAPTATION THAT ALLOWS IT TO SURVIVE IN ITS ENVIRONMENT (NAME THE ADAPTATION)	HAS AN ADAPTATION THAT ALLOWS IT TO SURVIVE IN ITS ENVIRONMENT (NAME THE ADAPTATION)
PLAYS A ROLE IN REPRODUCTION	PLAYS A ROLE IN REPRODUCTION	PLAYS A ROLE IN REPRODUCTION

MAKES SUCCULENT FRUITS	COMMONLY EATEN BY ANIMALS OR BIRDS (not insects)	IS MADE OF CELLS
MAKES FRUITS	MAKES SEEDS	MAKES DRY FRUITS
NEED A MAGNIFIER OR MICROSCOPE TO SEE IT PROPERLY	COMMONLY USED AS A FOOD SOURCE (for humans)	MAKES DRY FRUITS
NEED A MAGNIFIER OR MICROSCOPE TO SEE IT PROPERLY	DOES NOT HAVE A VASCULAR SYSTEM (or is not part of a vascular system)	DOES NOT MAKE FRUITS
HAS A "WOODY" STEM (not an herbaceous stem)	IS A DICOT	NEEDS SUNLIGHT (has a direct need for it)

MOSS	FERN	LIVERWORT
	frond — "fiddlehead" — rhizome — roots	
RAFFLESIA ("corpse flower")	AMAZON LILY	BLADDERWORT
QUERCUS ALBA (white oak tree)	*SOLANUM TUBEROSUM* (potato plant)	*SALIX BABYLONICA* ("Weeping willow" tree)
PINUS LONGAEVA (bristlecone pine)	*ACER SACCHARUM* (sugar maple tree)	*PRUNUS DOMESTICUS* (plum tree)
ATROPA BELLADONNA ("deadly nightshade")	*DAUCUS CAROTA* (carrot plant)	*HELIANTHUS* (sunflower plant)

"PLANT PILE-UP" page 3

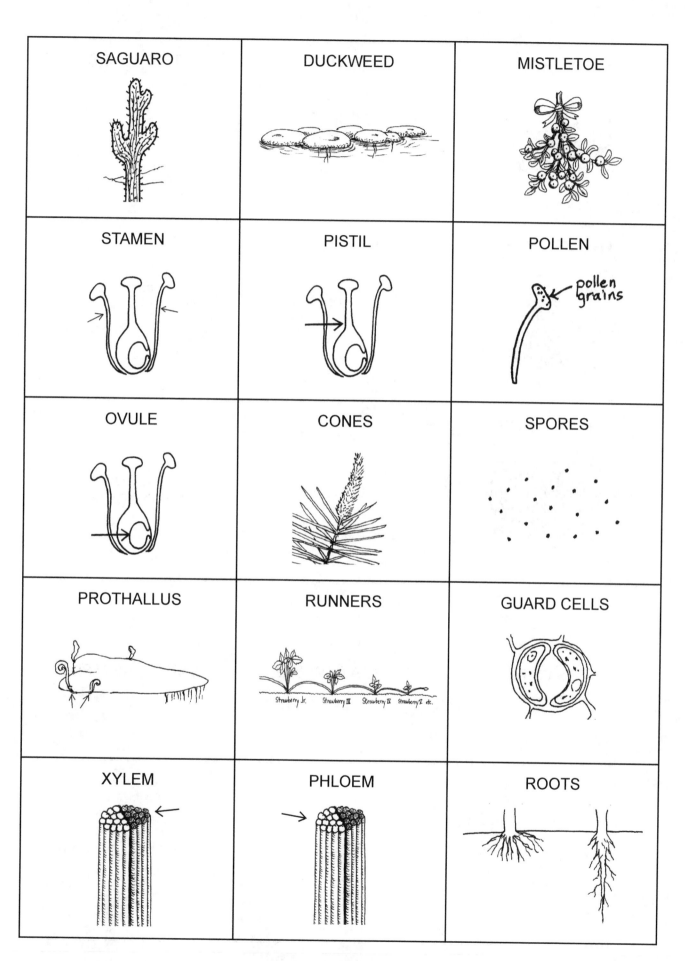

SAGUARO	DUCKWEED	MISTLETOE
STAMEN	PISTIL	POLLEN
OVULE	CONES	SPORES
PROTHALLUS	RUNNERS	GUARD CELLS
XYLEM	PHLOEM	ROOTS

STONE PLANT	SAPWOOD	TRICHOMES
GINGKO TREE	SEAGRASS	THYLAKOIDS
PALISADE LAYER	HAS LEAVES	NEEDS CARBON DIOXIDE
NEEDS WATER	START A NEW PILE	START A NEW PILE
START A NEW PILE	START A NEW PILE	START A NEW PILE

CORRECT (AND PLAUSIBLE) ANSWERS FOR "PLANT PILE-UP"

COMMONLY USED AS FOOD SOURCE FOR HUMANS: Potato, sunflower, maple tree (maple sugar), carrot, plum, roots, ovule (which turns into seeds/fruits), gingko (herbal medicine). If you live in an area of the world where duckweed is eaten regularly, then you can count this as a correct answer, also.

COMMONLY EATEN BY ANIMALS OR BIRDS: Seagrass, sunflower, duckweed, mistletoe, cones, oak tree (acorns are eaten by squirrels), maple tree (helicopter seeds are often eaten by squirrels or birds), pollen (bees). Creative but acceptable answer could also include palisade layer, thylakoids, guard cells, roots, xylem, phloem, as they are found in all kinds of leaves that are eaten by animals. For answers such as moss or saguaro, the player must be able to name an animal or bird that they know for a fact eats that plant. (Some bats feed on cactus fruits, for example.) Players' answers should demonstrate some kind of knowledge or good inference, not just a wild guess. (Even though the woodpecker might look like it is eating the sapwood, it is actually eating the insects in the wood, not the wood itself.)

DOES NOT HAVE A VASCULAR SYSTEM: Moss, liverwort, Rafflesia, pistil, stamen, ovule, pollen, spores, cones, prothallus, trichomes, thylakoids, palisade layer

DOES NOT MAKE FRUITS: Moss, fern, liverwort. Also these plant parts could be included as not being involved in fruit production: xylem, phloem, guard cells, palisade layer, thylakoids, sapwood, runners, trichomes, prothallus, cones, spores.

HAS CHLOROPLASTS: All plants are correct except Rafflesia; also palisade layer, prothallus, runners, guard cells.

HAS LEAVES: All plants except Rafflesia, moss and liverwort. (Saguaro spines can be classified as adapted leaves, and those two bumps that form the stone plant are leaves.) Runners usually have leaves attached, also.

HAS A WOODY STEM: Maple tree, willow tree, oak tree, plum tree, bristlecone pine tree, gingko tree

HAS A VASCULAR SYSTEM: Any plant except moss, liverwort and Rafflesia. Xylem, phloem, roots and guard cells are part of vascular systems. (A prothallus does not have a vascular system.)

HAS AN ADAPTATION THAT HELPS IT SURVIVE: Correct answers in this category will vary, and it will be up to the adult supervising the game to make final judgements. The obvious correct answers are plants that were mentioned in chapter 7 as having special adaptations. However, if a player is really thinking hard and can come up with another answer that has a good rationale behind it, the supervisor may allow that answer. If the player puts forth some real brain power to come up with a plausible answer (and it is plausible) their answer can be accepted.

IS MADE OF CELLS: Anything except the following: thylakoids, spores

IS A DICOT: Oak tree, maple tree, plum tree, willow tree, sunflower, potato, bladderwort, carrot, deadly nightshade, saguaro, duckweed, mistletoe, Rafflesia, stone plant

IS AN ANGIOSPERM (includes both dicots and monocots): Oak tree, maple tree, plum tree, willow tree, sunflower, bladderwort, carrot, potato, deadly nightshade, saguaro, duckweed, mistletoe, Rafflesia, stone plant, Amazon lily, seagrass

IS PERENNIAL: Oak tree, maple tree, willow tree, plum tree, gingko tree, deadly nightshade, saguaro, mistletoe, bristlecone pine, some tropical species of bladderworts, and possibly stone plants (which are so strange it is hard to categorize them as annual or perennial, but the plants do seem to persist from season to season).

IS PART OF VASCULAR SYSTEM: Xylem, phloem, sapwood, roots, guard cells (which regulate water vapor), runners (which are modified stems)

MAKES FRUIT: All angiosperms (see list for IS AN ANGIOSPERM) Remember, botanical fruits do not always look like the fruits we eat. You could also add pistil, ovule, stamen, pollen, as technically they "make" fruits.

MAKES FLOWERS: All angiosperms (see list for IS AN ANGIOSPERM).

MAKES DRY FRUITS: Oak tree (acorns), maple tree ("helicopters"), willow tree (seed pods), carrot (makes tiny seed pods), sunflower,

MAKES SEEDS: All angiosperms, plus the bristlecone pine (a gymnosperm).

MAKES SUCCULENT FRUITS: plum tree, deadly nightshade (berries), saguaro (cactus fruits), mistletoe (berries), gingko tree (although technically not an angiosperm it makes smelly fruits).

MAKES SPORES: All plants make spores. (Remember, we learned that although mosses and ferns have life cycles where the spores are more apparent, botanists discovered that pollen and eggs are produced by microspores and megaspores.) You might also want to include ovule and stamen as acceptable answers.

NEEDS CARBON DIOXIDE: All plants. Also, palisade layer (because of the chloroplasts) and thylakoids (carbon dioxide needed for photosynthesis occurring here).

NEEDS WATER: All plants and plant parts except spores. Also palisade layer, guard cells, and thylakoids because water is necessary for photosynthesis.

NEEDS SUNLIGHT: All plants, plus palisade layer and thylakoids.

NEED A MAGNIFIER OR MICROSCOPE TO SEE IT: Moss, (maybe liverworts—you decide), spores, pollen, guard cells, palisade layer, trichomes, thylakoids, and ovule. (Debatable but acceptable answers might also include duckweed, pistil, stamen, xylem, phloem.)

PLAYS A ROLE IN REPRODUCTION: Spores, pollen, pistil, stamen, ovule, prothallus, runners, cones

NOTE: If a question comes up that is not addressed here in these lists, Google it and you are likely to find an answer fairly quickly. (However, don't rely too much on sites like "answers.yahoo.com". Use Wikipedia (which is extremely reliable for botany), university websites, or websites created by plant experts.)

BOTANY SCAVENGER HUNT

LEAVES   (NOTE: Your specimens do not need to match these pictures. Yours might look very different but still qualify.)

Simple leaf with smooth edges	1	Simple palmate leaf	1	Furry or fuzzy leaf	1
Simple leaf with serrated edges	1	Compound palmate leaf	1	Thick, succulent leaf	2
Simple leaf with undulating edges	1	Simple pinnate leaf	1	Flat conifer needle (Test: won't roll between finger and thumb)	1
Simple lobed leaf	1	Doubly pinnate leaf	2	Round conifer needle (Test: will roll between finger and thumb)	1
Leaf with deltoid shape	2	Triply pinnate leaf	3	Conifer tuft containing 2 needles	1
Leaf with cordate shape	2	Opposite leaves	1	Conifer tuft containing 3 needles	2
Leaf with obcordate shape	3	Alternate leaves	1	Conifer tuft containing 5 or more needles	2
Leaf with linear shape	1	Leaves in spiral pattern	1	Leaf miner trail	3
Leaf with orbicular shape (round, but with stem parallel to lamina)	2	Leaves with whorl pattern	2	Leaf gall	3
Circular leaf (stem is perpendicular to lamina) underside shown	3	Variegated leaf (more than one color)	1	Leaf with fungus circles (spots cross over veins)	3

TOTAL POINTS EARNED ON THIS PAGE [   ]

STEMS

Term	Points	Term	Points	Term	Points
Tendril 	2	Stipules Occur at the base of some leaves. May look leafy or spiny. 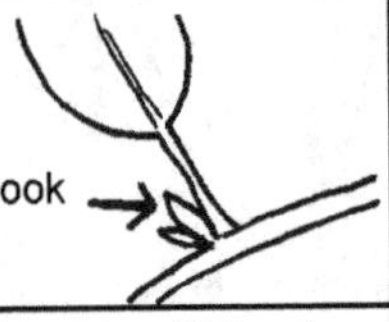	2	Stem gall 	3
Stolon ("runner") They can be at soil surface or slightly under. 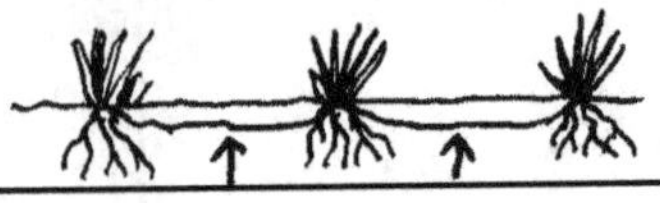	1	Apical (or "terminal") bud 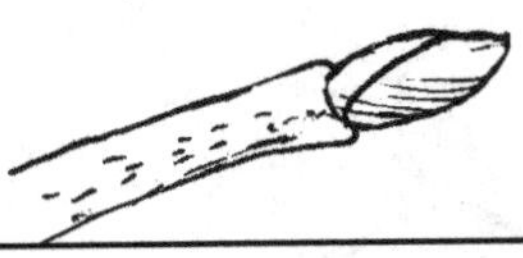	1	Axillary (or "lateral") bud 	1
Leaf scar 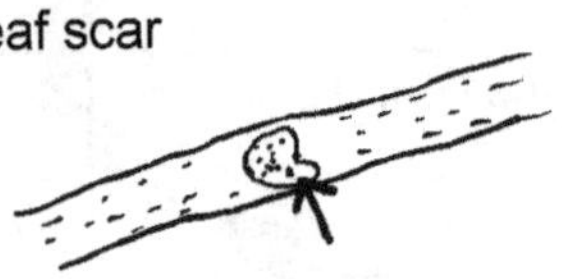	1	Fuzzy or hairy stem 	2	Hollow stem 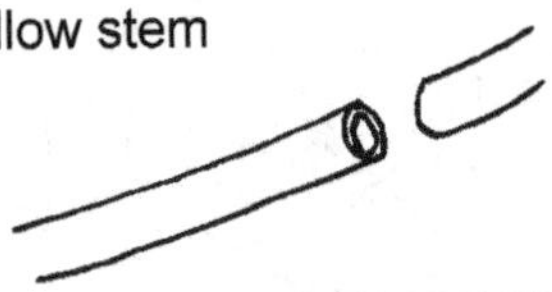	1

ROOTS / RHIZOMES

Term	Points	Term	Points	Term	Points
Tap root (but can't use carrot) 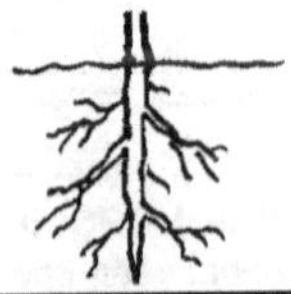	1	Tuber (but can't use potato) 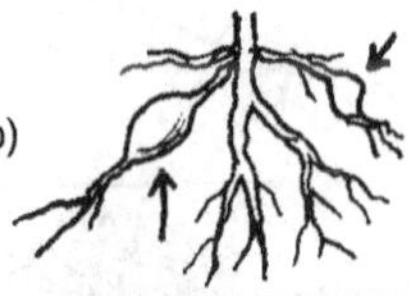	2	Rhizome (Modified stem that looks like a thick, clumpy root.) 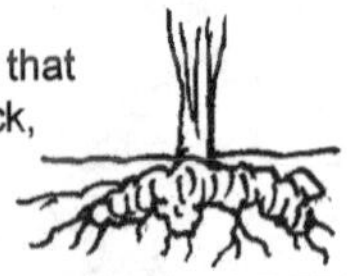	3
Fibrous root (but can't use grass) 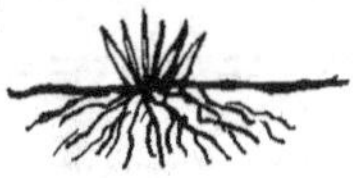	1	Nitrogen-fixing nodules 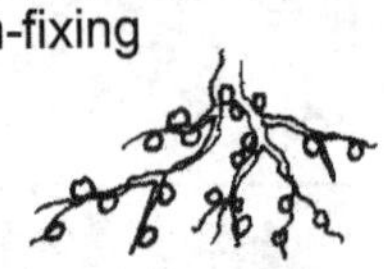	3	Bulb (but not onion, tulip or daffodil) 	2

REPRODUCTIVE STRUCTURES

Term	Points	Term	Points	Term	Points
Regular flower (has radial symmetry) 	1	Flower spire 	2	Seed case designed to float or fly 	1
Irregular flower (has bilateral symmetry) 	2	Cone 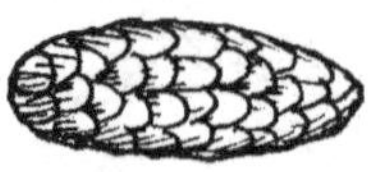	1	Seed case with hooks or barbs 	2
Composite flower (made of smaller flowers) 	1	A dry fruit (not from the store or your kitchen) 	2	Seed case thicker than this: 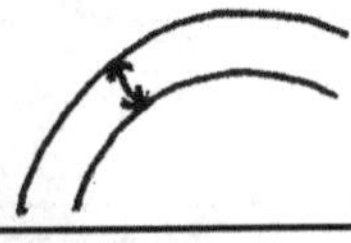	3
Umbrella-shaped flower 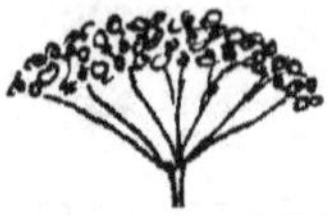	2	Moss sporangium 	3	Fern sori 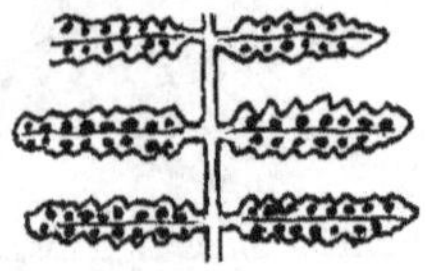	3

optional additional category

TOTAL POINTS EARNED ON THIS PAGE

TOTAL FROM FIRST PAGE

GRAND TOTAL

FINAL REVIEW   (Level 1)   Name _____

1) Which of these things is NOT a necessary ingredient for photosynthesis?
a) sunlight   b) sugar   c) carbon dioxide   d) water

2) This process is considered to be the "opposite" of photosynthesis because it uses sugar and oxygen instead of producing them.
a) respiration   b) perspiration   c) oxidation   d) transpiration

3) Where would you find chlorophyll molecules?
a) in thylakoids   b) in chloroplasts   c) in plant cells   d) all of there are correct

4) When a cell splits in half, this is called:
a) separation   b) doubling   c) mitosis   d) meiosis

5) Which organelle moves around inside the cell, "streaming" in a large circular pattern?
a) the nucleus   b) the chloroplasts   c) the ribosomes   d) the thylakoids   e) the vacuoles

6) Which one of these does not make seeds?
a) ferns   b) legumes   c) Gingko trees   d) lilies   e) monocots

7) Which one of these does not have a vascular system?
a) ferns   b) mosses   c) monocots   d) gymnosperms

8) Which one of these is not a monocot?
a) daffodils   b) lilies   c) tulips   d) roses

9) By what process do mosses and liverworts get water to their cells?
a) transpiration   b) photosynthesis   c) meiosis   d) osmosis

10) What type of cells transport water from the roots up to the leaves?
a) xylem   b) phloem   c) epidermis   d) cortex

11) Which one of these never contains chloroplasts?
a) guard cells   b) palisade layer   c) epidermis cells   d) cuticle   e) spongy mesophyll

12) Which one of these is NOT a female reproductive part?
a) ovule   b) anther   c) pistil   d) stigma

13) Which one of these would you find only in angiosperms?
a) seed   b) sperm   c) ovule   d) pollen tube   e) endosperm

14) Which one of these is a true vegetable?
a) tomato   b) squash   c) cabbage   d) corn   e) bean

15) Which one of these is NOT a plant pigment?
a) ethylene   b) xanthophyll   c) carotene   d) anthocyanin   e) chlorophyll

Matching:

16) _____ Another name for "seed leaf."

17) _____ The center of a dicot stem.

18) _____ Transports sugar up or down.

19) _____ The holes in the underside of a leaf.

20) _____ The waxy outer layer of a leaf.

21) _____ The proper name for a plant "hair."

22) _____ This is what forms when an egg and sperm join.

23) _____ This is what "heartwood" is made of.

24) _____ This is what forms when a sperm joins with polar nuclei.

25) _____ This is where you find pollen grains.

Possible answers:

A) cuticle
B) trichome
C) cotyledon
D) xylem
E) phloem
F) stomata
G) anther
H) pith
I) endosperm
J) zygote

TRUE or FALSE?

26) _____ Glucose is a type of sugar.

27) _____ Dicots have parallel veins and fibrous roots.

28) _____ Ferns have xylem and phloem.

29) _____ Ferns make egg and sperm cells.

30) _____ Photosynthesis does not occur in roots.

31) _____ Desert plants have fewer stomata than tropical plants do.

32) _____ Amazon lilies eat beetles.

33) _____ Plants can reproduce by means other than using egg and sperm.

34) _____ Seagrasses can get oxygen from water instead of air.

35) _____ Angiosperm ovules contain one female cell.

Nasturtium: one of the very few plants with truly circular leaves (the stem attaches to the leaf like an umbrella handle)

Fill in these blanks:

36) C3, C4 and CAM are all forms of _____.

37) The first virus ever discovered was on a _____ plant.

38) The tiniest flower in the world is found on a small aquatic plant called _____.

39) A stoma (one stomata) is surrounded by a pair of _____ cells.

40) A _____ is a lump that was caused by an invading insect, bacteria, or virus.

Match the words with the labeled parts in the diagram:

41) _____ pistil
42) _____ sepals
43) _____ anther
44) _____ stigma
45) _____ filament
46) _____ stamen
47) _____ style
48) _____ receptacle
49) _____ ovule
50) _____ ovary

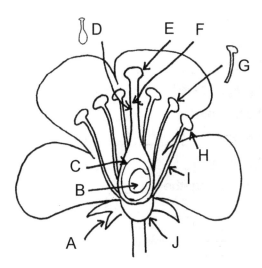

What are these things?

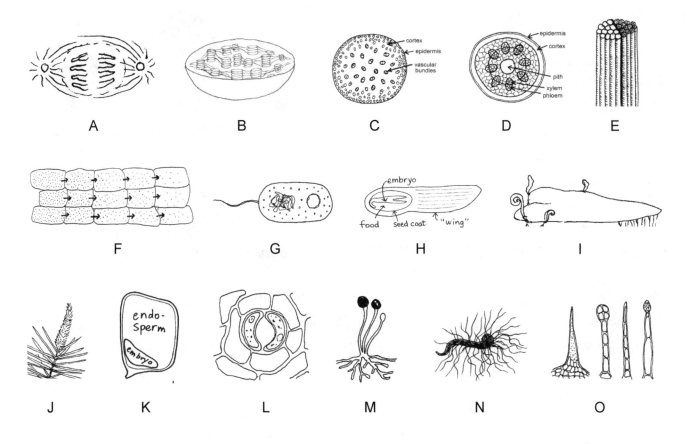

51) _____ monocot cross section
52) _____ osmosis in action
53) _____ corn seed
54) _____ mitosis in cell nucleus
55) _____ fern sperm

56) _____ dicot cross section
57) _____ crown gall bacteria
58) _____ pine seed
59) _____ guard cells / stoma
60) _____ vascular bundle

61) _____ fungus
62) _____ trichomes
63) _____ fern prothallus
64) _____ chloroplast
65) _____ male cone

We learned quite a few Latin word roots in this curriculum. How many can you remember?

66) light _____

67) greenish-yellow _____

68) container/vessel _____

69) naked _____

70) to make _____

71) joined together _____

72) side _____

73) tip _____

74) flat, or blade _____

75) tree _____

76) time _____

77) middle _____

78) one _____

79) two _____

80) outside or outer _____

81) skin _____

82) moss _____

83) leaf _____

84) seed _____

85) yellow _____

Here are the Latin words you can use:

angio	apex	bryo
chloro	chrono	dendro
dermis	di	epi
gymno	lamina	lateral
meso	mono	photo
phyll	sperm	synth
xantho	zygotos	

Can you match each tree to its scientific name?

white oak   sugar maple   plum tree

bristlecone pine   weeping willow

86) *Acer saccharum* _____

88) *Pinus longaeva* _____

90) *Prunus domesticus* _____

87) *Salix babylonica* _____

89) *Quercus alba* _____

(Notice how scientific names are always in italics.)

Can you fill in these word pairs?

91/92) The first division of the plant kingdom is _____ versus ___-_____.

93/94) Angiosperms are divided into two groups: _____ and _____.

95/96) The two major parts of an angiosperm seed are the e_____ and the e_____.

97/98) Seagrass leaves have neither c_____ nor s_____.

99/100) The two main types of vascular tissue are _____ and _____.

FINAL REVIEW   (Level 2)

Match each organelle to its function.

A) cytoplasm   D) Golgi bodies   G) ribosomes
B) cytoskeleton   E) chloroplasts   H) endoplasmic reticulum
C) nucleus   F) leucoplasts   I) vacuole
                                                            J) mitochondria

101) _____ The "center" of the cell. It contains DNA.

102) _____ A network of fibers that helps the cell to maintain its shape and serves as a "road system."

103) _____ The cell's "post office." It labels products and sends them where they need to go.

104) _____ The "powerhouses" of the cell. They generate energy in the form of ATPs.

105) _____ These are like storage tanks.

106) _____ These are like little factory workers, assembling proteins.

107) _____ This is where light energy is captured and turned into chemical energy.

108) _____ This is like an empty bubble.

109) _____ This is the fluid that fills the cells.

110) _____ This has many jobs. It manufactures proteins and lipids, helps the cell to maintain its shape, and helps to transport things around the cell. Some parts of it are covered with ribosomes.

111) What pops off ATP and releases energy?
a) an electron   b) a proton   c) a phosphate   d) an adenosine   e) an oxygen molecule

112) What does Rubisco do?
a) takes carbon dioxide out of the air   b) takes oxygen out of the air   c) makes PGALs

113) What changes ADP back into ATP?
a) nothing   b) high-energy electrons   c) photons   d) ATP synthase

114) How many carbon atoms are in a glucose molecule?   a) 1   b) 3   c) 4   d) 6   e) 8

115) Which one of these is NOT necessary for the light-dependent part of photosynthesis?
a) oxygen   b) carbon dioxide   c) water   d) electrons   e) protons

116) Which one of these is NOT necessary for the light-independent part of photosynthesis?
a) carbon dioxide   b) ATP   c) NADPH   d) photons

117) Which one of these is NOT produced by the light-dependent phase of photosynthesis?
a) oxygen   b) carbon dioxide   c) ATP   d) NADPH

118) Which one of these is NOT a simple fruit?
a) watermelon   b) squash   c) apple   d) cherry   e) strawberry

119) Which of the following does NOT transport seeds from one place to another?
a) animals   b) birds   c) humans   d) wind   e) water   f) rocks

120) What type of parasite is the Rafflesia plant?
a) hyperparasite   b) hemi-parasite   c) obligate parasite

TRUE or FALSE?

121) _____ The human digestive tract is very good at breaking apart plant cells.

122) _____ The inside of the thylakoid is called the lumen.

123) _____ Light is necessary for the Calvin Cycle.

124) _____ A plant's ability to respond to an aspect of its environment is called a tropism.

125) _____ Light stimulates plant cells to produce auxin.

126) _____ Spores do not contain embryos, therefore they can survive a lot longer.

127) _____ Spores are larger than seeds.

128) _____ All plants form nitrogen-fixing nodules on their roots.

129) _____ Pathogens can be used to control other pathogens.

130) _____ Mites belong to the spider family, therefore they are carnivorous and don't eat plants.

131) _____ Anthocyanin is poisonous.

132) _____ Acorns, peanuts and dandelion seeds are actually fruits.

133) _____ Planting marigolds will help to control root nematodes.

134) _____ Planting roses will help to discourage aphids.

135) _____ The Gypsy moth was brought to America intentionally.

Fill in the blanks.

136/137) Spores are produced for qu_____, seeds are for qu_____.

138) If it's not herbaceous, it's w_____.

139) If it's not gametophyte, it's s_____.

140) If it can't live on its own, it's a p_____.

Where would you be most likely to find these pests?

141) _____ Gypsy moths   A) raspberry leaves
142) _____ Aphids   B) tomato stems
143) _____ Weevils   C) oak trees
144) _____ "Cabbage whites" (butterflies)   D) broccoli plants
145) _____ Japanese beetles   E) cotton plants

146) This plant has the fastest trap mechanism in the world. _____   A) *Atropa belladonna*
147) This plant is poisonous. _____   B) bladderwort
148) This plant does not have leaves. _____   C) pitcher plant
149) This plant is a parasite on trees. _____   D) *Rafflesia*
150) This plant is carnivorous but has no spring mechanisms. _____   E) mistletoe

ANSWER KEY FOR FINAL REVIEW / TEST

Level 1: 1) B   2) A   3) D   4) C   5) B   6) A   7) B   8) D   9) D   10) A   11) D   12) B   13) E   14) C   15) A

16) C   17) H   18) E   19) F   20) A   21) B   22) J   23) D   24) I   25) G

26) T   27) F   28) T   29) T   30) T   31) T   32) F   33) T   34) T   35) F

36) photosynthesis   37) tobacco   38) duckweed   39) guard   40) gall

41) D   42) A   43) H   44) E   45) I   46) G   47) F   48) J   49) B   50) C

51) C   52) F   53) K   54) A   55) N   56) D   57) D   58) H   59) L   60) E   61) M   62) O   63) I   64) B   65) J

66) photo   67) chloro   68) angio   69) gymno   70) synth   71) zygotos   72) lateral

73) apex   74) lamina   75) dendro   76) chrono   77) meso   78) mono   79) di   80) epi

81) dermis   82) bryo   83) phyll   84) sperm   85) xantho

86) sugar maple   87) weeping willow   88) bristlecone pine   89) white oak   90) plum tree

91-92) vascular, non-vascular   93-94) monocots, dicots   95-96) embryo, endosperm

97-98) cuticle, stomata   99-100) xylem, phloem

Level 2:   101) C   102) B   103) D   104) J   105) F   106) G   107) E   108) I   109) A   110) H

111) C   112) A   113) D   114) D   115) B   116) D   117) B   118) E   119) F   120) C

121) F   122) T   123) F   124) T   125) F   126) T   127) F   128) F   129) T   130) F

131) F   132) T   133) T   134) F   135) T

136) quantity   137) quality   138) woody   139) sporophyte   140) parasite

141) C   142) B   143) E   144) D   145) A

46) B   147) A   148) D   149) E   150) C

BIBLIOGRAPHY

I've listed the books in the order of how much I used them, not in alphabetical order.

Biology of the Cell (Fourth Edition) by Sylvia S. Mader. Published by Wm. C. Brown Publishers, © 1993. ISBN 0-697-20857-5.

Biology (Tenth Edition) by Sylvia S. Mader. Published by McGraw Hill Higher Education, © 2010. ISBN 978-0-07-352543-3

What's Wrong With My Plant (And How Do I Fix It?) by David Deardorff and Kathryn Wadsworth. Published by Timber Press in Portland and London, © 2009. ISBN 978-0-88192-961-4

Science Explorer: From Bacteria to Plants, (a science text for grade 7), published by Prentice Hall, © 2005 by Pearson Education, Boston. ISBN 978-0-558-65259-3

How Did We Find Out About Photosynthesis? by Isaac Asimov. Published by Walker and Company, New York, © 1989. ISBN 0-8027-6886-5.

Botany for All Ages by Jorie Hunken. Published by Globe Pequot Press, © 1993. ISBN 978-1564402813

100 Flowers and How They Got Their Names, by Diana Wells. Published by Algonquin Books of Chapel Hill, © 1997. ISBN 1-56512-138-4

Ferns: Plants Without Flowers, by Bernice Kohn. Published by Hawthorn Books, Inc., New York. © 1968.

Seeds and Fruits, by Holding B. van Dobbenburgh. Published by Smithmark Publishers, New York, © 1995. ISBN 0-8317-6122-9

Looking at Plants by David Suzuki. Published by John Wiley & Sons, © 1991. ISBN 0-471-54049-8

Here are some websites I used, in addition to the books. (The site addresses are written in Times New Roman font to avoid confusion between 1's and l's.)

General info:

Wikipedia.com (many articles)

       I will not list all the Wikipedia articles I consulted, as there were probably hundreds of them. I have found Wikipedia to be very accurate when compared to other web resources, including ".edu" sites. (In fact, it seems that some sites now copy and paste the Wiki articles. I kept running into the exact same paragraphs on many different sites.) Far from being unscholarly, Wiki articles are now so scholarly they are sometimes hard to read if you don't already know a lot of technical terms. I had to click on a lot of linked articles to find definitions.

Mosses:

http://umanitoba.ca/Biology/BIOL1030/Lab7/biolab7_2.html

Mosses, Ferns, cross sections:

http://people.bethel.edu/~johgre/bio114d/lowervasculars.html

Ferns:

http://www.deanza.edu/faculty/mccauley/6a-labs-plants-02.htm
http://www.bbg.org/gardening/article/growing_ferns_from_spores
http://universe-review.ca/R10-34-anatomy2.htm#ferns

Stem cross section, including fern:
http://sols.unlv.edu/Schulte/Anatomy/Stems/Stems.html

List of monocots:
http://www.plantbiology.siu.edu/Greenhouse/MonocotList.html

Gymnosperms:
http://hcs.osu.edu/hcs300/gymno.htm
http://web.gccaz.edu/~lsola/NonFlwr/conif105.htm

Gymnosperms and angiosperms:
http://faculty.clintoncc.suny.edu/faculty/michael.gregory/files/bio%20102/bio%20102%20lectures/seed%20plants/seed%20plants.htm

Flower structure:
http://www.differencebetween.com/difference-between-carpel-and-vs-pistil/
http://www.culturaapicola.com.ar/apuntes/libros/Polinizacion/flower.html
http://www.botany.uwc.ac.za/ecotree/flowers/flowerparts2.htm
http://www.finegardening.com/how-to/qa/hollies-fruit.aspx
http://www.whatcom.wsu.edu/ag/homehort/plat/viburnum2.html

Fruits:
http://scidiv.bellevuecollege.edu/rkr/biology213/assignments/pdfs/FruitLabKey.pdf
http://chemistry.about.com/od/chemistryexperiments/ss/ethyleneexp.htm
http://www.catalyticgenerators.com/whatisethylene.html

Pollination:
http://plantphys.info/plants_human/pollenemb.shtml

Flower dissection:
http://www.fs.fed.us/wildflowers/teacher/documents/k5_DesertGardeners_flowerDissection.pdf
http://www.fairchildgarden.org/uploads/docs/Education/Downloadable_teaching_modules/flower%20power/Flower%20Dissection%20LabII.pdf
http://www.cbsd.org/sites/teachers/hs/jucollins/Lists/Advanced%20Science%20Calendar/Attachments/240/flower_dissection.pdf

Seed dispersal:
http://www.theseedsite.co.uk

Plant adaptionas:
http://www.mbgnet.net/bioplants/adapt.html
http://www.countrysideinfo.co.uk/wetland_survey/adaptns.htm
http://www.dep.state.fl.us/coastal/habitats/seagrass/
http://www.seagrasswatch.org/seagrass.html
http://reefkeeping.com/issues/2006-10/rhf/index.php

World Record plants:

http://waynesword.palomar.edu/ww0601.htm
http://www.adventureandscience.org/high-plants.html

Poisonous plants:

http://aggie-horticulture.tamu.edu/earthkind/landscape/poisonous-plants-resources/common-poisonous-plants-and-plant-parts/
http://www.poisoncontrol.org/plants.html
http://cal.vet.upenn.edu/projects/poison/common.htm
http://webecoist.momtastic.com/2008/09/16/16-most-unassuming-yet-lethal-killer-plants/
http://www.terrapermadesign.com/wp-content/userfiles/Trees-with-Edible-Leaves.html
http://artofmanliness.com/2010/10/06/surviving-in-the-wild-19-common-edible-plants/
http://www.rawfoodsupport.com/read.php?4,24008
http://www.rosefloral.com/blog/poisonous-plants
http://alloveralbany.com/archive/2008/05/09/tulips-really-are-edible-sort-of
http://www.chop.edu/service/poison-control-center/resources-for-families/berries-and-seeds.html

Plant Diseases:

http://www.hickorytech.net/~flapper/thistlecontrol.html
http://www.buzzle.com/articles/plant-diseases-caused-by-fungi.html
http://dspace.jorum.ac.uk/xmlui/bitstream/handle/123456789/937/Items/S250_1_section3.html?sequence=4
http://www.fs.fed.us/ne/morgantown/4557/gmoth/
http://utahpests.usu.edu/htm/utah-pests-news/up-summer12-newsletter/root-knot-nematodes/

Photosynthesis videos I watched:

http://www.youtube.com/watch?v=ixpNw6mx3lk&feature=related
http://www.youtube.com/watch?v=m8v7prlscM0&feature=related (Brightstorm.com)
http://www.youtube.com/watch?v=2IygaV0_-B0&feature=relmfu (Brightstorm.com)
http://www.youtube.com/watch?v=hj_WKgnL6MI (N. Dakota State Univ., Virtual Cell series)
http://www.youtube.com/watch?v=3UfV060N27g&feature=channel&list=UL (N. Dakota State Univ.)
http://www.youtube.com/watch?v=-rsYk4eCKnA&feature=relmfu (Khan Academy)
http://www.youtube.com/watch?v=o1I33Dgcc_M&feature=related
http://www.youtube.com/watch?v=uwOCkEf37Lc&NR=1&feature=endscreen (Univ. of Kent)

LAPBOOK PATTERNS

NOTE: If you would like to print out these pattern pages instead of photocopying them out of the book, you can download the PDF files for the images by going to www.ellenjmchenry.com. Click on FREE DOWNLOADS, then on PLANTS, then on "Printable pages for *Botany in 8 Lessons*." After downloading this file, you can print the pages using your computer printer or you can ask a print shop to print them for you.

COVER DESIGNS for your lapbook are avaialable as part of the digital download "Printable pages for *Botany in 8 Lessons*" at www.ellenjmchenry.com. (Click on FREE DOWNLOADS, then on PLANTS.)

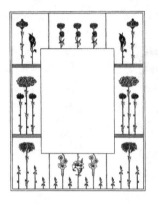    

NOTE: Don't limit yourself to the project ideas presented here. Be sure to add some of your own creations, as well!

GENERAL INSTRUCTIONS FOR LAPBOOK

These lapbook patterns are "modular" in design. Each project fits into either one half of a page or one quarter of a page. This makes it easy to mix and match (and to add your own ideas, too). You don't have to spend much time planning the overall design of the book. You already know everything will fit. A bit predictable, yes, but very easy. A few possible arrangements are shown here.

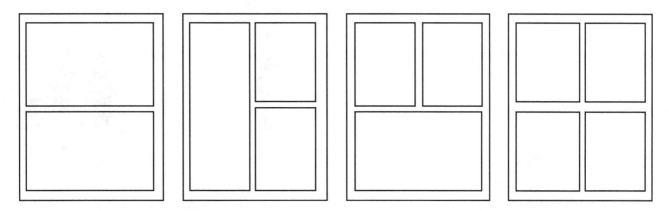

It's up to you how to make the blank lapbook. You can use cardboard, poster board, card stock (very heavy paper), file folders, or anything else you have on hand. It's also up to you to decide how complex to make it. You can do just two pages that open up like book, you can make a tri-fold, or you can do something fancy with flaps that fold in from the top and bottom. You can make it all one piece or you can use individual panels with taped seams.

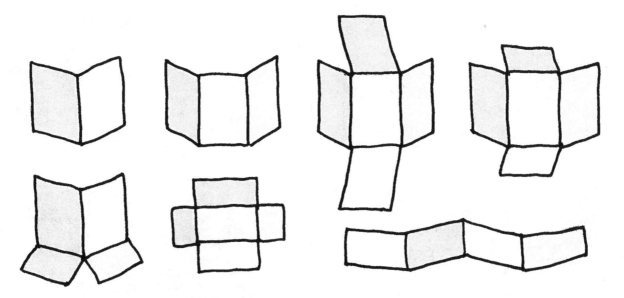

NOTE: In the patterns that follow, the outside dimensions are slightly smaller than a half-page or a quarter-page, so that there is a bit of "breathing room," so to speak, between the projects. The projects should not touch each other when they are glued into place. You might want to keep this in mind if you decide to add your own projects.

THE WORLD'S MOST AMAZING PLANTS

TALLEST TREE	**OLDEST TREE**
LARGEST SEED	**SMALLEST SEED**
FASTEST GROWING PLANT	**SMALLEST ANGIOSPERM**
MOST POISONOUS PLANT	**LARGEST FRUIT**
LARGEST LEAF	**PLANT FOUND AT HIGHEST ELEVATION**

"Hyperion," a redwood in California, 379 ft tall (115.5 m).

"Methuselah," a bristlecone pine in California, 6000 years old.

"Coco de Mer," which grows in the Seychelles Islands

Seeds of the orchid family, which are as long as a hair is wide.

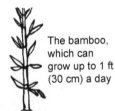

The bamboo, which can grow up to 1 ft (30 cm) a day

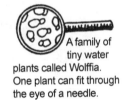

A family of tiny water plants called Wolffia. One plant can fit through the eye of a needle.

The castor bean, estimated to be 6000 times more poisonous than cyanide.

The pumpkin, with a world record of 1818 lbs (825 kg).

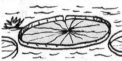

The Amazon water lily. One lily pad can reach 8 ft (2.5 m) in diameter.

A species of moss grows on Mt. Everest at an elevation of 6480 meters.

LAPBOOK IDEA #1: "RECORD-HOLDING" PLANTS

You will need:
- Copy of this pattern page (card stock or regular paper)
- Glue stick
- Scissors
- X-acto knife or razor blade to cut flaps
- Optional: colored pencils

How to assemble:

1) Cut out both long rectangles.

2) Cut the flaps using a sharp knife or razor blade.

3) Apply glue stick very carefully to the back of the flap page, making sure you don't get any glue on the backs of the flaps. Stick the flap page onto the picture page. (Add color if you wish.)

    Option: Print two copies of the page, one on colored paper (I recommend a pastel color) and one on white. Use the colored flap rectangle and the white picture rectangle. The colored flaps will contrast nicely with white pictures underneath.

Alternative method of assembly:

    If cutting (or pre-cutting) the flaps with a sharp knife is not an option for you, just cut out the flaps from the flap page, leaving some extra space at the top of each flap. Paste the flaps (with glue on just the top edges!) over the correct pictures on the picture page. Cut out the title and transfer it to the top of the picture page. The flaps won't stay flat quite as well using this method, but this is a minor problem considering that it would possibly will allow the project to be done entirely by the student(s).

LAPBOOK IDEA #2:
DESIGN A FLOWER STAMP

You will need:
- A copy of this pattern (or make your own if you would rather have a more square shape)
- Art supplies
- Optional: images of real flower stamps (many are available online using Google search)

    Flowers are a very popular theme for stamps. If possible, look at some real stamps that feature flowers. Then choose your favorite flower and make it into a stamp. Don't forget to include in your design the name of the country (doesn't have to be your country!) and the number of cents the stamp is worth.

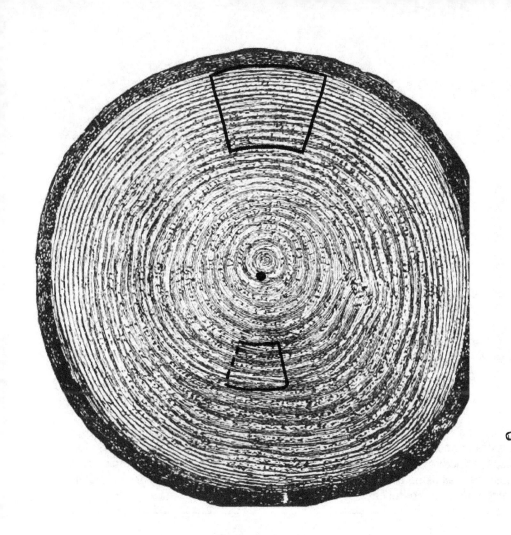

TREE
TRUNK
TRIVIA

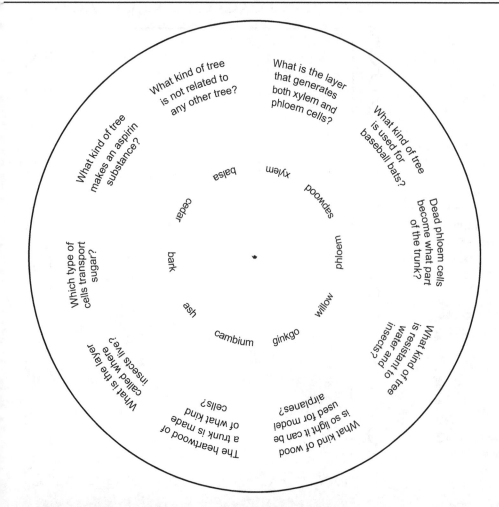

What is the layer that generates both xylem and phloem cells?

What kind of tree is not related to any other tree?

What kind of tree makes an aspirin substance?

What kind of tree is used for baseball bats?

Dead phloem cells become what part of the trunk?

Which type of cells transport sugar?

balsa
xylem
cedar
sapwood
bark
phloem
ash
willow
cambium
ginkgo

What kind of tree is resistant to water and insects?

What is the layer called where insects live?

The heartwood of a trunk is made of what kind of cells?

What kind of wood is so light it can be used for model airplanes?

LAPBOOK IDEA #3: "TREE TRUNK TRIVIA" WHEEL

You will need:
- Copy of this pattern page on card stock (or regular paper if you can't get card stock)
- Scissors
- X-acto knife or razor blade to cut flaps
- Paper fastener

How to assemble:

1) Cut the page in half across the middle line and cut out the wheel.

2) Use the sharp knife or razor to cut out the question window, to make the answer flap, and to cut along the flat side on the trunk section.

3) Punch a small hole in the two center dots (middle of wheel and middle of trunk). Put the wheel behind the trunk page, match up the centers and secure with a paper fastener. Slip the edge of the wheel through the slit on the side of the trunk.

This window should be cut out completely.

Cut a slit along this edge.

Wheel will stick out here.

This window should be cut as a flap that can open and close.

Remember, you can download printable digital patterns for all these projects at www.ellenjmchenry.com.
Click on FREE DOWNLOADS, then on PLANTS, then on "Printable pages for *Botany in 8 Lessons.*"

LAPBOOK IDEA #4: ENVELOPES FOR VARIOUS COLLECTIONS

Here is a pattern for a large envelope that can be used to store things you have collected during the unit—pressed flowers or leaves, pictures of plants, drawings, magazine clippings, etc. There is a pattern for a small envelope on the next page.

You will need:
- Copy of this pattern page printed onto card stock (or regular paper can be used)
- Glue stick or white glue (use white glue very sparingly!)
- Scissors, and an X-acto blade or razor blade

How to assemble:
Print the pattern page onto the paper you would like to make into an envelope. You can even use a fancy printed piece of paper (the type of paper used for scrapbooking). The back side of the pattern will be the outside of your envelope, so if your paper has a top side and a reverse side, make sure this pattern gets printed onto the reverse side.

Cut on the solid line and fold on the dotted lines. Cut the slot line at the bottom with an X-acto blade or a razor blade.

TIP: If you are working with heavy paper, scoring on the dotted lines will make them much easier to fold. To score the paper, lay a ruler along the line and run either the scissor blade or the X-acto blade VERY LIGHTLY along the line, just enough to scratch the paper but not cut it.

Fold the envelope along the middle line, then fold the edges around to the back and glue them in place. If you are using liquid glue, don't use too much. No leaking or seeping! If you are using a glue stick, use plenty.

Fold the top flap over to the front. The half-circle should tuck into the slot.

You can decorate or label the envelope in whatever way is appropriate for the contents.

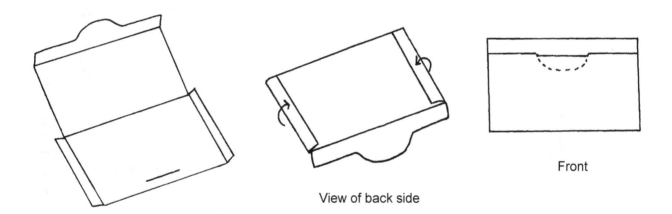

View of back side   Front

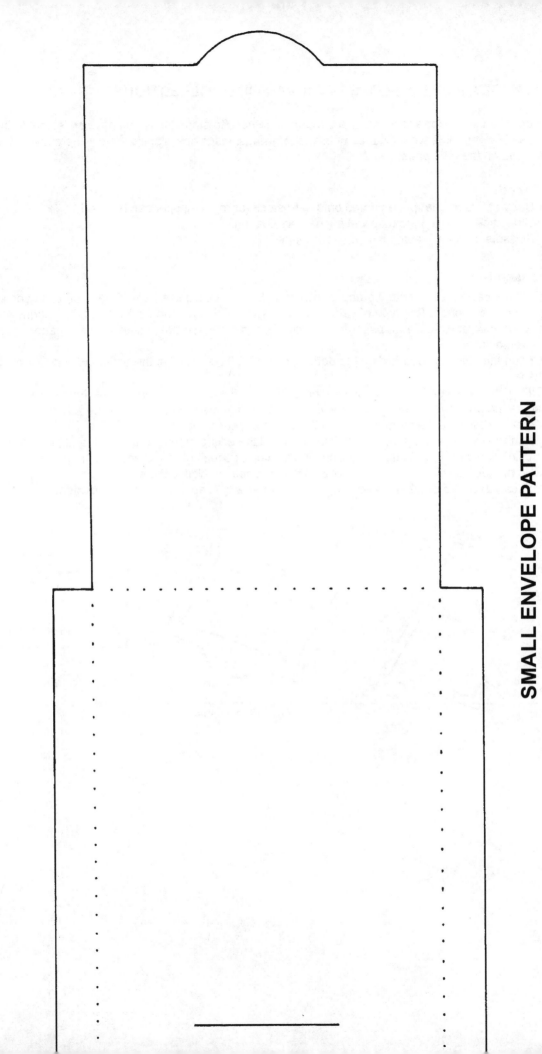

SMALL ENVELOPE PATTERN

This assembles in the same way the large envelope does. You can use the instructions for the large envelope.

LAPBOOK IDEA #5: PORTRAITS OF MONOCOT AND DICOT SEEDLINGS

You will need:
- • Copies of these frame patterns (or make your own pattern)
- • Seedlings to observe
- • Pencil, or colored pencils

What to do:

Sketch two portraits: a monocot seedling and a dicot seedling. Make sure the cotyledons (seed leaves) can be seen. If the seedlings are growing in dirt, take them out of the dirt and rinse them off so you can see all of the roots. Work carefully to make the drawings as accurate as possible. The drawings can be left as pencil sketches, or can be traced over with a fine tip ink pen.

Don't forget to write either MONOCOT or DICOT in the white spaces at the bottom of the frames.

You can cut out the frames and use them separately, or you can leave them together as a half page. You can also make two copies of this page and use the same pattern twice, for both the monocot and dicot.

Option: If you need to save space in your lapbook, you can draw both seedlings in one frame (assuming that both of them are tall and thin).

LAPBOOK IDEA #6: PHOTOSYNTHESIS REVIEW LEAF (WITH PULL-OUT TABS)

You will need:
- Copy of the pattern page (on card stock, if possible)
- Scissors and a craft knife or razor blade
- Optional: colored pencils

How to assemble:

1) If you want to add color, do this first.
2) DON'T cut out the leaf. Cut out the rectangle around the leaf.
3) Use a sharp craft knife or razor blade to cut the six slits in the sides of the leaf (the thin lines with hash marks on either end).
4) Cut out the six tabs.
5) Insert the tabs into the slits. You will have to fold the ends of the tabs temporarily to get them through the slit. After the tab is inserted, unfold it.

6) When you glue this into your lapbook, be very careful not to get glue near the flaps. Apply glue only around the edges.

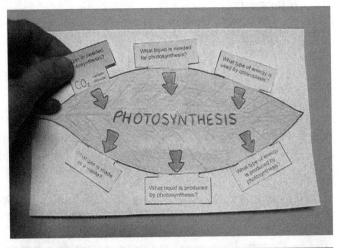

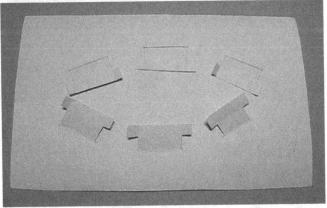

This is how the tabs look on the back.

LAPBOOK IDEA #7: PERSONALIZE YOUR LAPBOOK WITH PHOTOGRAPHS

You will need:
- Photos you've taken while doing this unit study

What to do:
Personalize the lapbook with some photos you've taken while doing various botany activities. They could be photos taken while playing games, doing the scavenger hunt, setting up experiments, going on a field trip, or doing outside gardening. Bear in mind your format when sizing and trimming the pictures. Photos are usually oblong in the horizontal direction and your lapbook may have empty spaces that are oblong in the vertical direction. One solution would be to scale down the photos and put two of them onto quarter page space. If you have a lot of photos, you could make a little booklet. However you do it, photos scattered throughout will make the lapbook into a more cherished item as the years go by, as it will contain sentimental childhood photos. (If you really don't want to create something that will become a "sacred" item that can't be disposed of, skip this idea and don't include any photos.)

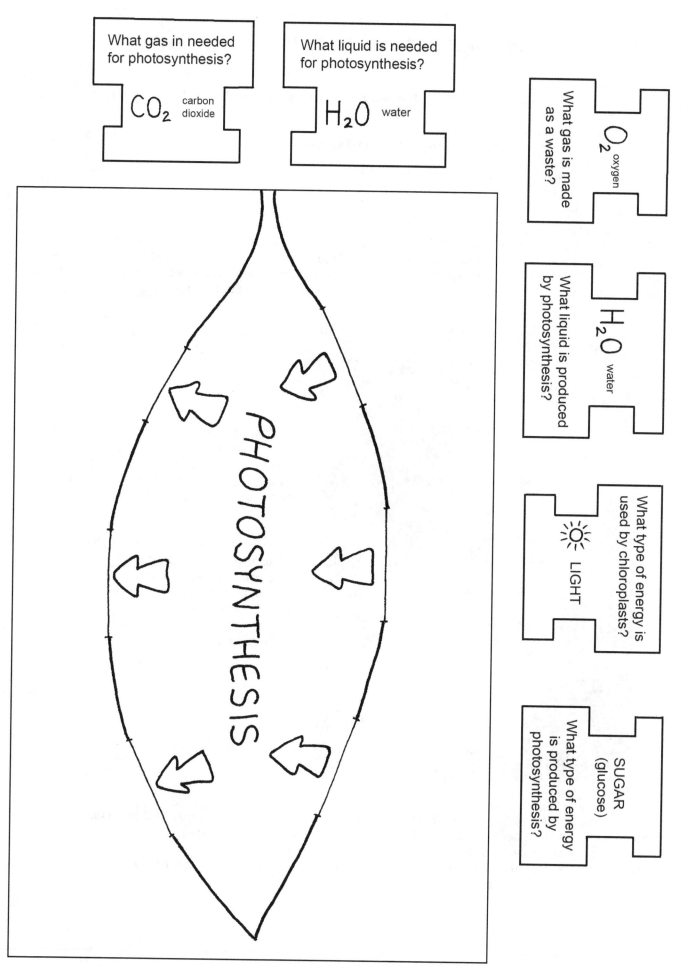

What gas in needed for photosynthesis?

CO_2 carbon dioxide

What liquid is needed for photosynthesis?

H_2O water

What gas is made as a waste?

O_2 oxygen

What liquid is produced by photosynthesis?

H_2O water

What type of energy is used by chloroplasts?

LIGHT

What type of energy is produced by photosynthesis?

SUGAR (glucose)

PHOTOSYNTHESIS

205

LAPBOOK IDEA #8: POP-UP LEAF CROSS SECTION

You will need:
- A copy of this pattern page printed onto card stock (or regular paper if card stock is unavailable)
- Scissors
- Glue stick (or white glue)
- Green marker or colored pencil (or piece of green paper)
- Pencil and ink pen
- Optional: colored pencils

How to assemble:

1) Cut out the two rectangles.

2) Do all coloring and labeling before any folding or gluing. The rectangle right under "FLAP A" should be colored green. This rectangle will represent the top side of the leaf. If you don't want to use marker or colored pencil, you could also cut out a piece of green paper this size and glue it on. If you'd like to add one extra touch of realism, you can sketch light outlines of where cells can be seen through the cuticle.

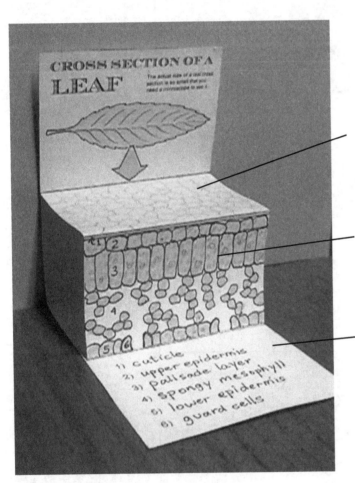

3) Color the top light green. You can lightly sketch in cell shapes (seen through the cuticle) or you can leave it plain green. (Another option is to cut a piece of light green paper this size and glue it on.)

4) Draw these layers using the little dots as guidelines for where to begin and end each layer. These cells can be colored or they can have green chloroplasts drawn inside of them.

5) Write the names of each layer.

6) Fold the background rectangle in half. Make fold lines where indicated on the cross section rectangle. Notice that the thin cross section of the cuticle appears on the front side of the pop-up.

7) Glue the flaps as indicated, so that they are on the inside of the pop-up (not visible). Before the glue dries completely, fold the pop-up in half and make sure it will close properly. Adjust the flaps if it does not. (Or, adjust the fold line on the corner that sticks out.)

FLAP A

. . . .

FOLD LINE

1
2

3

4

5 6

FLAP B

CROSS SECTION OF A
LEAF

The actual size of a real cross
section is so small that you
need a microscope to see it.

GLUE FLAP "A" HERE

. . . .

GLUE FLAP "B" HERE

1)

2)

3)

4)

5)

6)

LAPBOOK IDEA #9: LEAF ID WRAP-UP

You will need:
- A copy of this pattern page
- Scissors and glue stick
- A piece of thin string or thread that is about 6 ft (2 meters) long
- A piece of thin cardboard (an old cereal box is ideal)

How to assemble:
1) Cut out the rectangular pattern with the leaves printed on it. The blank pattern is an extra in case you get really inspired by this activity and want to make another one with your own pictures on it.
2) Fold the paper in half and cut a piece of thin cardboard that will fit perfectly inside this folded paper. Glue the cardboard inside using a glue stick. (Glue stick is recommended so that the paper does not wrinkle.)
3) Cut the notches on the sides.
4) Punch the hole next to the word "lobed." Put one end of the string through this hole and tie securely.

How it works:
     Start with the word "lobed." Find the picture that you think matches this word and pull the string so that it goes through the notch next to that picture. Wind the string around the back and then up through the notch next to the word "linear." Now take the string over to the notch that is next to the picture that you think goes with the word "linear." Then make the string go around the back again and then into the notch that says "pinnate." Continue like this until you have the string wrapped around the card nine times. The last wrap should leave the string on the back side of the card, but ending right behind the word END. Pinch that corner so the string stays in place, then turn the card over. If you guessed correctly, all of your strings will match up with the lines on the back of the card. If you see some lines that don't match your strings, unwind the string and try again.
     (If you find that your string is too long, trim it to the right length.)

Storage in the lapbook:
     Print this "envelope" pattern (preferably onto heavy paper) and then cut and assemble it as shown. It will fit exactly on one quarter of a page in your lapbook. Put the "leaf wrap" into the pocket. During storage, the string can be wound around the card so that the strings do not overlap very much, thus avoiding a big lump.

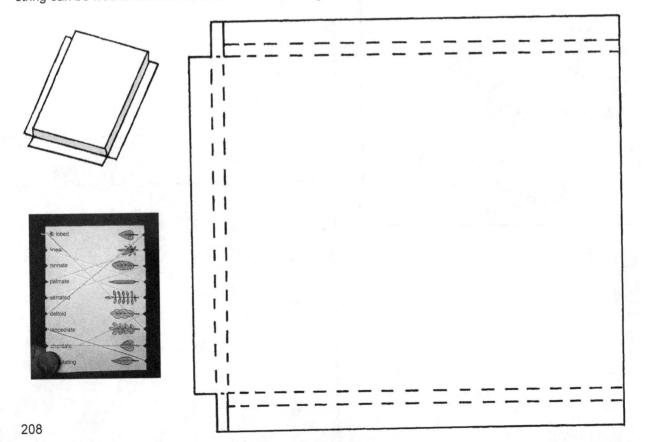

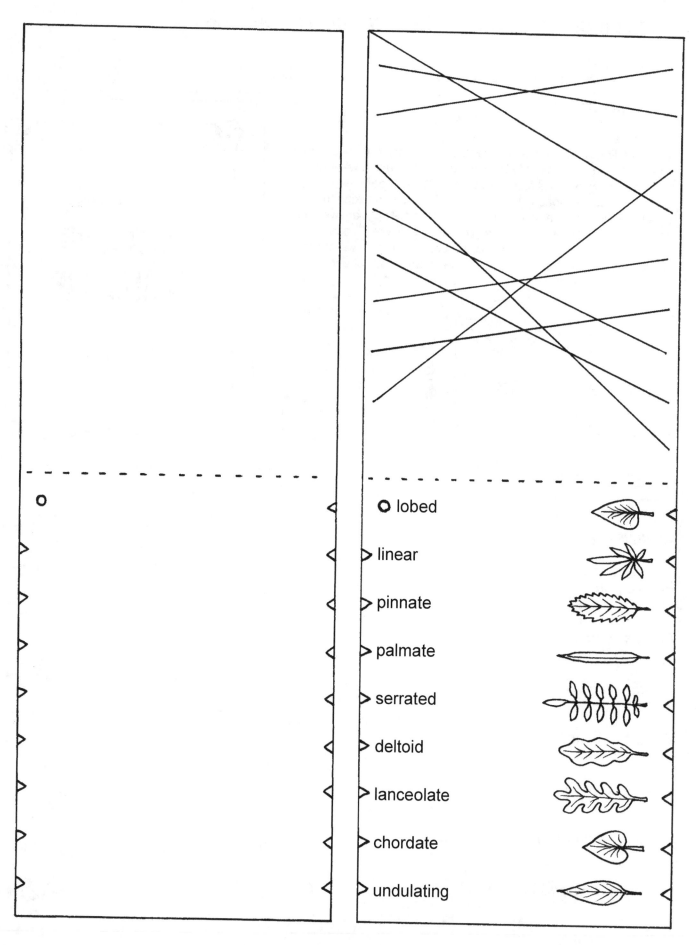

○ lobed

linear

pinnate

palmate

serrated

deltoid

lanceolate

chordate

undulating

LAPBOOK IDEA #10: *GENUS SPECIES* MATCHING CHALLENGE

You will need:
> • A copy of this pattern page, scissors, glue stick, pen or pencil

How to assemble:

Cut out the rectangle below. Make squiggly lines between the names on the left and the correct answers on the right. You can make the lines go however you want, but don't make them so complicated that you can't manage to follow them. You might want to make the lines lightly in pencil first, then go over them in pen.

When it is done it will be a quiz. The person taking the quiz puts his finger on a name on the left, guesses the right answer, then traces the squiggly line all the way over to see where it ends up.

You can paste this into the lapbook as an open half page, or you can fold it in half so that it only takes up a quarter page. You can use this cover design or make one of your own.

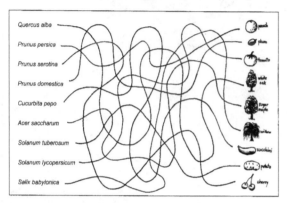

Sample showing what to do. Your lines can be very different from these, but you get the idea.

Genus species

MATCHING CHALLENGE

WARNING: Latin inside!

Quercus alba

Prunus persica

Prunus serotina

Prunus domestica

Cucurbita pepo

Acer saccharum

Solanum tuberosum

Solanum lycopersicum

Salix babylonica

peach

plum

tomato

white oak

sugar maple

willow

zucchini

potato

cherry

LAPBOOK IDEA #11: "SECRET LIFE" DIAGRAM OF THE INSIDE OF A FLOWER

You will need:
- A copy of this pattern page
- Scissors
- Pencils, pen, colored pencils
- Glue stick

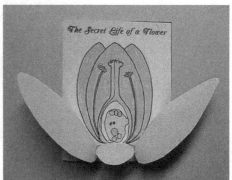

How to assemble:

1) Cut out the rectangle below and draw an ovule inside the ovary. Include the six female cells and the polar nuclei. Draw the stamens next to the pistil. If you wish, you may also add color to the petals. Just make sure the color does not obscure any color and/or labeling you did on the pistil and stamens.
2) Optional: Add pollen grains and a pollen tube.
3) Cut out the piece with the sepals. Color this piece green.
4) Put glue on the back of the sepals and stick under the pistil so that the oval flap covers the bottom of the pistil. You will be able to fold back this oval flap to reveal the ovule underneath.
5) Cut out the large petals and color them if you wish. Place them over the base picture so that you have a left and right petal flap. The petals will overlap quite a bit. Put glue on the back of the flaps and secure in place.

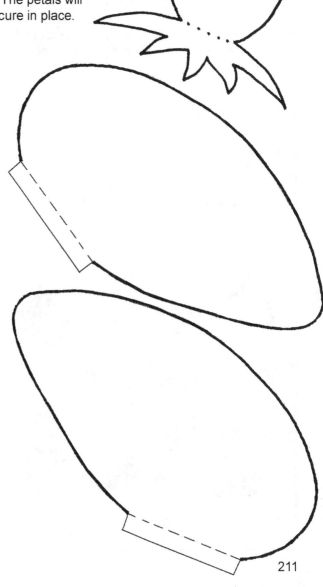

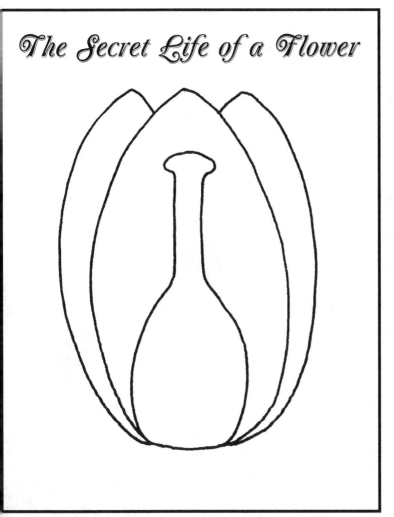

The Secret Life of a Flower

LAPBOOK IDEA #12: SKETCHBOOK OF FRUITS

Can you think of a more classic subject to paint or draw than fruit? Most artists draw fruit, or bowls of fruit, at some ponit in their career. In this activity, the students will keep a fruit sketchbook, but they will be allowed to include any kind of botanical fruit. Remember, botanical fruits include nuts, many "vegetables," and seeds from flowers and weeds. Maple tree "helicopters" and those fluffy white dandelion seeds are also fruits. If it's got a seed, it's a fruit.

You will need:
- Two copies of the blank page pattern (or make your own pages by cutting paper in half, folding, stapling, then trimming it to size
- Scissors
- Pencils, pen, colored pencils
- Fruits, or pictures of fruits (remember to include nuts, seeds, and vegetables that are botanical fruits)
- Optional: copy of the image below as a cover design (or make your own!)

How to assemble:
Make copies of the this pattern page. Or, as stated above, just cut pieces of paper in half, then fold, stack, and staple them. This pattern will give you a booklet that is a little bit smaller than a quarter page, so that when you glue the booklet into your lapbook, the sketchbook doesn't bump into the other projects in the book. If you make a booklet simply by folding pieces of paper, consider whether you want to trim down the final size a bit, or leave it as a full quarter page. You can make the sketchbook as thin or thick as you like, depending on how much sketching you want to do.

Sketch lots of fruits. Look at real fruits whenever possible, but you could also use images from books or the Internet, especially for fruits from other parts of the world. Make sure to observe and draw shadows and highlights, as these are what make objects look three-dimensional.

SKETCHING HELP:

If you would find it helpful to watch some "how to" drawing videos, there are some videos posted at the bottom of the Botany playlist.

LAPBOOK IDEA #13: DRAW A CELL

You will need:
- A copy of the cell outline below (or make your own)
- Scissors
- Pencil and pen, colored pencils if you wish

What to draw:

1) The large empty blob is the cell's vacuole. Label it.

2) The large circle (with the endoplasmic reticulum attached to it) is the nucleus of the cell. Draw some DNA inside of it. You can draw DNA as a mass of squiggly lines. Label the nucleus.

3) Add some more endoplasmic reticulum to the other side of the nucleus. Choose one side of the ER to be the smooth ER and the other side to be the rough ER. On the rough ER, add some little dots all along the sides of the squiggles. These will represent ribosomes. Label the smooth and rough ER. (The ribosomes sticking to the ER makes the ER look "rough" when viewed under a microscope, thus the name. There isn't anything actually rough about the rough ER.)

4) The cell needs more chloroplasts. The chloroplast is the organelle with the thylakoid "pancake" stacks inside of it. Label the chloroplast, then draw at least six more. You can draw more than six, but leave space for some other organelles. Put at least a few thylakoid stacks in each one. (The chlorophyll molecules are too small to see at this scale.)

5) Now add some Golgi bodies. That's the organelle that looks like a stack of pancakes but is not inside the chloroplast. (Don't forget to label one of them.) The Golgi body is like the post office of the cell, packaging and labeling things that need to be delivered various places. You only need to add one or two more Golgi bodies.

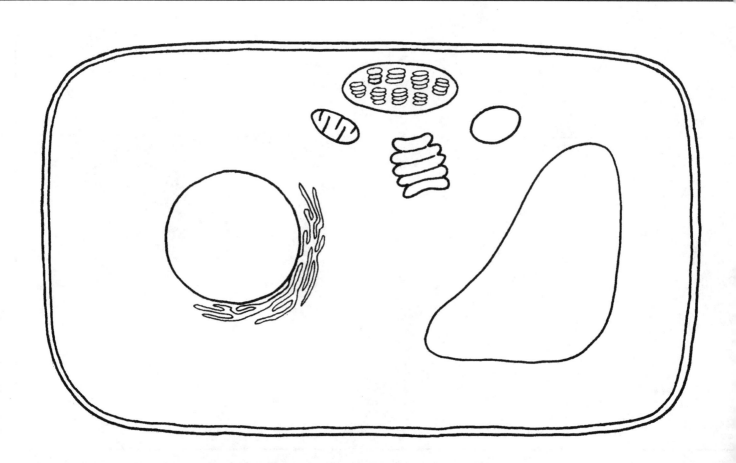

6) Draw some more mitochondria. The mitochondrion is the oval with half-lines across it. The mitochondria really do look a bit like this when viewed under the microscope. The half-lines represent the internal structure. Remember, the mitochondria are where the ATP synthase generators are located. However, at this scale, the ATP synthases are invisible. Don't forget to label one of your mitochondria.

7) The last major organelle you need to add is some leucoplasts (the plain oval). "Leuco" means "white" so don't color them. However, you might want to add some dots or circles inside of them to represent the substances they are storing. Leucoplasts are like warehouses that store the proteins, fats, or carbohydrates that the cell manufactures. Label a leucoplast. (You could color the substances they are storing.)

8) Now that you have the major organelles in place you can decide whether you want to add some cytoskeleton lines. If you feel that your cell is pretty full and you want to stop at this point, you may do so. If you want to add the cytoskeleton, get a ruler and draw light lines that go behind the organelles. You don't want the lines to obscure the beautiful organelles you have just drawn, so don't draw any cytoskeleton lines on top of the organelles. Keep the lines very light. If you make the lines too dark, it will make your cell look very confusing.

9) Check to see if you have everything labeled. You may want to add CELL WALL and CYTOPLASM.

10) Add color if you wish. Real cells are colorless except for the chlorophyll and perhaps some other pigments. But you may take artistic license and color the organelles different colors. (Just be consistent and make all the same types of organelles the same color.)

11) You can paste this into the lapbook as a half-page picture, or you can fold it in half to save space. If you decide to fold it, label the front with something like "INSIDE A PLANT CELL."

Here are some micrograph pictures of real plant cells:

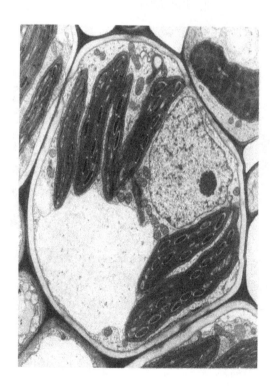
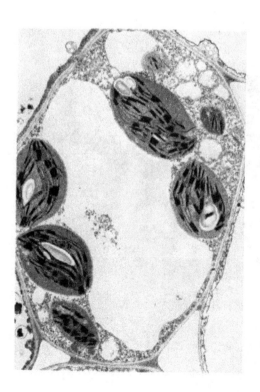

LAPBOOK IDEA #14: "FOLD-OUT" OF FAVORITE FLOWERS

You will need:
- A copy of the pattern page (any type of paper you choose, either white or colored paper)
- Scissors
- Glue stick
- Small pictures of your favorite flowers (Pictures from the "Flower Flip" game are just the right size.)

How to assemble:

1) Copy the pattern onto your choice of paper, cut out, and fold on the dotted lines.

2) Cut out pictures of your favorite flowers and glue them into the "booklet" as shown in the photos. You can draw your own pictures, you can use pictures from a garden catalog, you can print some using Internet photos, or you can go to www.ellenjmchenry.com and use the pictures from the Flower Flip game (click on FREE DOWNLOADS, then on PLANTS).

How it will look when it is all folded up.

Open the cover, then the righthand flap.

Then open the bottom and top flaps.

View from the back.

My
Favorite
Flowers

217

LAPBOOK IDEA #15: MAKE A CACTI POP-UP PICTURE

You will need:
- Copies of the pattern pages (card stock is best)
- Scissors
- Glue stick or white glue
- Clear tape
- Colored pencils or crayons

How to assemble:

1) Do any coloring you want to do. (Colored pencils are recommended.)
Note that the prickly pear cactus has three fruits on it. Color the fruits red.
You might want to add a very yellow sun in the sky.
2) Use the lines provided to write some information you have learned about
cacti or other desert plants.
3) Cut out the pieces. The desert scene will be the "lid"and the piece with the
writing lines will be the "base."
4) Tape the top and bottom pieces together so that the desert scene will form the
background of the scene and the information will be on the bottom.
5) Fold the glue tabs at the bottom of the cacti, then glue them onto the indicated
rectangles on the bottom of the scene.
6) Fold the support pieces on the dotted lines. Glue the narrower piece between the barrel cactus and the
prickly pear cactus. Glue the wider supports between the barrel and the saguaro, and the saguaro and the
background. It doesn't matter exactly where you glue the supports, as long as they are parallel to the bottom of
the scene. Before the glue is completely dry, gently fold down the scene and pull it back up again. Make any
adjustments necessary (and re-glue) if the supports are too crooked.

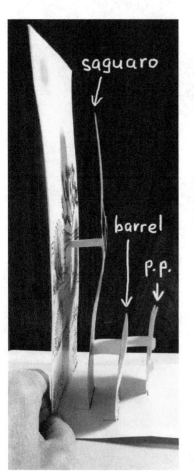

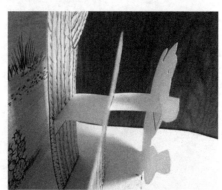

ADDITIONAL IDEAS:

1) If you made an expandable
model in chapter 7 (activity 2) you
could glue it above the information
section.

2) You could make your own cactus
scene from scratch, without these
patterns. All you have to do is
make sure that the support pieces
are the same width as the distance
that the pop-up piece is from the
background.

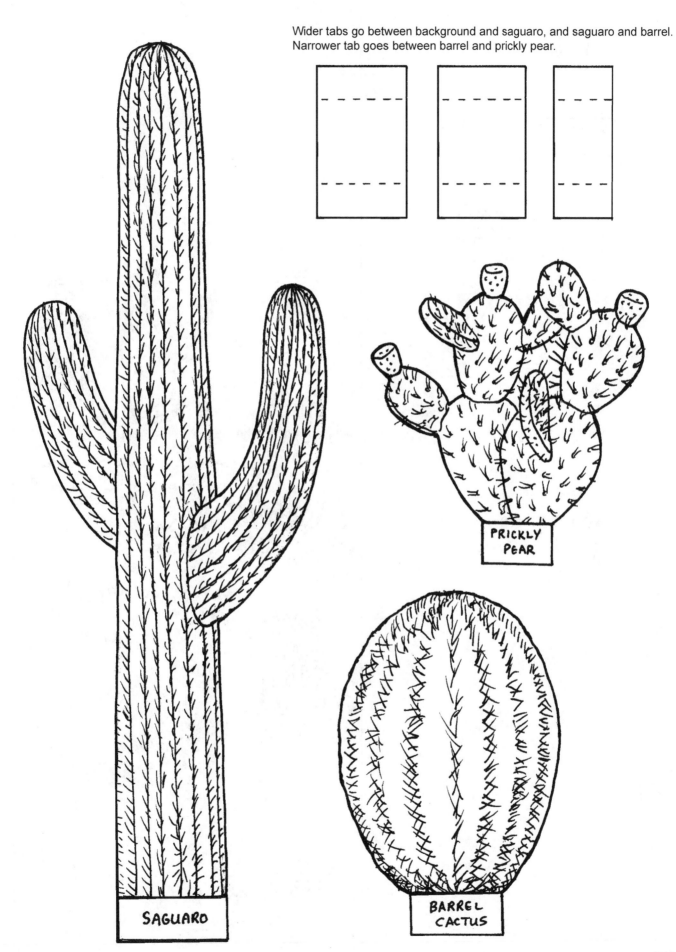

Wider tabs go between background and saguaro, and saguaro and barrel.
Narrower tab goes between barrel and prickly pear.

PRICKLY PEAR

SAGUARO

BARREL CACTUS

SAGUARO

BARREL
CACTUS

PRICKLY
PEAR

FACTS ABOUT DESERT PLANTS:

_____
_____
_____
_____
_____
_____
_____
_____
_____
_____
_____

"CONSUMABLE" PAGES

The following pages can be cut out of the book.   They are provided as a convenience to those of you who are in circumstances where printing color copies is very difficult.

If you need additional copies, you can download the PDF files for these images and print them on your own printer or at a print shop. These free downloads are at www.ellenjmchenry.com. Click on FREE DOWNLOADS, then on PLANTS, then on "Printable Pages for *Botany in 8 Lessons*."

You might want to have your students label the atoms:

C= carbon, N= nitrogen, H= hydrogen, P= phosphorus, O= oxygen

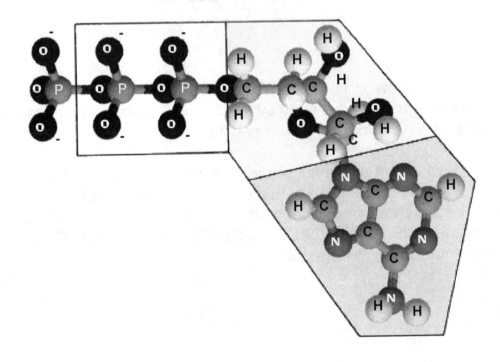

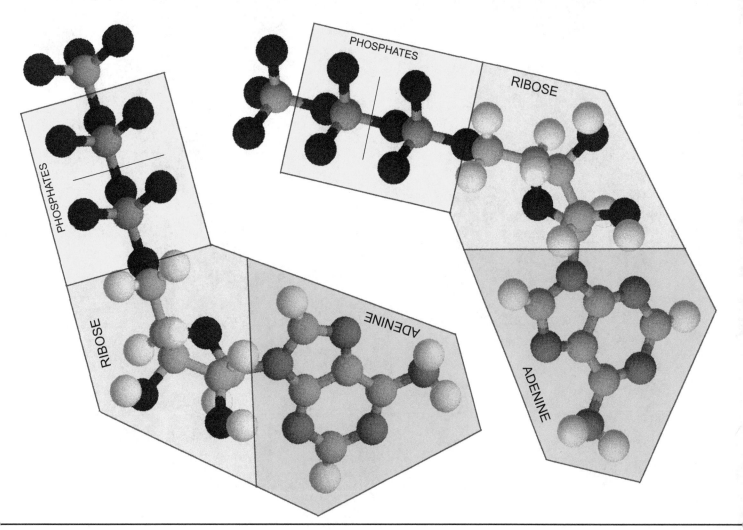

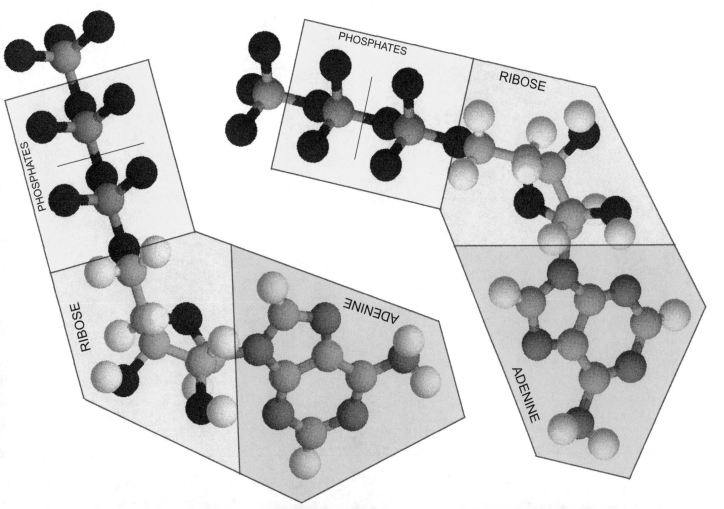

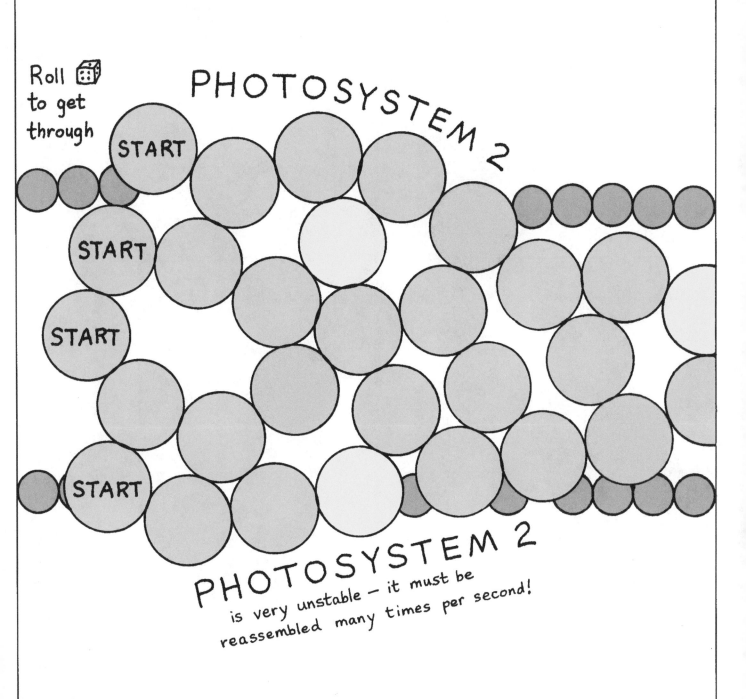

Roll 🎲 to get through

PHOTOSYSTEM 2

START
START
START
START

PHOTOSYSTEM 2
is very unstable — it must be
reassembled many times per second!

Water molecules
float here

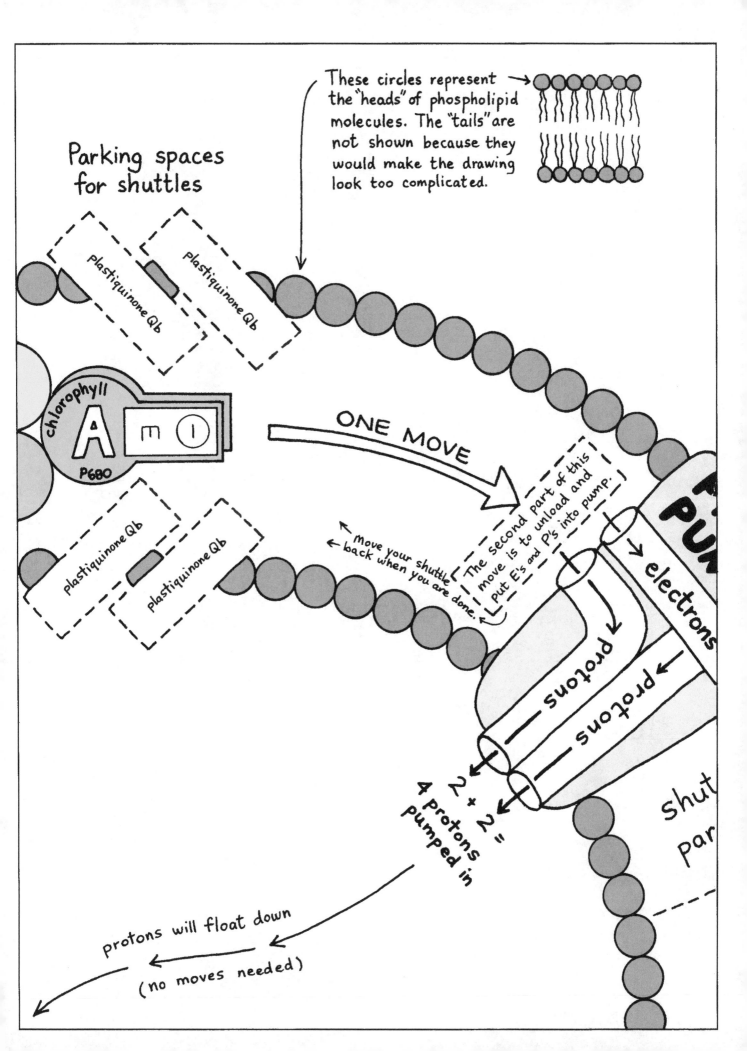

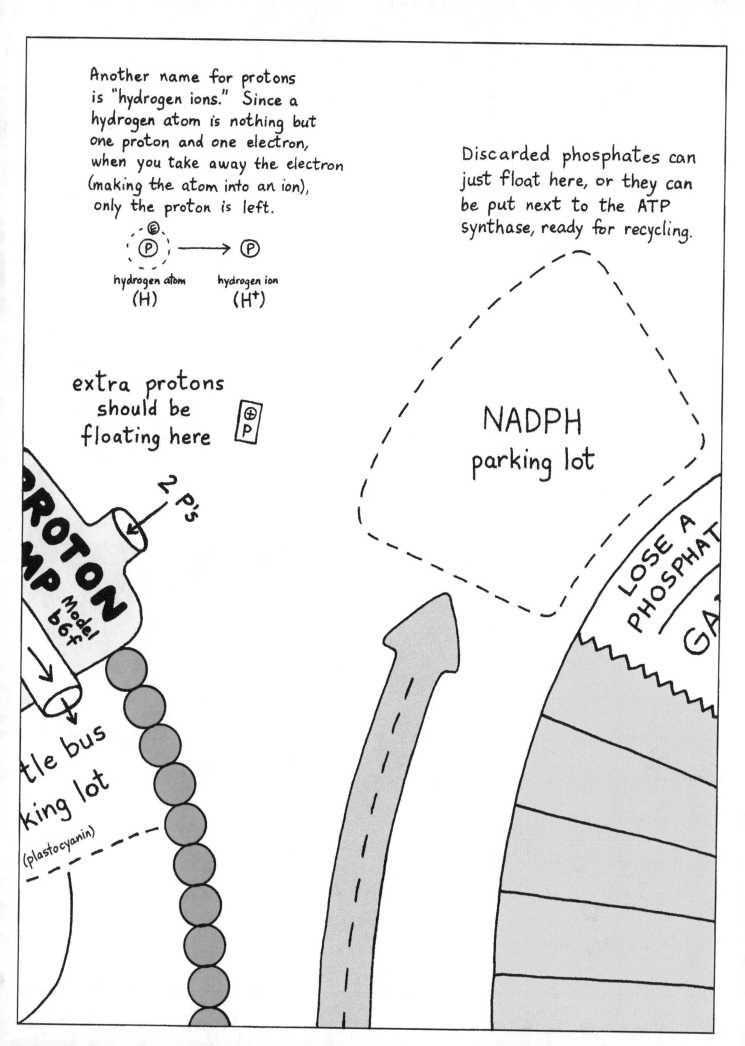

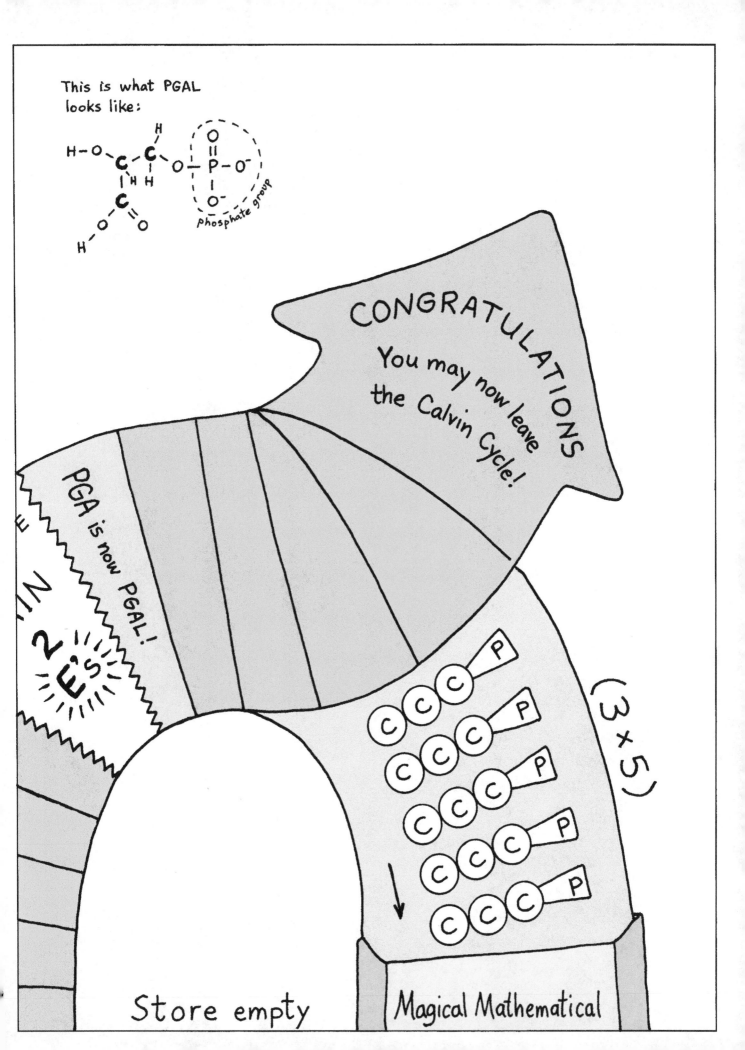

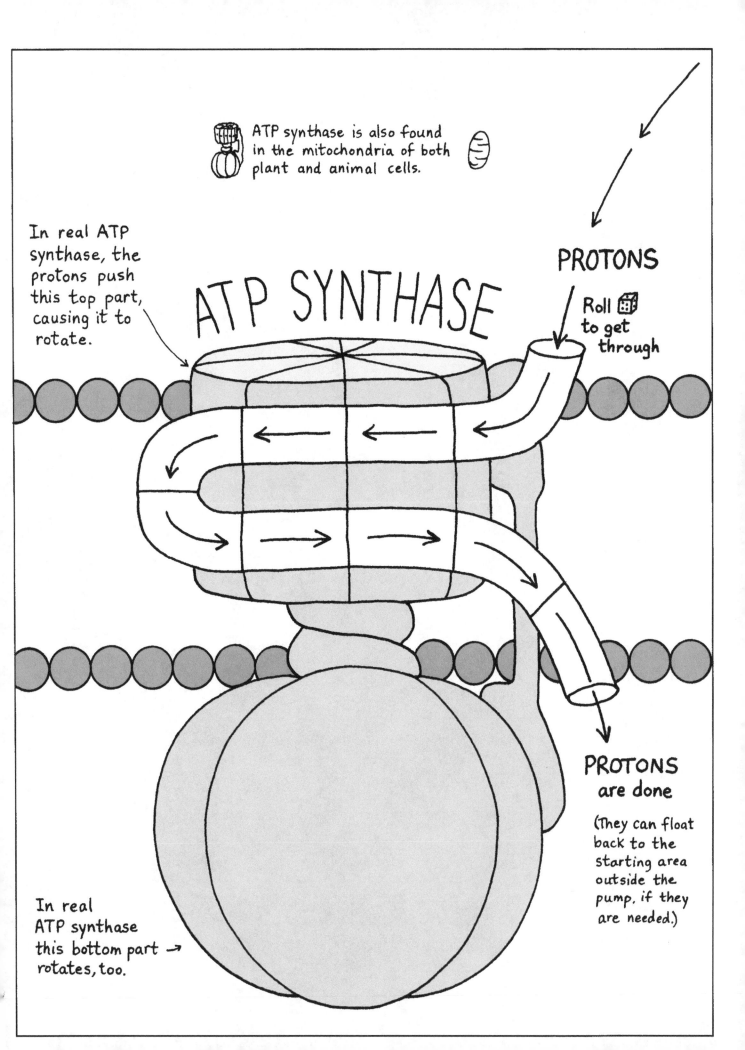

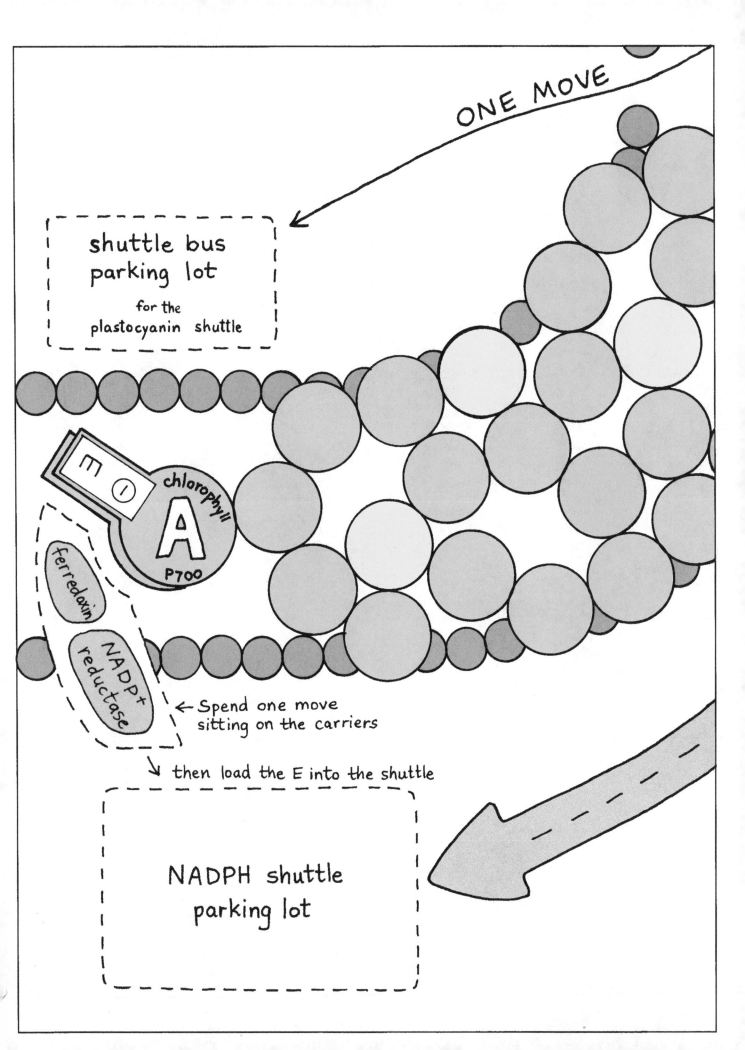

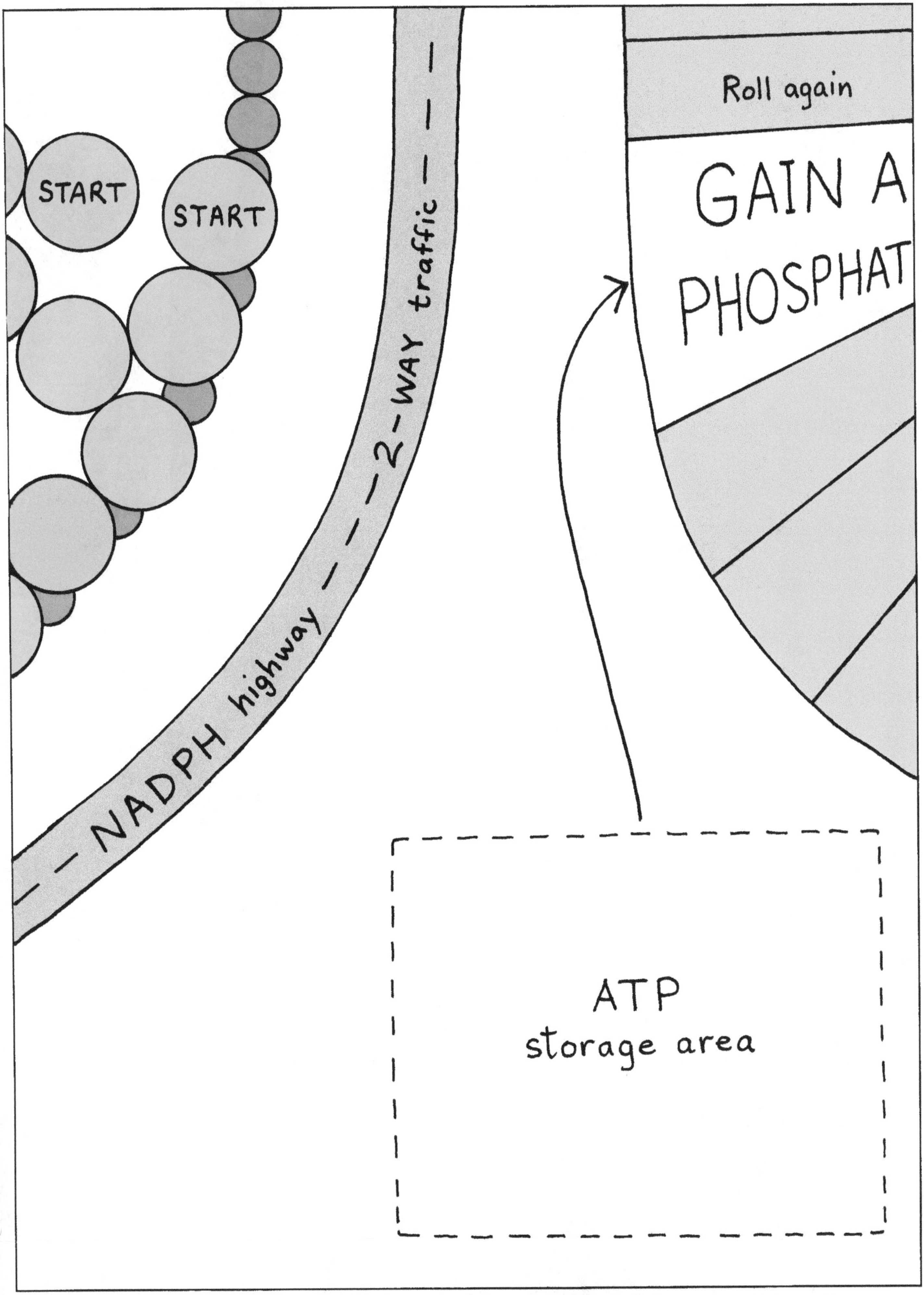
Roll again
GAIN A
PHOSPHAT
START
START
2-WAY traffic
NADPH highway
ATP
storage area

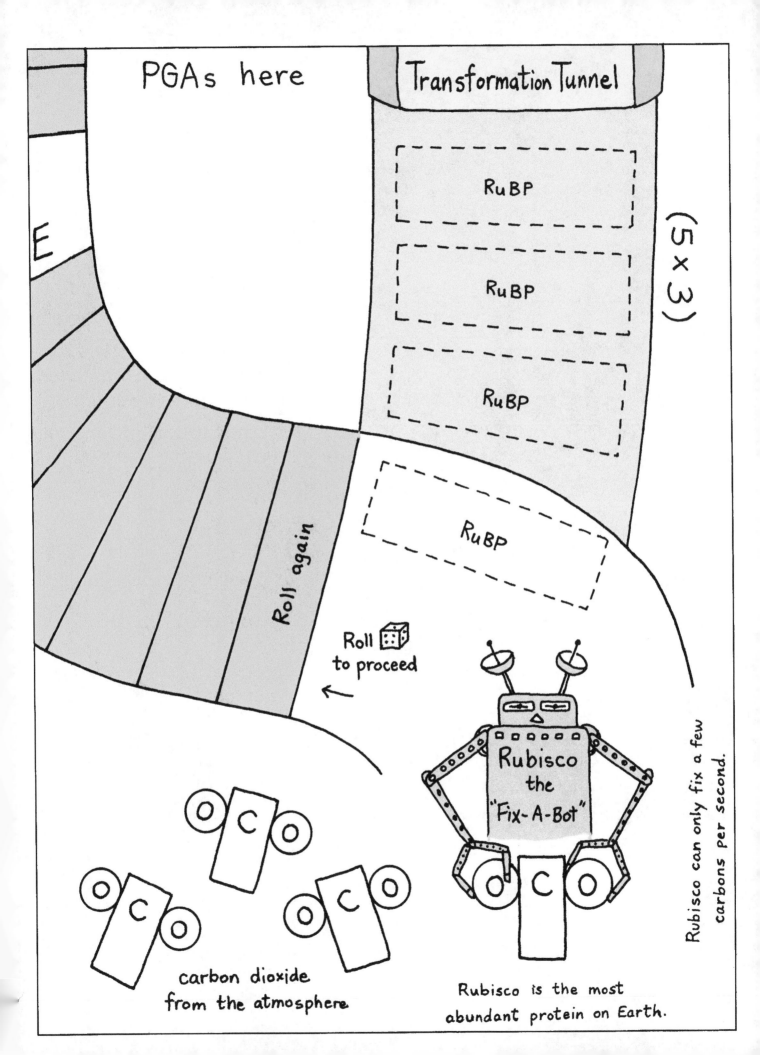

WANTED

WANTED

CPSIA information can be obtained
at www.ICGtesting.com
Printed in the USA
BVHW011418130220
572005BV00005B/7

9 780988 780804